Edward Caldwell Rye

British Beetles

an introduction to the study of our indigenous Coleoptera

Edward Caldwell Rye

British Beetles
an introduction to the study of our indigenous Coleoptera

ISBN/EAN: 9783337300739

Printed in Europe, USA, Canada, Australia, Japan

Cover: Foto ©Suzi / pixelio.de

More available books at **www.hansebooks.com**

BRITISH BEETLES:

INTRODUCTION TO THE STUDY OF OUR

INDIGENOUS COLEOPTERA.

By E. C. RYE,

MEMBER OF THE ENTOMOLOGICAL SOCIETIES OF FRANCE AND STETTIN.

SECOND EDITION,

REVISED AND IN PART RE-WRITTEN

BY THE

Rev. CANON FOWLER, M.A., F.L.S.,

SECRETARY TO THE ENTOMOLOGICAL SOCIETY OF LONDON, AND EDITOR (FOR COLEOPTERA) OF THE "ENTOMOLOGIST'S MONTHLY MAGAZINE."

LONDON:
L. REEVE & CO., 5, HENRIETTA STREET, COVENT GARDEN.
1890.

PREFACE.

The large amount of subject-matter and the comparatively limited space at my disposal render it impossible that the present volume should assume the most useful form, viz. that of a complete *Dictionary*. Neither is it desirable that it should be a mere *Grammar*, consisting solely of dry rules. It must, therefore, be somewhat on the scheme of a *Delectus*; combining extracts from the biographies of individual objects with principles of classification and hints for obtaining further knowledge.

It is difficult, if not impossible, to introduce the "popular element" (so attractive a bait for study) into a book treating on Beetles. Unlike butterflies and moths, they are not familiar objects; or, if so, are not considered friendly: nor is much known of their earlier stages, on account of the difficulty of rearing them in confinement; damp, darkness, and quiet being necessities for their development. Neither do they, like bees, ants, &c., exhibit any wonderful instincts in their perfect state: so that little remains to notice beyond their actual structure; which is, luckily, so varied and adapted to their numerous ways and means of life as to afford a never-ending subject for discovery, instruction, and delight. Here, however, we are met by fresh difficulties in the path of investigation; since the two points of size and colour,—usually of primary importance to beginners in any study of natural objects,—are of less help than usual in the Order *Coleoptera*, owing to their frequent instability; and the detail of minute differences necessitates the use of peculiar terms, incapable of conversion into "plain English."

Nevertheless, the field for observation is so extensive,—the cost of implements so small,—the collection of material alike so easy and so conducive to health,—and the material itself so readily manipulated (owing to the hard integuments of most species of beetles), and affording scope for so many interesting observations,—that few who have commenced can abandon the pleasing labour.

The student desiring further acquaintance with the principles of classification, &c. (too generally neglected by English Coleopterists), will do well to consult the works of Lacordaire and Westwood mentioned in the present volume; from which authors the majority of the characters in it are taken.

E. C. RYE.

284, *King's Road, Chelsea, London, S.W.,*
February, 1866.

PREFACE TO THE SECOND EDITION.

On the exhaustion of the first edition of this work three courses were open to the publishers : firstly, to reprint it exactly as it stood; secondly, to issue an entirely different work on the same lines; and thirdly, to produce it in a revised form, as Mr. Rye himself had intended to have done, if he had lived. The first course was open to great objection, as some of the early chapters, together with the greater part of the classification, were out of date; and at the same time it seemed a great pity to adopt the second course, as Mr. Rye's work is far too good to be lost. At the request of the publishers, I undertook to carry out the last alternative, although not without many misgivings, as Mr. Rye had a peculiar style of his own which might make any additions appear like patchwork. I have, however, endeavoured as far as possible to keep to the style and to a great extent to the actual wording of the first edition. The first chapter has had to be entirely re-written, and many alterations and additions have been made in others; the classification and arrangement has, moreover, been considerably modified; the length of the work has thus been increased, but, to counterbalance this, the catalogue, which is useless as it stands, has been omitted, as the publishers hope shortly to issue a new and revised catalogue in a separate form.

The fact that a new edition of the work has been called for serves to show that the interest taken in British Beetles is considerably on the increase, and it is hoped that its re-issue may lead many more to take up the study concerning which Mr. Rye in his preface says " that few who have commenced can abandon the pleasing labour."

W. W. FOWLER.

The School House, Lincoln,
    July 20, 1889.

CONTENTS.

CHAPTER I.
On the Relations and Divisions of the Class Insecta . 1

CHAPTER II.
Remarks upon the Structure, Metamorphoses, etc., of Coleoptera 16

CHAPTER III.
On the Terms used in Descriptions of Coleoptera . . 23

CHAPTER IV.
On the External Anatomy of the Coleoptera . 29

CHAPTER V.
Books useful to the Student of British Coleoptera . 37

CHAPTER VI.
Instruments, etc., required for Collecting, Mounting, and Preserving Coleoptera 41

CHAPTER VII.
Hints on Collecting 48

CHAPTER VIII.
On the Sections and Families of the Coleoptera . . 51

CHAPTER IX.
The Geodephaga, or Land Carnivorous Beetles . 56

CHAPTER X.
The Hydradephaga, or Aquatic Carnivorous Beetles . 75

CHAPTER XI.
The Palpicornia, or Hydrophilidæ 84

CHAPTER XII.
The Staphylinidæ, or "Rove-Beetles" 88

CHAPTER XIII.
The Necrophaga, or Carrion and Burying Beetles and their Allies 115

CHAPTER XIV.
The Lamellicornia, or "Chafers" 146

CHAPTER XV.
The Sternoxi, or "Skipjacks" and their Allies . 162

CHAPTER XVI.
The Malacodermata 172

CHAPTER XVII.
The Longicornia 190

CHAPTER XVIII.
The Eupoda, or Phytophaga 202

CHAPTER XIX.
The Heteromera 219

CHAPTER XX.
The Rhynchophora, or "Weevils" 243

CHAPTER XXI.
The Stylopidæ 273

Index 276

LIST OF PLATES.

Plate I.
1. Cicindela sylvatica.
2. Lebia crux-minor.
3. Brachinus crepitans.
4. Clivina collaris.
5. Carabus nitens.
6. Licinus silphoides.

Plate II.
1. Callistus lunatus.
2. Anchomenus sexpunctatus.
3. Pterostichus picimanus.
4. Amara fulva.
5. Dichirotrichus obsoletus.
6. Bembidium pallidipenne.

Plate III.
1. Dytiscus punctulatus (*male*).
2. Agabus maculatus.
3. Hydroporus rivalis.
4. Haliplus obliquus.
5. Pelobius Hermanni.
6. Gyrinus bicolor.

Plate IV.
1. Atomolos emarginatus.
2. Bolitobius atricapillus.
3. Quedius cruentus.
4. Creophilus maxillosus.
5. Xantholinus fulgidus.
6. Pœderus caligatus.

Plate V.
1. Dianöus cærulescens.
2. Oxyporus rufus.
3. Homalium planum.
4. Phlœobium clypeatum.
5. Prognatha quadricornis.
6. Micropeplus margaritæ.

Plate VI.
1. Necrophorus mortuorum.
2. Eumicrus tarsatus.
3. Anisotoma cinnamomea.
4. Hister bimaculatus.
5. Soronia punctatissima.
6. Cicones variegatus.

Plate VII.
1. Cryptophagus scanicus.
2. Mycetophagus multipunctatus.
3. Byrrhus fasciatus.
4. Helophorus rugosus.
5. Hydrobius fuscipes.
6. Trichius fasciatus.

Plate VIII.
1. Phyllopertha horticola.
2. Typhæus vulgaris.
3. Aphodius inquinatus.
4. Dorcus parallelopipedus.
5. Agrilus biguttatus.
6. Melasis buprestoides.

Plate IX.

1. Elater sanguinolentus.
2. Eros Aurora.
3. Drilus flavescens (*male*).
4. Telephorus clypeatus.
5. Clerus formicarius.
6. Hylecœtus dermestoides (*male*).

Plate X.

1. Hodobia imperialis.
2. Crypticus quisquilius.
3. Helops pallidus.
4. Orchesia undulata.
5. Notoxus monoceros.
6. Metœcus paradoxus (*male*).

Plate XI.

1. Sitaris muralis.
2. Œdemera cærulea (*male*).
3. Rhinosimus viridipennis.
4. Brachytarsus scabrosus.
5. Rhynchites æquatus.
6. Hypera trilineata.

Plate XII.

1. Otiorrhynchus picipes.
2. Balaninus villosus.
3. Cryptorrhynchus lapathi.
4. Cionus blattariæ.
5. Cossonus linearis.
6. Hylesinus vittatus.

Plate XIII.

1. Xyloterus lineatus.
2. Platypus cylindrus.
3. Callidium alni.
4. Acanthocinus ædilis (*male*).
5. Saperda scalaris.
6. Molorchus umbellatarum.

Plate XIV.

1. Strangalia armata (*var.*).
2. Hæmonia Curtisii.
3. Criocoris asparagi.
4. Cryptocephalus bilineatus.
5. Chrysomela distinguenda.
6. Calomicrus circumfusus.

Plate XV.

1. Phyllotreta ochripes.
2. Aptoropoda graminis.
3. Cassida sanguinolenta.
4. Tritoma bipustulata.
5. Coccinella 22-punctata.
6. Endomychus coccineus.

Plate XVI.

1. Corylophus cassidioides.
2. Ptenidium apicale.
3. Lathridius lardarius.
4. Pselaphus Heisii.
5. Euplectus nanus.
6. Claviger foveolatus.

BRITISH BEETLES.

(*COLEOPTERA.*)

CHAPTER I.

ON THE RELATIONS AND DIVISIONS OF THE CLASS INSECTA.

As this volume is intended solely for the use of *beginners* in Entomology, and especially those who desire to be acquainted with the leading groups and peculiarities of structure, &c., of Beetles (or *Coleoptera*), as exhibited by our British species, it is perhaps advisable to commence with a brief statement of the relative position in the scale of creation held by the class *Insecta*, in which either the *Hymenoptera* or the *Coleoptera* are usually accorded the place of honour.

The Animal Kingdom is divided into two great divisions or sub-kingdoms: the VERTEBRATA, or animals with a spinal column (comprising *Mammalia, Aves, Reptilia,* and *Pisces,* or Beasts, Birds, Reptiles, and Fishes, a fifth class, *Amphibia,* containing the frogs and toads, newts, &c., being by many authors separated from the *Reptilia*), and the INVERTEBRATA, in which the spinal column is wanting: these divisions are useful to the ordinary student for all practical purposes, but cannot be retained, in the present state of our knowledge, as scientifically accurate, as the *Tunicata* (containing the Ascidians), and the curious little Lancelet (*Amphioxus*) form more or less strong connecting links, and cannot be definitely classed with either division.

For a full account of the classification of the Animal Kingdom which is now generally followed, the student is referred to the Elementary Text Book of Zoology by Dr. C. Claus (translated by Sedgwick and Heathcote in 1884) and to the second edition of Professor Rolleston's "Forms of Animal Life," by Mr. W. Hackett Jackson (1888) : in a work like the present it is, of course, only possible to give a very short account indeed of the chief divisions, which may either be regarded as seven in number, viz.—the *Protozoa, Cœlenterata, Vermes, Echinodermata, Arthropoda, Mollusca* and *Chordata* (the last of these including the whole of the Vertebrata and the *Tunicata* and *Amphioxus* before referred to), or perhaps more correctly as ten, the list standing as above with the omission of the *Chordata* and the addition of the *Molluscoidea, Tunicata* (or *Urochorda*), *Cephalochorda*, and *Vertebrata*.

The PROTOZOA are the lowest forms of life; in the simplest cases they are composed of a nearly or altogether structureless jelly-like substance, with no definite body cavity, and no marked alimentary apparatus: the best-known members of this section are the *Amœba*, or Proteus-animalcule, which is a mere microscopic lump of jelly which moves along by thrusting out and withdrawing portions of its body substance ; the *Foraminifera*, which have the power of protecting their bodies by a hard shell usually composed of carbonate of lime; and the *Infusoria*, which include several well-known microscopical objects such as the *Vorticella*, or Bell Animalcule, the *Paramœcium*, or Slipper Animalcule, and others; the *Bacteria* also, which have obtained such a bad reputation as being at the bottom of all putrefaction and probably of all infectious diseases, must be classed with the latter members of the division.

The CŒLENTERATA differ from the preceding section in that they have a body cavity which serves alike for circulation and digestion; there is, however, only one opening to the body; no circulatory system, and in most cases no traces of a nervous system are present; of the *Cœlenterata* proper the best known examples are the Sea-anemone, the Jelly-fish, and the various species of so-called coral "insects;" the Sponges, which used to be classed with the *Protozoa*, are now regarded as forming a sub-group of the present division, called *Porifera*.

The VERMES are very variable in structure; in fact it is hard to find any reliable character to distinguish them, except the fact that jointed lateral appendages or limbs are always wanting; as a rule, there is a distinct digestive canal, but in the *Cestoda* it is not even indicated, and in the male Rotifers it is rudimentary; a vascular system is usually present, but is occasionally wanting; a nervous system is always traceable, but is very differently constituted in the thirteen classes of which the division is composed; the body is usually elongate, flat or cylindrical, sometimes without rings, sometimes ringed, sometimes divided into distinct segments; the best known members of the division are the Earth Worm, Leech, Tape Worm, and Liver Fluke.

The ECHINODERMATA, which are often placed before the *Vermes* in an ascending scale, may be defined as animals with a radiate arrangement, the rays being usually five in number; they possess a skin bearing spicules and more or less hardened by calcareous deposits, a digestive canal, a nervous system, a true vascular system, and a curious system of canals called a "water-vascular" system, which has a locomotive and often a respiratory function; the Star-fishes and Sea-urchins (Echini) are well-known examples.

The ARTHROPODA have a segmented body with jointed appendages or limbs; they possess a brain and a ventral nerve cord; a complete alimentary canal is always present, and the organs of circulation, respiration and sense, although very variable, are more or less perfectly developed; the division is usually regarded as containing four subdivisions, the *Crustacea*, *Arachnida*, *Myriapoda*, and *Insecta*; a fifth is now added, the *Protracheata*, containing the curious genus *Peripatus*, with which however we need not here trouble ourselves.

The *Crustacea* are characterized by the possession of *branchiæ* or gills, by means of which they breathe; they have two pairs of antennæ, and numerous paired legs are present on the thorax and usually also on the abdomen; the body is covered by an integument, which is often very hard, and is chiefly composed, in this case, of carbonate of lime; wings are never present; the eyes are often situated on stalks, and this character is used in subdividing the section. The Crab, Lobster, Cray-fish, Prawn, Shrimp, and Woodlouse are well-known members of this class, which has inhabitants of the sea, fresh water, and dry land.

The *Arachnida*, which include the Spiders Scorpions, and Mites, are very closely allied to the *Crustacea*, and possess most of their characters, but differ in not being provided with branchiæ, and in the fact that the number of locomotive limbs is only eight; the body is composed of two distinct parts, the head (or *cephalo-thorax*) and abdomen, in some cases even these being joined so closely together as scarcely to admit of distinction. In others, as for example the Scorpions, the abdomen is composed of many rings, and the palpi are developed so as to look like two additional legs. They are all without antennæ and wingless, and do not undergo the complete metamorphoses of insects, being mostly hatched at once from the egg, and growing afterwards only in size; they breathe either through internal air-gills (pulmonary sacs), or by tracheæ, or by both combined: the tracheæ vary from two to eight in number, and open into spiracles (or breath-holes) on the lower part of the abdomen or sides of the head; the covering of the body is mostly leathery (but harder in the Scorpions), and the eyes vary in number from two to eight, being placed in different positions on the head or *cephalo-thorax;* the sexes are always distinct, as in the insects; the spiders are all predaceous animals, and in most cases are furnished with special glands that secrete a viscid fluid, which hardens rapidly on exposure to the air, and which is cast into a proper thread-like shape by being passed through certain conical or cylindrical organs called "spinnerets;" by means of this property they are enabled to construct webs for the capture of their prey.

The *Myriapoda*, as their name implies, are characterized by the possession of very numerous pairs of legs; the head is separate and distinct, and bears one pair of antennæ; the remaining segments are similar; respiration is always effected by means of tracheæ: the best-known members of the section are the Centipedes and Millepedes; Dr. Claus (vol. i. p. 514) says that "of all the Arthropoda the Myriapoda present the greater resemblance to the Annelids (among the *Vermes*), in the serial similarity of the segments, in the possession of an elongated, sometimes cylindrical, sometimes flattened body, and in the mode of locomotion. In fact they bear much the same relation to the Annelids that the Snakes do to the vermiform fishes amongst the Vertebrata."

The *Insecta*, by far the most numerous in species of any corresponding group throughout the animal kingdom, have in their perfect state six legs only, which are borne on the segments of the thorax, and are never attached to the abdomen; some of these are occasionally abnormal or undeveloped, but never more than six are present; the head, thorax, and abdomen are always distinct, a point which separates the section from the *Arachnida* (which, moreover, are furnished with eight legs), and from the *Crustacea*, moreover, they differ in always breathing atmospheric air through lateral spiracles by ramified tracheæ (or air-pipes); a single pair of antennæ is present, and two compound eyes usually composed of a large number of facets; as a rule there are two pairs of membranous wings, which are borne by the two hinder segments of the thorax; these are sometimes only two in number, and are often entirely absent: in the *Coleoptera* the front pair are chitinous and cover the posterior pair, which are, as a rule, ample and membranous, but are sometimes absent or rudimentary; the circulatory, alimentary, and nervous systems are very distinct.

The sixth division of the Invertebrata, the MOLLUSCA, may be defined as soft-bodied animals, with a ventral foot and usually a calcareous univalve, bivalve, or tubular shell; they have no articulated limbs; a compact heart is always present, driving the blood through the vessels into the organs; the nervous system in its highest development consists of three principal ganglia, or groups of ganglia, which are reduced to one in the lower forms; the nutritive organs occupy the greater part of the body; in habit the species are both terrestrial and aquatic, the land species breathing air, and those that live in the water having branchiæ or gills; the latter are by far the most numerous portion, some inhabiting salt water, others fresh: the *Mollusca* are divided into several groups, but we need not go into them further than to say that the best known are perhaps the Snail, Whelk, Oyster, Cuttle-fish, Nautilus, and the Ship-worm or Teredo; the tiny Pteropods, which form the chief food of the whale, also belong to this section.

We need not here do more than just notice the MOLLUSCOIDEA, which contain the Polyzoa (Sea-mats, &c.) and the Brachiopoda; by the most recent authors they appear now to be included under or placed in proximity to the *Vermes*.

The TUNICATA are exceedingly interesting as forming one of the connecting links between the Vertebrates and the Invertebrates: this is, however, chiefly noticeable in their early development, which presents a great resemblance to that of *Amphioxus* and through this genus to that of the lower Vertebrates; in their perfect state the Ascidians would not be supposed to occupy at all a high position, being barrel-shaped or sac-shaped animals, with the body completely surrounded by a gelatinous or cartilaginous mantle; the Tunicata are all marine, and some of them are strongly phosphorescent.

The CEPHALOCHORDA are distinguished by having "no paired limbs; no skull or vertebral arches; no jaw arches; no differentiated brain, sympathetic nervous system, or organ of hearing; no heart, spleen, kidneys, or sexual ducts;" the notochord, which answers to the backbone of the Vertebrata, extends from nearly one end of the body to the other; there is but one genus contained in the group—*Amphioxus*—with species found near the coast in various parts of the world. The animal, when adult, lives buried in the sand with the mouth aperture just exposed. (*Vide* Rolleston's "Forms of Animal Life," 2nd edition, p. 437.)

The members of the last division of the Animal Kingdom, the VERTEBRATA, are characterized by the possession of an internal skeleton, which is bony or cartilaginous; dorsal processes of this skeleton enclose the nervous centres (the brain and spinal chord), and ventral processes (ribs) enclose the cavity containing the heart and lungs; two pairs of limbs, at least, are present; the nervous system, and the various systems of circulation, digestion, respiration, &c., are developed in a greater or lesser degree of perfection; in a work like the present there is no need to discuss the various sections of this the most important division of the Animal Kingdom.

The word "insect," meaning "divided," is applicable to nearly all the *Arthropoda*, so far as a name extends, but it has, in many languages, been given to the class to which it now belongs; the Latin *insecta*, Greek *entoma*, French *insecte*, and German *insecten*, having all the same signification. At one time the *Crustacea*, *Arachnida*, and *Myriapoda* were included with the *Insecta* under the same name, as they possess several characters in common; as a rule we may say that in no other animals do so many external changes take place as in the *Insecta;* first the egg, then the caterpillar, moulting its skin and changing appearance and size several times, next the pupa or chrysalis, and finally the imago or perfect insect: yet even this cannot be laid down as a general rule, as the metamorphoses of one or two groups are incomplete, and in the aberrant groups *Collembola* and *Thysanura* are practically nil; it must be admitted, however, that these last-mentioned groups are by many authors regarded as outside the pale of the *Insecta*, and are only placed among them in order that they may not be omitted altogether. It may be remarked that the great number of species of insects, their multiplicity of form, and the high development of parts in some, accompanied by the habitual exercise of the most profound instinct, would almost seem to warrant their holding a better rank than at present accorded to them; with regard to the Ants, Sir John Lubbock ("Ants, Bees, and Wasps," p. 1) remarks as follows:—" The Anthropoid apes no doubt approach nearer to man in bodily structure than do any other animals; but when we consider the habits of Ants, their social organization, their large communities and elaborate habitations; their roadways, their possession of domestic animals, and even, in some cases, of slaves, it must be admitted that they have a fair claim to rank next to man in the scale of intelligence;" it must, however, be remembered that the highest type of a group is often far more developed than many of the lower examples of the next above it, and that nature never works in a continuous or even line; hence the fact that all classification *must* be more or less provisional and artificial.

With regard to the classification of the *Insecta*, the student is referred to the valuable article on "Insects" by Mr. McLachlan in the edition of the "Encyclopædia Britannica" which has just been completed; the section is divided by him as follows:—

Metamorphoses complete (*Metabola*).
- COLEOPTERA.
- HYMENOPTERA.
- DIPTERA.
  - *Diptera Genuina.*
  - *Pupipara.*
  - *Aphaniptera.*
- LEPIDOPTERA.
- NEUROPTERA.
  - *Trichoptera.*
  - *Planipennia.*

Metamorphoses incomplete (*Hemimetabola*).
- ORTHOPTERA.
  - *Pseudo-Neuroptera.*
  - *Neuroptera Genuina.*
- HEMIPTERA.
  - *Heteroptera.*
  - *Homoptera.*

No metamorphoses (*Aberrant Insecta*).
- COLLEMBOLA.
- THYSANURA.

In a work like the present it is of course impossible to discuss these at length, but two or three of the leading characters may perhaps in each case be pointed out.

COLEOPTERA. Wings four, under pair often aborted,

upper pair modified, hard and horny in texture and forming sheaths (or *elytra*) for the lower; mouth mandibulate; metamorphoses complete, but the pupa has the outlines of the undeveloped image visible (v. p. 16).

HYMENOPTERA. Wings four (frequently absent in ants and certain Ichneumonidæ), membranous, without scales, and transparent; mouth mandibulate; metamorphoses complete, but the pupa as in the preceding order: the chief divisions are the Aculeate Hymenoptera, in which the females and workers are provided with a sting connected with a poison gland, or at all events with a poison gland ("Ants, Bees, and Wasps"), and the Non-aculeate Hymenoptera, in which no poison gland or sting is present (Saw-flies, &c.).

DIPTERA. Anterior pair of wings only present, posterior pair replaced by knobbed processes called "halteres;" which have usually, but perhaps wrongly, been considered as their homologues; wings membranous, bare, and transparent; mouth with the parts modified, forming a sucker; metamorphoses complete.

The *Diptera genuina* comprise all the species ordinarily known to us as "Flies" (House-flies, Meat-flies, Daddy Long Legs, Midges, &c.).

The *Pupipara* are a small group in which the larvæ and pupæ are developed in the body of the mother; they are all parasitic, and include the Bird-flies, Sheep-tick, and the Bat-parasites (Nycteribia).

The *Aphaniptera*, including the Fleas and the Chigoe or Jigger, are by many authors considered a distinct order, as they differ from the true Diptera in the well-defined thoracic divisions and developed labial palpi, as well as in their laterally compressed form.

LEPIDOPTERA. Wings four (sometimes rudimentary or absent in the female), more or less thickly clothed with scales; mouth haustellate or suctorial; metamorphoses complete.

NEUROPTERA. Wings four in number, membranous, and for the most part densely reticulate, more or less clothed with hairs, but without true scales; mouth mandibulate; metamorphoses complete, but the pupa as in the *Coleoptera* and *Hymenoptera*.

The *Trichoptera* (or Caddis-flies) have the mouth parts rudimentary (except the palpi) and the clothing of hairs very distinct; with one or two exceptions they are aquatic in their habits.

The *Planipennia* have strongly-developed mandibulate mouths, the wings more thickly reticulate, and the clothing of hairs absent or almost wanting; the best known are the Ant-Lions, the Lacewing-flies, and the Panorpidæ or Scorpion-flies.

ORTHOPTERA. The arrangement of this group has been much disputed; as here constituted it includes several divisions that have ordinarily been considered to belong to the *Neuroptera*; the group is defined by Mr. McLachlan as follows: "Typically with four densely reticulate unequal wings (or apterous), whereof the anterior are more or less coriaceous, the posterior folded under them and membranous; in the most typical groups they are deflexed and closely applied to the body longitudinally in repose. Mouth mandibulate. Metamorphoses incomplete;" in the first group, however, which are separated from the true *Neuroptera* on the ground of their incomplete metamorphosis, and are termed *Pseudo-Neuroptera*, all four wings are equally membranous; this group includes the Dragon-flies,

Termites or. White Ants, the Ephemeridæ or Mayflies, and the Psocidæ, which latter often commit great ravages in collections of insects.

The *Orthoptera genuina* consist of groups which for the most part are sharply defined; the best known are the Blattidæ or Cockroaches (erroneously termed "beetles" by ordinary observers), the Forficulidæ or Earwigs (which form the order *Euplexoptera* of Westwood), and the Grasshopper, Cricket, and Locust tribes; they also include the curious Leaf-insects and Walking-stick insects (Mantidæ and Phasmidæ).

RHYNCHOTA or HEMIPTERA. Mouth suctorial, consisting chiefly of an elongate articulate tube, which is more or less pointed at the end for piercing; metamorphoses incomplete.

The first division, *Heteroptera* (or true Bugs), have the anterior wings horizontal, and composed of two parts, one coriaceous, and the other membranous; the Water-scorpion, the Water-boatman, and the curious spider-like Gerridæ (which may be seen on almost all stagnant water in summer) are the best examples; the ordinary Bed-Bug is a somewhat aberrant member of the group; in the *Homoptera* the wings, if present, are usually deflexed and meet at an angle, like the roof of a house; the *Cicadæ*, the Cuckoo-spit insect, the *Aphides*, and the abnormal *Coccidæ*, or Scale-insects, may be mentioned as examples.

The *Anoplura*, or true Lice, are usually included in the *Hemiptera* as a degraded form, whereas the *Mallophaga*, or Bird-lice, as being furnished with mandibles, are classed with the *Pseudo-Neuroptera*.

The *Collembola* (*Poduridæ*) and the *Thysanura* (including *Lepisma*) are, as above stated, extremely aberrant members of the order *Insecta*, even if they can be included within it at all, and need not be further noticed.

There only remain the *Achreioptera*, containing *Platypsylla* (a parasite on the beaver) and the *Strepsiptera* (parasitic on bees, of which the best-known member is *Stylops*); these, however, are now usually regarded as abnormal members of the Coleoptera, and as representatives of the latter occur in Britain, they will again be noticed in due course.

The foregoing system of classification of the *Insecta* will be found quite sufficient for all practical purposes, but a more intricate and more scientifically correct arrangement is proposed by Brauer (Systematisch. Zool. Studien, S.B., Akad. Wien., xci., Abth. i. 1885; *vide* Rolleston's " Forms of Animal Life," 2nd edition, pp. 509—511); it is based on recent advances in anatomy and physiology which it would take a great deal too much space to discuss in a work like the present; in this classification the *Collembola* and *Thysanura* are separated off as a primitive group of the Insecta, in which the wings have never been developed, and the remainder are divided into sixteen classes or characters depending chiefly on the formation of the mouth parts, the anatomy of the genital organs, and the completeness or incompleteness of the transformations, all taken together, instead of a predominant importance being given to one particular character, as has too often been the case in the older systems; these sixteen divisions are as follows:—1. *Dermaptera* (Earwigs); 2. *Ephemeridæ* (May Flies); 3. *Odonata* (Dragon Flies); 4. *Plecoptera* = (*Perlariæ* or *Orthoptera Amphibia* (Stone Flies)); 5. *Orthoptera* (Cockroaches, Leaf In-

sects, Walking-stick Insects, Grasshoppers, Crickets);
6. *Corrodentia* (White Ants, *Psocidæ*, Bird Lice);
7. *Thysanoptera* (*Thrips* and its allies); 8. *Rhynchota*
= *Hemiptera* (including *Heteroptera*, *Homoptera*, and
ordinary Lice (*Pediculidæ*); 9. *Neuroptera* (Ant Lion,
Lace Winged Fly, &c.); 10. *Panorpatæ* (Scorpion
Flies); 11. *Trichoptera* (Caddis Flies); 12. *Lepidoptera* (Butterflies and Moths); 13. *Diptera* (Two-winged Flies); 14. *Siphonaptera* = *Aphaniptera* (Fleas);
15. *Coleoptera* (Beetles); 16. *Hymenoptera* (Gall Flies,
Saw Flies, Ants, Bees, &c.). The *Strepsiptera* are
included by Brauer in this system under the *Coleoptera;* Professor Westwood, however, is still of opinion
that they should be retained as a separate order; no
one, apparently, now recognizes the *Achreioptera* as
distinct from the *Coleoptera*.

CHAPTER II.

REMARKS UPON THE STRUCTURE, METAMORPHOSES, ETC., OF COLEOPTERA.

The *Coleoptera*, or Beetles, are insects whose outer wings are not evidently veined, but are more or less horny (or chitinous) like other parts of the external covering of the body; the hinder edges of these wings when closed are nearly always brought together over the back of the individual by close apposition in a straight line termed the "suture." These hard wings are called elytra or wing-cases, and usually cover and conceal membranous wings having a few veins and folded either transversely or longitudinally; but these lower wings are not infrequently atrophied or absent. The elytra are sometimes reduced in size so as not to entirely cover the back, and in such cases it also occasionally occurs that they do not meet together by a straight suture. The maxillæ and mandibles (or jaws) move transversely and separately. The metamorphosis is complete, but the integument or skin of the pupa is not a hard encasement, but a more or less elastic membrane enwrapping the parts of the undeveloped imago, and allowing their outlines to be more or less completely perceived.

They pass through the ordinary metamorphoses of

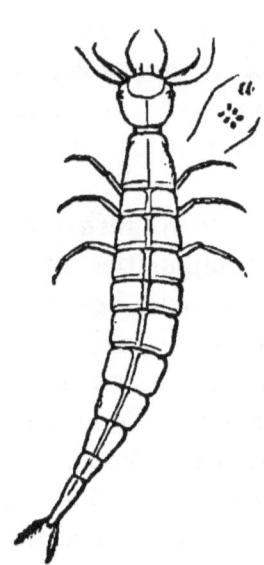

Fig. 1.
Full-grown larva of *Dytiscus marginalis*, a common Water Beetle (*nat. size*).
a. Group of ocelli forming one of the eyes.

Fig. 2.
Pupa of *D. marginalis* (*nat. size*).

egg, larva, and pupa, before arriving at the perfect state. The eggs, which are usually oblong, or oval, and soft, are laid in places where the larva, when hatched, will be likely to obtain proper food, according to the habits of the different species. The larvæ are very variable in form, but are mostly linear, with a horny front and head, the latter having strong jaws, rudimentary eyes, antennæ, and palpi; they have, as a rule, six hard front legs, and appendages on the upper side, with a fleshy tubercle on the under side, of the last segment. The legs are sometimes wanting entirely, or replaced by fleshy tubercles. The body is composed of the head, and, usually, twelve segments, to the first three of which the horny legs are attached, one on each side; and there is usually a spiracle, or breathing-hole, on each side of all the segments, except the second, third, and last. The number of these segments is reduced in the perfect insect, as some of them are incorporated in the generative organs, &c.: in a very large number of cases there is a cylindrical anal appendage present, which is often reduced to a wart-like prominence, and which in many instances serves as a "proleg," or additional organ of locomotion; the apical segment is usually terminated by two appendages of greater or less length, and often jointed, called "cerci."

The pupa is generally soft, and formed underground, often in a cell or case; but many peculiarities in the early conditions of species will be noticed hereafter, when the families in which they occur are described. It may be here stated that the best way to rear either the larvæ or pupæ of beetles is to endeavour to keep them in as nearly as possible the same condition, &c., as that in which they are found. They should not be kept in-doors, but exposed to the natural temperature; and are best kept in large porous earthenware vessels, containing damp earth, &c., and covered either with glass or perforated zinc. Larvæ, however, are hard to rear, as they live for so long a time, in some cases nearly three years.

Want of space prevents us from detailing the numerous interesting points of the internal anatomical structure in the *Coleoptera*: these will be found discussed in any of the more detailed works relating to the order; there are present a distinct *alimentary canal* (with a mouth and vent) which dilates in the carnivorous beetles to form a gizzard; a *circulatory system* consisting of a heart, or an organ answering to a heart, divided into several chambers arranged longitudinally and opening one into another; a *nervous system* variable but usually formed of a series of ganglia or nervous centres united by one or two cords of nerve; and a *respiratory system* made up of the external spiracles or stigmata, and the internal tracheæ or air-tubes; in rare cases gills or *branchiæ* are present in certain larvæ (o.g. *Gyrinus, Berosus*, &c.).

The attachments and development of the muscles of the Cockchafer, a good type of the beetle tribe, are admirably described and figured in Strauss-Dürckheim's "Considérations générales sur l'Anatomie comparée des Animaux articulés" (Paris, 1828).

Presuming that the student now has a general idea of what is signified by the word *Coleoptera*, we will, before entering more fully into the subdivisions of that order, proceed to make some observations upon certain points which it will be necessary for him to master,—such as the definition of a species, &c., the terms used in descriptions, the names of external parts of the body, the best books of reference, and the instruments required, &c.

A "species," the most simple lasting alliance of specimens that is usually recognized (commonly termed a "sort" or "kind"), may be defined as an imaginary congregation of individuals, possessed, during all the stages of their existence, of an identity of habit and structure, and of which the sexes confine themselves to each other in breeding.

A "genus" consists of an assemblage of such species, usually somewhat alike in habits, as possess in common either *one* well-defined structural character, or *several* of a minor nature, unaccompanied by any radical points of separation.

In a similar way, subfamilies, families, tribes, sections, orders, and classes are constituted; the points of affinity in each become more and more remote as the groups are wider in extent, but all unite in some particular characters by which they may be known from other portions of the animal kingdom. It must however be admitted that the greater part of these relations and differences are to a very large extent artificial, and adopted more for the sake of convenience than because they are known to be scientifically correct; in the case of the *Coleoptera*, with which we have more particularly to deal, it is perfectly impossible to arrive at any satisfactory conclusion as regards their definite arrangement, and the confusion is increased a hundredfold by the fact that authors have often used the same characters as specific in one group and generic in another; it is, in fact, perfectly impossible to define in words what constitutes a genus, a species, or even a variety.

The beginner must in a great degree dismiss size and colour from his mind in investigating Beetles critically, and rather rely upon structure and sculpture, —as the former are bad guides, though good companions. An examination of the number and shape of the joints of all the tarsi, and the structure of the antennæ and palpi, will usually afford a sufficient clue as to the section in which any individual species should be placed: further characters are to be sought in the relative length of the thorax and elytra, the development of the different limbs, the existence or non-existence of wings, and, above all, in the parts of the mouth, and the formation of the under-skeleton: the latter character is now regarded as one of the most valuable, but the formation of the mouth organs is still in many cases a very reliable character; these organs are extremely variable, and in order to be properly examined they require to be carefully dissected; this is by no means a difficult operation; if we examine the under side of the head of any beetle, we shall find that nearer to or further from the front there is a suture; this suture is called the *mental suture*, or more generally, though erroneously, the *gular suture;* the true gular sutures, however, are situated at each side of the mental suture; now if with a needle (ground down to an edge on a fine hone and fixed by sealing-wax into a piece of wood such as a match stem) we divide this mental suture, and in the case of a larger insect the gular sutures as well, we shall be able to separate and examine in detail all the mouth organs; as a rule, when the mental suture is severed, the mentum, labium, and maxillæ may at once be removed in one piece, and may afterwards be easily separated, especially if a little water is spread over them by a camel's-hair brush: for dissecting small insects a lens mounted on a stage is very useful, or, if it can be procured, a Zeiss's dissecting microscope, or any microscope that leaves the hands free and does not invert the image of the insect.

The compound microscope is often indispensable for the mere superficial examination of exceedingly small beetles; and such points as the sexual characters, form and number of the joints of the tarsi and palpi, &c., are best seen under it when damped with clean water or benzine, or carbolic acid and spirits of wine mixed in the proportion of one to twenty.

The scrutiny of *specific* characters is at once more general and more close than for any other purpose, and necessitates inspection and comparison of the form of many parts of the body; the relative length and breadth of joints of the limbs, the degree of punctuation generally, the amount of pubescence, the greater or less elevation, depression, angulation or rounding of the thorax and elytra, the structure of the surface, and the sexual characters, being the chief points to be noticed. Species, also, that resemble each other very much on the upper side frequently differ considerably on the under surface. Occasional differences, owing to want of maturity, accidental abrasion, or slight varieties,—the frequent want of similarity in sexes of the same species,—and the absolute difficulty of *seeing* minute specimens in the same light and level, do not tend to decrease the natural difficulties of this branch of the study.

CHAPTER III.

ON THE TERMS USED IN DESCRIPTIONS OF COLEOPTERA.

BEFORE acquiring a facility of noticing what are termed the salient diagnostic characters of a Beetle, it will be necessary, for the purposes of comparing notes with other observers, to know the usual meaning given to certain terms of description, and the parts of the external anatomy of the perfect insect : we will therefore now give a short list of such words as are either not usually met with in common parlance, or have a particular signification. These will be kept separate from the parts of the body, which will be sufficiently explained by the cuts.

Ab, in composition, means a departure from.
Aciculate. As if scratched with a needle.
Aculeate. Produced to a point.
Acuminate. Terminated in a point.
Alutaceous. Covered with minute cracks; like mud, or mosaic.
Anal. Relating to the extreme end of the abdomen.
Apex. The extremity. In Coleoptera, the part farthest from the centre.
Apical. Relating to the extremity.

Apod. Without legs.
Approximate. Brought near to one another.
Apterous. Wingless.
Articulation. Joint.
Articulated. Jointed.
Base. The root or bottom. In Coleoptera, the part nearest to the centre; thus, in the thorax, that part next the elytra; and *vice versâ.*
Basal. Appertaining to the base.
Bi-, in composition, means a reduplication.
Calcar. A spur, strong spine, or pointed process.
Callose. Furnished with a callosity or slight projection or elevation.
Canaliculate. Furnished with one or more channelled furrows.
Carina. A keel or elevated line.
Castaneous. Chestnut-coloured.
Catenulate. Chain-like.
Ciliate. Fringed with hairs; as the eyelid.
Clava. The club, knob, or apex of antennæ, usually more or less abrupt.
Clavate. Clubbed.
Concolorous. Uniform in colour; used in comparison of parts.
Conic. Tapering, like a cone, from base to apex.
Connate. Soldered together.
Cordate. Heart-shaped.
Coriaceous. Leathery.
Corneous. Of the consistence of horn.
Costate. With elevated ridges.
Crenate. Cut into segments of small circles.
Crenulate. The diminutive of *crenate.*
Cretaceous. Chalky.

Cursorial. Adapted for running.
Deflexed. Bent down.
Dentate. Toothed.
Disc. The middle, most elevated part.
Emarginate. Notched.
Entire. Without notch or projection.
Farinose. Mealy.
Fascia. A coloured band.
Ferruginous. Brick-red; rust-red.
Filiform. Thread-shaped.
Flabellate. Fan-shaped.
Fossorial. Adapted for digging.
Fovea. A large depression on the surface.
Funiculus. The joints between the base and club of the antennæ.
Fuscous. Brown, or tawny-brown.
Fusiform. Spindle-shaped.
Geniculate. Elbowed, or kneed.
Gibbous. Hump-backed, very convex.
Glabrous. Unpunctured, smooth, and hairless.
Granulate. With small rounded-off elevations.
Gressorial. Adapted for walking.
Hirsute. Set with thick long hairs.
Hispid. Set with short bristles.
Humerus. The shoulder.
Humeral. Relating, or near to the shoulder.
Hyaline. Glassy.
Imbricate. Overlapping one another like tiles on a roof.
Incrassate. Thickened.
Infuscate. Darkened.
Interstices. The spaces between punctures or striæ.
Iridescent. Exhibiting prismatic colours.

Laminate. Plated.
Lateral. Appertaining to the side.
Linear. Line-like; narrow, elongate.
Lineate. Striped longitudinally.
Lobe. A lappet or division.
Lunulate. Crescent-shaped.
Maculate. Spotted (not necessarily with *round* marks).
Margin. Outer edge.
Moniliform. Bead-shaped.
Natatorial. Adapted for swimming.
Necrophagous. Feeding on dead animals.
Normal. Usual or natural.
Ob-, in composition, means reversed, as *Obovate*, reversed ovate.
Obsolete. Indistinct.
Ocellus. An eye-like spot.
Ocelli. Small eyes, usually on the top of the head.
Ocellated. Marked with spots having a round centre and a light-coloured outer ring.
Ochraceous. Brownish-yellow.
Ovate. Egg-shaped.
Palmate. Widened and divided like the hand.
Patella. A little cup.
Pectinate. Toothed like a comb.
Phytophagous. Plant-feeding.
Pilose. Hairy.
Pitchy. Brown with a tinge of black.
Pubescent. Downy.
Punctate. Impressed with punctures.
Puncture (or *Punctuation*). A small depression in the surface, often round.
Pygidium. Last dorsal segment of abdomen.
Quadrate. Square.

Raptorial. Adapted for preying.
Reflexed. Bent up; opposed to *Deflexed*, bent down.
Reniform. Kidney-shaped.
Reticulate. Covered with a network of scratches or cross striæ.
Rufous. Red tinged with yellow.
Rugose. Wrinkled.
Rugulose. Slightly wrinkled.
Saltatorial. Adapted for leaping.
Scansorial. Adapted for climbing.
Scape. The long joint at the root of the antennæ.
Scrobes. Lateral furrows on the rostrum holding the base of the antennæ when at rest.
Scutellar. Appertaining to, or near to the scutellum.
Securiform. Hatchet-shaped.
Serrate. With teeth like a saw.
Setaceous. Gradually diminishing to the tip like a bristle.
Setose. Set with stiff bristles, or setæ.
Simple. With no unusual addition; un-spined, un-notched, un-dilated,—as the case may be.
Sinuate. Slightly waved.
Spiracle, or *Stigma.* Breathing-hole.
Squamose. Scaly.
Stria. An impressed or elevated line, usually the former.
Striate. With thin longitudinal grooves: usually applied to the elytra.
Strigose. Streaked or scratched.
Sub-, in composition, means *almost.*
Subulate. Suddenly pointed and lessened.
Sulcate. Furrowed.
Superficies. Upper surface.

Suture. Junction of the wing-cases.
Testaceous. Yellow with a tinge of brown; not a bright yellow.
Tomentose. Cottony.
Transverse. Broader than long.
Truncate. Abruptly cut straight across.
Tubercle. A small abrupt elevation: usually like a blunt tooth.
Typical. That which presents the best abstract idea of any particular thing.
Unicolorous. Of one colour.
Variolose. Covered with impressions or pits like the markings left on the face by small-pox.
Versicolorous. Variously coloured.
Vesicant, Vesicatory. Raising a blister (applied to *Mylabris, Cantharis,* &c.).
Villose. Covered with long raised closely-set hairs.
Xylophagous. Wood-feeding.

Very many of the above terms are used in conjunction with each other, and then have a modified meaning, the predominating part of which rests with the last word used; thus " pitchy-testaceous " means a yellow colour with a tinge of dark-brown.

CHAPTER IV.

ON THE EXTERNAL ANATOMY OF THE COLEOPTERA.

It will be necessary to enter somewhat fully into the position and names of the various parts of the external anatomy of Beetles, as they are constantly referred to in all works, either of description or classification; and the common Water-beetle (*Dytiscus marginalis*), before alluded to, will act very well as a type, owing to its large size, and the well-defined outline of its component parts: it cannot, however, be taken as a perfect standard, as its paraglossæ and metathoracic epimera are obsolete, and its hinder coxæ are enormously developed. The body is usually considered to be divided into three segments, with their respective appendages: viz. the head, with the eyes, antennæ, and mouth-apparatus; the thorax, with the elytra, wings, and legs; and the abdomen, with the organs of generation. These segments are in reality composed of numerous separate parts, which we will now proceed to mention; there is, however, no occasion to enter very fully into the details of external structure, for which the student can refer to several of the larger works; but the principal parts of the body, with the names by which they are now usually known, must be enumerated,—it being absolutely necessary to understand them in working from descriptions.

The head, bearing the eyes, antennæ, and organs of mastication, &c., is the first to be considered. The accompanying cut of the head of a Water-beetle will show the chief points to be noticed on the upper side: here, *a* is the *labrum* or upper lip; *b*, the *clypeus* or shield of the mouth, often bearing tubercles or even horns; *c* and *d* are the *mandibles* or upper jaws (these are dissected out in the figure, and *d* is reversed); *e e*, the eyes; *f*, the base of the antennæ; *g*, the *vertex* or crown, and *h* the *occiput*.

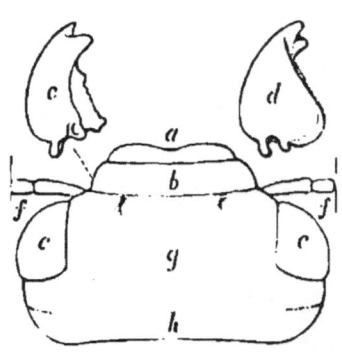

Fig. 3.
Upper side of head of *D. marginalis* (*highly magnified*).

The mandibles are hard and sharp, often (as in the male of the Stag-beetle) very much developed. The eyes, which are composed of many facets, situated on the side of the head, and usually large, are normally two in number, being however in some cases aberrant; for instance, in *Dorcus* (the small Stag-beetle), each eye is almost divided into two, being interrupted by the lateral ridge of the head; and in the *Gyrini* (the "Whirlwigs"), it is distinctly divided by a deep broad channel, containing the antenna, so that the insect is four-eyed, having two on the upper and two on the under surface,—an admirable structure for species that pass their lives on the top of the water, and need extra sharpness of vision, partly to save themselves from foes above, and partly to detect their own food below. There are also in some few beetles two *ocelli*, or additional eyes, small, and not composed of facets, on the back of the head; these are especially noticeable in *Homalium*, a genus of the *Brachelytra*. The antennæ are long flexible instruments, through which the insect certainly receives a considerable amount of sensation, either by actual contact or atmospheric influence. They are nearly always composed of eleven joints, though some of them are often indistinct, being clubbed together, and in a few species the absolute number varies in the sexes; for instance, in the male of *Ischnomera melanura* there are twelve joints, though the normal number is found in the female. They are inserted into a cup-like socket in the head, and have often the first or basal joint long, and the second short; but their variations in structure are too numerous to be specified here.

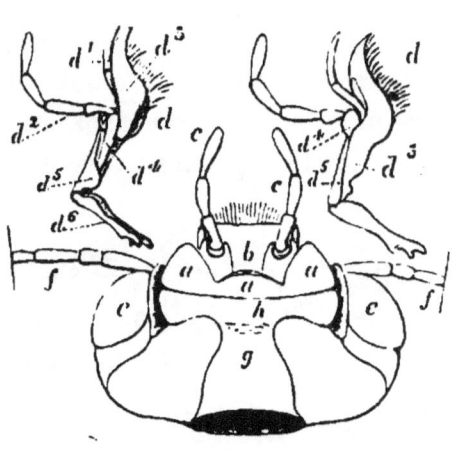

Fig. 4.
Under side of head of *D. marginalis* (highly magnified).

Fig. 4 shows the under side of the head; *a*, *b*, and *c* forming the *labium* or lower lip, whereof *a* is the *mentum* or chin, *b* the *ligula* or tongue, and *c c* the *labial palpi* or lip feelers; *d d* are the *maxillæ* or lower jaws (which are dissected out, and show the upper and under sides), composed of the following pieces:—d^1, the *galea* or palpiform lobe; d^2, the *maxillary palpus* or jaw feeler;

d^3, the *lacinia* or blade; d^4, the *palpifer*; d^5, the *stipes* or stalk, and d^6, the *cardo*, base, hinge, or insertion, by which the lower jaw is attached to the inner side of the head. There are two small organs, the *paraglossæ*, which in *Dytiscus* are soldered to the sides of the *ligula*: these are very conspicuous in many *Coleoptera*, and will be seen in Fig. 5 (the *labium*, or lower lip, of *Pterostichus niger*, a very common black ground-beetle), in which a is the

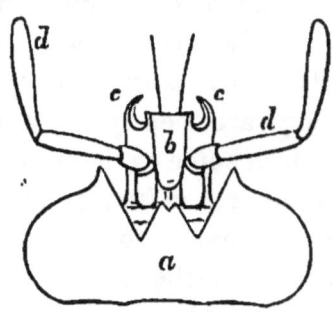

Fig. 5.
Labium of *Pterostichus niger*.

mentum, and b the *ligula*; $c\ c$ are the paraglossæ, and d the labial palpi.

The next segment is the thorax, which is divided into three parts, the *prothorax*, *mesothorax*, and *metathorax*. The first of these, the *prothorax*, is considered to consist of two portions,—the upper side, called *pronotum*, and the under side, or *prosternum*. The *pronotum* is that part to which the word *thorax* is exclusively applied in descriptions, and is much developed in the *Coleoptera*. In Fig. 6, a is the anterior, b the posterior, and c the lateral margin; d, the medial line (of which the front extremity is called the *apex*, and the hinder the *base*); $e\ e$ are the anterior, and $f\ f$ the posterior angles, and g the disc.

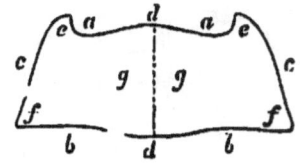

Fig. 6.
Pronotum of thorax of
D. marginalis.

Both this and the following upper thoracic segment

EXTERNAL ANATOMY OF THE COLEOPTERA. 33

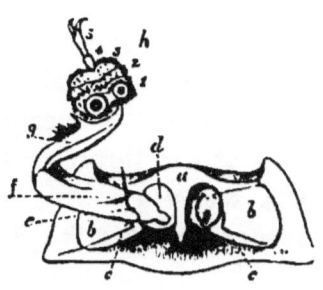

Fig. 7.
Prosternum of thorax of
D. marginalis.

are considered each to be normally composed of four separate pieces,—the *præ-scutum*, *scutum*, *scutellum*, and *post-scutellum*; but these are all joined together, with no trace of suture in the *pronotum* of the *Coleoptera*.

The *prosternum* bears the two front (or anterior) legs, and is divided into three parts, viz. (Fig. 7) *a*, the *sternum*; *b b*, the *episterna*, and *c c*, the *epimera*. The *coxa*, or hinge-plate of the leg, is seen at *d*; *e* is the *trochanter*; *f*, the *femur*, or thigh; *g*, the *tibia*, or shank; and *h*, the *tarsus*, or foot, of which the joints are separately numbered. The first three joints in the male of *Dytiscus marginalis* are widened into a round plate, provided with suckers beneath, as will be seen by Fig. 7; in which, with the other cuts of the thoracic segments, only one of the limbs is represented. All these figures are, of course, considerably magnified.

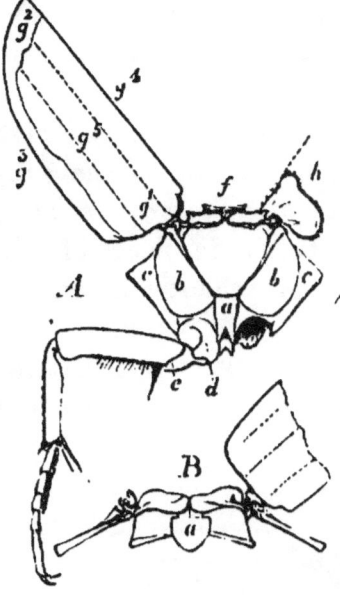

Fig. 8.
A. Mesothorax of *D. marginalis*, seen vertically.
B. Ditto, seen from above.

The *mesothorax*, which bears the wing-cases, or elytra, and the intermediate

D

or middle pair of legs, is also divided into two portions —the upper, or *mesonotum*, and lower, or *mesosternum*. In Fig. 8, B is the *mesonotum*, seen from above, *a* being the *scutellum* referred to in descriptions. Strictly speaking, there is a *scutellum* to each of the three segments of the thorax; but it is the *scutellum* of the *mesonotum* which is invariably meant by this word, when no other reference is made. The *mesonotum* is also seen sideways at *f*, in Fig. 8, A, with one of the *elytra*, of which g^1 is the base, g^2 the apex, g^3 the lateral margin, g^4 the suture, and g^5 the disc. On the other side is the *alula*, or winglet, *h*, which is attached to the body and the under side of the base of the wing-case: it is a thin membrane, exposed in flight, and either covering, or a continuation of, the mesothoracic spiracle.

The *mesosternum*, to which the middle pair of legs is attached, is composed of similar pieces to the *prosternum*, viz. (8, A), *a*, sternum; *b b*, *episterna*; and *c c*, *epimera* (the two last being the thin side-pieces of B in Fig. 8); *d* is the *coxa*, and *e* the trochanter of one of the legs.

The *metathorax*, likewise divided into upper (*metanotum*) and lower (*metasternum*) surfaces, carries the wings and hinder legs.

Fig. 9.—Metanotum of thorax of *D. marginalis*.

The *metanotum* (Fig. 9) is composed of the usual

four dorsal pieces, and bears one of the wings on each side: these wings are membranaceous, often very large, and lie in a small compass under the elytra when not required for flight, the membrane being thickened where contact takes place on the wing being folded.

The *metasternum* (Fig. 10) is usually composed of the sternum (*a*), the *episterna* (*b b*), and the *epimera*; but in *Dytiscus* and some (*Geodephaga*) the latter are wanting, being replaced by the largely developed *coxæ* (*d d*) of the hinder legs, of one of which *e* is the *trochanter*. The *parapleura*, or *paraptera* (*c c*), are side-pieces, which in some beetles are very conspicuous.

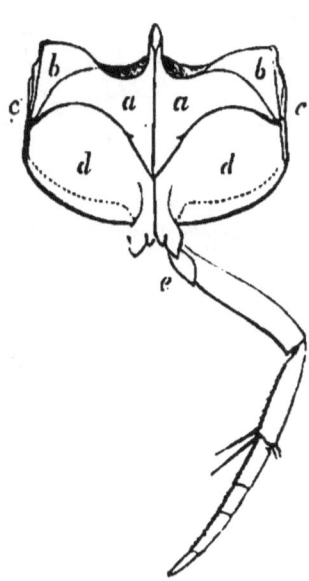

Fig. 10.
Metasternum of thorax of
D. marginalis.

The remaining part is the abdomen, the upper side of which, being covered by the elytra, is softer than the lower, or ventral surface; the apical segments on the upper side, however, where not covered by the wing-cases, are much harder than the protected portion of the abdomen, and are called the *pygidium* and *propygidium*. The entire abdomen is divided into segments, fitting like those of a telescope, and usually nine in number: in Fig. 11 only six are visible, the extreme apical one, comprising the generative organs, being retracted within the sixth (which, in the male, is usually notched, or otherwise altered in outline and surface), and the remainder being only seen on the upper side. The abdomen also contains the greater number of *spiracles*, or breathing-holes, situated in a row on the upper surface of the sides; these spiracles, nine or ten in number, are placed as follows:—one, the largest, between the *prothorax* and *mesothorax;* another between the *mesothorax* and *metathorax*, covered in reposo by the wing-cases, but exposed in flight; a third between the *metathorax* and first segment of the

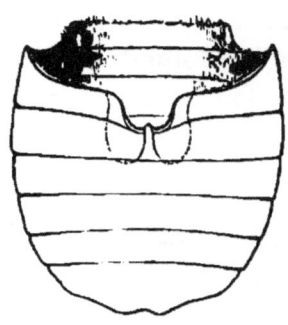

Fig. 11.
Under side of abdomen of *D. marginalis*.

abdomen, and the remainder between every two of the other abdominal rings, with the exception of the last pair.

CHAPTER V

BOOKS USEFUL TO THE STUDENT OF BRITISH COLEOPTERA.

WHEN the first edition of this book was published, there was no work on British Coleoptera that had appeared since the publication of Stephens' Manual of British Coleoptera (London, 1839, one vol.), which formed an abridgement of the " Illustrations of British Entomology: Mandibulata" (1828) by the same author: so many species had been added since the appearance of these works, and they were in themselves so full of errors and so confused in nomenclature, that they were practically of little or no use: the same remark applied to the letter-press of the " Genera of British Insects " of Curtis, but the plates of this work are still as valuable as ever, and are models of what plates ought to be.

In 1874, Mr. Janson published " A Handbook of the Coleoptera of Great Britain and Ireland," by H. E. Cox, which has been, and still is, of great service to students, but is very incomplete as containing no reference to habits and localities; these are supplied in Fowler's " Coleoptera of the British Islands " (Reeve and Co.), of which three volumes have already appeared, and the remaining two are either in the press or in course of preparation.

For general information and reference, the "Introduction to the Modern Classification of Insects," by J. O. Westwood (London, 1839), is still unequalled, and must be consulted by all beginners: the chief drawback against it is that it is scarce and very expensive; if the portions relating to the various orders could be republished and sold separately, it would be of very great advantage to Entomologists in general, and would tend more than anything else to make them students rather than mere collectors; Burmeister's "Manual of Entomology," translated by Mr. Shuckard (London, 1836), will be found of great service on structural points, although in some ways it is considerably out of date. There are a large number of valuable monographs on different British groups by various authors, which will be found in the Transactions of the Entomological Society, the Entomologist's Monthly Magazine, and other publications.

The following foreign works will be found to be of the greatest service:—

"Faune des Coléoptères du Bassin de la Seine," by L. Bedel. Vol. I. Carnivora—Palpicornia, 1881; Vol. VI. Rhynchophora, 1888: this is one of the most original and valuable works on the Coleoptera that has appeared for some time.

"Faune Entomologique Française: Coléoptères," by Fairmaire and Laboulbène: Paris, 1854: not completed.

"Histoire naturelle des Coléoptères de France," by Mulsant and Mulsant and Rey: Paris and Lyons, 1840—1887.

"Naturgesichte der Insecten Deutschlands: Coleoptera," by Erichson, Schaum, Kraatz, Von Kiesenwetter, Reitter, Weise, &c. : still in progress.

"Bestimmungs-Tabellen der Europäischen Coleopteren," by Reitter and others: Berlin: still in progress.

"Skandinaviens Coleoptera," by C. G. Thomson: Lund, 1859—1868. 10 vols.

The works of Lacordaire (continued by Chapuis) and Duval are also of the greatest service, especially on account of their plates.

The following works are necessary to students studying the life history of the Coleoptera :—

"De Metamorphosi Eleutheratorum Observationes," by J. C. Schiödte, 1861—1883: for accuracy of observation and delicacy of plates this work has no equal.

"Larves des Coléoptères," by E. Perris: Paris, 1877.

"Catalogue des Larves des Coléoptères," by Chapuis and Candèze : Liége, 1853.

As regards classification, the most valuable work now in course of progress is the "Biologia Centrali-Americana, Coleoptera," by Sharp, Bates, Gorham, Champion, Matthews, Jacoby, &c.; this splendid publication is, however, far beyond the ordinary student, but must be consulted by any persons who intend to write on the groups there referred to: the Classification of the Coleoptera of North America, by Leconte and Horn (Washington, 1883), will also be found of very great assistance in many points.

The Transactions of the various Entomological Societies that have been formed in different countries (notably the French "Annales") contain a large number of monographs and descriptions.

Foreign works may be obtained from R. Friedländer and Sohn, Berlin, N.W. 6, Carlstrasse, 11; from Ed. André, 21, Boulevard Bretonnière, à Beaune (Côte d'Or); or from E. Reitter, Entomologe, Moedling, Vienna, either of whom will send priced catalogues: they may also be ordered from Messrs. Williams and Norgate, Henrietta Street, Covent Garden.

CHAPTER VI.

INSTRUMENTS, ETC., REQUIRED FOR COLLECTING, MOUNTING, AND PRESERVING COLEOPTERA.

THE instruments required by the Coleopterist for capturing his game are very few, and may be briefly summed up as follows :—A stout folding "umbrella" net to fit in a glazed cover. This may be purchased at any of the dealers in objects of natural history (as, for instance, Cooke, of New Oxford Street, or Watkins and Doncaster, 36, Strand); if the side-pieces are made of metal, instead of whalebone, it will also serve for sweeping.

A small round sweeping-net is, however, also necessary; the frame should be a thoroughly well-made folding ring, fitting by a good screw into a stout stick; such a frame is best obtainable at a gunsmith's: it costs about three times as much if thus made to order, but never wears out like the ordinary more slender rings; the collector should provide himself with two nets, one of rough calico for land work, and another of coarse cheese-cloth for water work: if these are furnished with brass rings of about three-quarters to one inch in diameter, sewn round a little below their upper edge, they can be changed in a few seconds: an old umbrella will serve all the purposes of a beating-net, especially if lined above the wires, and the butt of the sweeping-net may be used as a beating-stick: in this way beating, sweeping, and water-collecting may all be carried on at the same time; if, however, the collector is making his expedition chiefly in search of water beetles, he should provide himself with a net shaped like the prawning-nets often seen at the seaside, with a flat metal edge for scraping attached to a semicircular frame, the metal edge being bored with holes for the attachment of the net, which is joined to the frame and the flat scraper; such a net is often indispensable for the capture of *Hydrænæ, Octhebii,* and other Hydrophilidæ which attach themselves closely to the moss, &c., at the sides of pools and ponds.

A strong knife, with blade fixed to the handle, and carried in a sheath, for cutting tufts of grass, &c.

A very stout steel "pick;" or, if that cannot be got, a long and strong chisel—for ripping off bark and penetrating wood. If the collector really meditate doing any good with wood-feeding beetles, no weapon of attack is too large or strong.

A sheet or two of stout brown paper, upon which tufts, &c., can be shaken.

A square piece of mackintosh or India-rubber cloth, to kneel upon when working in wet places.

A collecting bottle or two of stout clear glass, with no internal bottom elevation, and wide-mouthed. If one side be pasted over with paper, it considerably lessens the chance of fracture. It should have a good cork, which must be perforated by two or three inches of a wide quill; this quill may project slightly below the lower end of the cork, and of course very much on its upper side, and may be kept tight by sealing-wax round its insertion. Through the quill a soft wooden plug is passed, not reaching below the lower end, and having a knob at the top, which can be seized in the teeth when both hands are occupied: specimens can then be bottled without the risk of losing those already captured; and it is best to give the quill a tap before withdrawing the plug, so as to dislodge any would-be fugitives. The safest way in taking small insects is to touch them with a wet finger, transfer them to the back of the hand, and get the mouth of the quill (which may be cut obliquely) over them while they are drying their legs, &c. One bottle of the sort above mentioned should have blotting-paper or a piece of muslin put into it, so as to afford foot-hold and hiding places for the captives; if this be done, they will seldom attack each other. Another and rather larger bottle should be also taken; this should be half filled with the bruised and cut-up leaves of the *young* shoots of the laurel, which will almost instantly kill most of the larger and more rapacious species. Great caution must be taken in collecting, for any of the *Adephaga*, or larger *Brachelytra*, or *Telephori*, if put into the bottle without laurel, would maim or destroy all its other occupants. Both bottles are best secured by fastening one end of a long piece of string round their necks, and tying the other to the button-hole of the coat. Collectors usually also take with them one or two strong little test-tubes, with corks fitted, in which to place any very choice captures.

A depôt of the above-mentioned laurel leaves should be kept in a wide-mouthed tightly corked bottle, or earthenware jar, or in a tin canister, into which the beetles are put, after being killed, on returning from an excursion. Those in the first-mentioned bottle can be turned into quite boiling water, taken out as soon as possible with a wide camel's-hair brush, and laid to dry on blotting-paper. It is as well, also, to put the boetles out of the other bottle into the boiling water; as some of the larger species, and many of the weevils, &c., are not always effectually killed by the laurel, especially if it be not fresh. The more delicate specimens, and especially those with long pubescence, should be mounted at once; the remainder can be placed in little muslin bags or screws of paper, and placed in the laurel depôt or relaxing-jar, with a note of the localities, &c., of capture. The effect of the laurel is to preserve them from decay, and in a good condition for mounting, for a long period; but, if left too long, they get discoloured, half rotten, and too weak to handle with safety. It should be remarked that beetles *killed* in laurel become very stiff, and impossible to mount, until they have been kept for three or four days *in* laurel, when the rigidity of their muscles relaxes.

For mounting or setting out the specimens, the following apparatus is necessary :—

A frame with canvas or perforated-zinc back and door for setting-boards, which are oblong pieces of wood covered with cork and fitting into grooves; in the bottom may be a drawer for pins, &c.

A bottle of gum tragacanth (called also "gum dragon"). The thin clear pieces are the best, and can be obtained at any chemist's. Two or three bits, of the size of the thumb-nail, with a very few small pieces of clear gum-arabic to give consistency, if put into a wide-mouthed bottle and covered with cold water, will swell to a very large bulk; more water can be added at discretion, and the gum stirred until it appears melted; it should be quite white, and too stiff to come out of the bottle readily. By making a little at a time, it keeps its colour, not having time to get dirty or sour before it is used; or it may be preserved and kept for a very long time by the addition of a little spirits of wine or quite clear glacial carbolic acid.

Some camel's-hair brushes, fine-pointed but stiff.

"Setting-needles," made either of fine pins slightly hooked at the tip, or "bead" needles. These may be stuck into paint-brush sticks, or have a knob of sealing-wax at their upper end for a handle.

Small pins, and good white card of moderate stoutness, and not too smooth; if too thin, it curls up with the gum, and should then be damped on the under side.

When setting out specimens, a glass of cold water and some clean blotting-paper should be kept handy, to be used in cleaning them. They should be placed on their backs, and their legs brushed out with a clean brush; some gum is then to be put on the card (which can be either cut into long narrow strips of the required depth, or into straight-sided narrow pieces, one for each beetle) and the insect placed on it, when the legs, antennæ, and palpi must be put into the desired position with a clean brush or the setting-needle. The body should not be touched with the gum brush, and care should be taken to get the head, thorax, and elytra straight on the card; the limbs ought to be properly set out, but no part should be pulled to an unnatural extent. After being mounted, the specimens must be left on the setting-board for at least a fortnight; thorough drying being essential for their preservation. The larger insects should be pinned through the *right* wing-case, and never through the thorax, and their legs may be kept in position with smaller pins whilst drying. Some, such as the Oil-beetles, require stuffing; and many others of the very large species dry all the better for having the contents of the abdomen removed, and the cavity dried with bits of blotting-paper and filled up with cotton wool. Each specimen should have a number written on the under side of the card or on a small label attached to the pin, by means of which a record can be kept in a journal of the date, place, and circumstances of its capture.

Examples of both sexes of each species should, where practicable, be mounted on their backs, to show the under side; it is, however, very easy to float off specimens set in the ordinary way, and reverse or recard them as desired.

When the insects are quite dry, they should, if mounted in a row, be separated, and all superfluous card cut away from each specimen,—care being taken, however, to leave ample room *behind* for the pocket-glass to go all round the body. Not more than one example should be allowed on one card, and the cards (which look best when those on which the specimens of any one species are mounted are all of the same size) should be oblong, with parallel ends and sides; and pinned in the middle of, and close to, the hinder margin. If elevated about three parts up the pin, they are more secure from dirt and mites, and easier to examine; and No. 17 pin (Messrs. D. F. Tayler and Co., New Hall Works, Birmingham) is perhaps the most useful size.

For examining specimens, a good pocket-glass of two or three powers is necessary, and a Stanhope or Coddington or Browning's platyscopic lens will be required for the very minute species. A square bung to stick the pins into is very handy, and a pair of insect pliers almost indispensable.

Insects that have become dry, or old specimens, may be relaxed in a jar of damp sand, or by immersion in water; they can then be set by gumming them on card, and as soon as the gum is dry, damping one side only, and putting the limbs out; afterwards serving the other side in the same way. If required, the body or any of the limbs can be kept in position by small card-braces with pins through them.

A mixture of carbolic acid and spirits of wine in the proportion of 1 to 18 or 20 is most useful in cleaning old beetles, and restoring their colours; benzine is also of great service in removing grease, especially if mixed with a little carbolic acid; this grease is very apt to appear in imperfectly dried specimens, especially if they have been left for too long a time in laurel.

The collection may be arranged in a cabinet or in corked store boxes [1]: the latter are in some respects preferable, as a box can be easily intercalated, whereas a cabinet drawer cannot; at the same time the specimens are less likely to get disturbed in a cabinet, in which they are always in a horizontal position.

---

[1] I have the whole of my collection in corked store boxes, which I obtained from Mr. E. W. Janson, 35, Little Russell Street, Bloomsbury, W.C.; these are perfectly air-tight, and are the best and cheapest store boxes I have ever seen the price was three guineas per dozen.—W. W. F.

CHAPTER VII.

HINTS ON COLLECTING.

In the body of this work the most usual haunts of the different families will be pointed out; but a few general remarks on collecting may also be of service.

The best time for beating is at the end of May and beginning of June, and the most productive trees are young oaks, hazels, poplars, and sallows. Sweeping commences when the beating-net is no longer useful, and continues all through the summer and autumn; patches of wild flowers on the edges of woods and fields, damp meadows, and water plants, being all good for this work. In early spring and summer many good things are to be found in sand-pits, especially if they have straight cut sides; the reason being that the insects fly in the evening wildly, hit against the steep banks, and fall half-stupefied.

The very best times in the year for collecting are in the early warm days of spring up to the middle of June, and late in the autumn, at the end of September: this is easily accounted for, as most insects come out of the pupa condition about the latter time, hybernate during the winter months, and come out again in the next spring. Hence there are absolutely more beetles to be had in December (though of course in a state of inactivity) than in August; during which month the spring insects die away, and those coming to maturity are either in the pupa state or not yet sufficiently hardened.

In the winter, very many beetles can be obtained by cutting isolated tufts of grass, pulling moss, &c., and shaking them over brown paper; the proceeds need not be examined on the spot, but can be taken home in a bag and carefully investigated indoors at leisure. In this way, by a judicious selection of likely-looking spots, a few hours' work out of doors will often furnish occupation for several evenings.

In the autumn, examining fungi and puff-balls, and sweeping among dead leaves under trees are very productive; and later still, the leaves (especially the black, damp, bottom layers) may be sifted or shaken over the brown paper with great results. On the seashore, heaps of decaying seaweed harbour many species, and dead fish or birds become capital traps; but a "keeper's tree" in a wood, with dead vermin nailed to it, is the luckiest thing to find. Many species come to the running sap of the stumps of felled trees, and a great number haunt the wet burrows of the caterpillar of the Goat Moth in the solid wood; whilst ants' nests, both in woods, tree trunks, and sandy places, produce a large number both of specimens and species, many of them being very rare.

Tapping rotten twigs and sticks, and shaking the damp bottom layers of grass and rubbish heaps and hay-stacks, will produce many species in profusion.

It is, however, manifestly impossible to give full directions, in our limited space, for the pursuit of a race so numerous and varied in habit: the young collector will soon acquire the requisite "cunning" by diligent observation, and the natural habitats of the different groups will be alluded to in their proper places.

Finally, with regard to localities, it may be remarked that a chalky or sandy soil is very productive, whilst a clay basis is usually quite the reverse; that woods, marshes, mountains, and heaths are far better for collecting purposes than cultivated lands; and that beetles are, as a rule, more plentiful in the extreme south, north, and coast-lines of our island, than in the midland counties.[1]

[1] In "The Entomologist" (March, 1882—April, 1883) I published a series of papers on "Natural Localities of British Coleoptera," which may perhaps be found of service by collectors.—W. W. F.

CHAPTER VIII.

ON THE SECTIONS AND FAMILIES OF THE COLEOPTERA.

According to the system adopted by many modern writers, the *Hymenoptera* are placed at the head of the Insecta as containing among its members those insects that appear to be endowed with the highest intellectual faculties (e.g. Ants and Bees); by many, however, the priority is assigned to the *Coleoptera*, which are in some points the most highly developed in structure, and in number of species probably excel any of the other orders; upwards of 150,000 at least must now be known, and numbers of new species are constantly being found in all quarters of the globe.

The general structure is very marked, in spite of the ever-varying forms that are discovered; with one or two exceptions (such as *Platypsylla* and *Stylops* before referred to) a beetle is always recognized as a beetle in the perfect state; in the larval state the case is very different, and no one, for instance, would recognize the larvæ of *Gyrinus, Haliplus, Meloë,* and the Curculionidæ as in any way connected with one another.

When, however, we come to the classification of the *Coleoptera*, we are met by very great difficulties, which arise from the fact that it is quite impossible to divide them with accuracy into any definitely defined groups; if we attempt to do so, there will always be found intermediate forms that might as well be placed in one group as another: in classifying any section of the Animal Kingdom, or even the various sections of the Animal Kingdom itself, the difficulty will and must always be met with to a greater or a less degree; "synthetic" forms, as they are called, will always be found that upset our preconceived ideas; linear classification is impossible, and the best symbol that could be adopted for any classification would be a large circle with its circumference intersected and divided by smaller circles, which are themselves in the same way intersected and divided.

Now in the case of the *Coleoptera* the difficulties are increased by the enormous amount of material already known, as well as by the new forms that are being continually added; any arrangement must therefore be regarded as, in the present state of our knowledge, unsatisfactory, artificial, and provisional, and every defined group must be allowed to contain a certain number of exceptions.

The system of Latreille, founded on the number of the joints of the tarsi, has been the one which has perhaps, up to recent times, been most generally adopted; under this system many allied families, the most fully developed, possessing five joints to all the tarsi, have been termed the *Pentamera;* those with five joints to the front and middle legs, and only four to the hinder, *Heteromera;* those with *apparently* only four to all the tarsi, *Tetramera;* and those with *apparently* only three to all the tarsi, *Trimera*.

This arrangement, although well marked, and in most cases apparently natural, cannot be strictly adhered to; as in the first section there are numerous species *not* possessing five joints to all the tarsi, and in the two last there is really a small joint at the articulation of the apical joint of the tarsi which escaped the notice of the original founder; in fact, so artificial is the system that many modern writers ignore the larger divisions altogether, and regard the order as composed of upwards of a hundred families without collecting them into the larger groups: for the sake of convenience, however, they may be divided as follows for the ordinary student:—

I. The *Carnivora* or *Adephaga*, sometimes styled *Filicornia*, which fall into two distinct sections (connected, however, by intermediate families).
   i. The *Geodephaga*, or Land Carnivorous Beetles.
   ii. The *Hydradephaga*, or Water Carnivorous Beetles.
II. The *Hydrophilidæ* or *Palpicornia*, often regarded as a section of the unwieldy group *Clavicornia*.
III. The *Clavicornia*, which are in this work divided, for convenience sake only, into two sections.
   i. The *Staphylinidæ* (Rove-Beetles), or, as they have been often termed, *Brachelytra*.
   ii. The *Necrophaga*, or Carrion-feeders and their allies.
IV. The *Lamellicornia*, or Chafers and their allies.
V. The *Serricornia*, divided into two sections.
   i. The *Buprestidæ* and *Elateridæ*, or Skip-Jacks and their allies.
   ii. The *Malacodermata*, or Soldier-Beetles and their allies.

VI. The *Longicornia*.
VII. The *Phytophaga*, or *Chrysomelidæ* and their allies, sometimes called *Monilicornia*.
VIII. The *Heteromera*.
IX. The *Rhynchophora*, or Weevils.
X. The aberrant Coleoptera, or *Strepsiptera*.

The *Rhynchophora* are placed at the end of the normal Coleoptera, as containing the most archaic forms, and as differing in some important points from all of them, and the *Heteromera* have been located at the end of the other series, as affording by their varied forms a sort of epitome of them all; this latter division is usually retained by all authors, as being the most constant of all the divisions under the tarsal system: at the same time it must be remembered that certain heteromerous species (with the tarsi 5–5–4-jointed) are found in the other groups.

(As I do not wish to make Mr. Rye at all responsible for the classification here adopted, I prefer to quote his arrangement. After noticing the fact that there are numerous species in the *Pentamera* not possessing five joints to all the tarsi, and the presence of an extra minute joint in the *Tetramera* and *Trimera*, he proceeds as follows (First Edition, p. 42):—

"Nevertheless, nearly every one of the species in the arrangement followed in this work, from *Cicindela* to *Octotemnus*, will be found to be pentamerous;[1] the Heteromerous section is preserved; the species of the *Rhynchophora*, *Longicornes*, and *Eupoda* answer to the *Tetramera*, and the remainder constitute the *Pseudotrimera* of Westwood, equivalent to the three-jointed beetles above mentioned.

"It will be seen, then, that our *Coleoptera* are divided into

---

[1] This can hardly be allowed; the chief sub-family of the *Staphylinidæ*, for instance, the *Aleocharinæ*, is now divided almost entirely on the *difference* in the number of the tarsal joints.

eleven great sections, viz. the *Adephaga*, or Carnivorous Beetles; the *Brachelytra*, 'Rove-Beetles' or 'Devil's Coach-horses;' the *Necrophaga*, or Carrion-feeders (equivalent to the *Clavicornes* and *Palpicornes* of French authors); the *Lamellicornes*, or Chafers and their allies; the *Sternoxi;* the *Malacodermi;* the *Heteromera;* the *Rhynchophora;* the *Longicornes;* the *Eupoda*, and the *Pseudotrimera*. These again are divided into sub-sections, families, &c., whose characters will be given in due order."—W. W. F.)

CHAPTER IX.

THE GEODEPHAGA, OR LAND CARNIVOROUS BEETLES.

SECTION I. The ADEPHAGA possess an outer or palpiform lobe or *galea* to the maxillæ, in addition to the four-jointed maxillary palpi (Fig. 4, d^1, p. 31), and are readily separated into two sub-sections; the first of which, the GEODEPHAGA, contains terrestrial, and the second, the HYDRADEPHAGA, aquatic species.

Sub-section 1. GEODEPHAGA, *M'Leay*.

This sub-section, although not employed in the most recent Continental systems of classification (wherein its families are not distinguished, as a group, from those of the *Hydradephaga*, its aquatic representative), will be retained in the present work, being generally used in British catalogues, &c., and forming a natural division, of which the members are readily separated from other beetles.

It consists, as the name imports, of the predaceous ground-beetles,—recognizable by their hard, well-developed mandibles or jaws; their legs eminently constructed for rapid movement combined with strength, and with all the tarsi five-jointed; and by their antennæ being slender, nearly always lessened towards the tip, and rarely inclined to be moniliform (i.e. with the joints like beads): they have, also, the mentum (or chin) more or less deeply notched (Fig. 5, *a*, p. 32); an outer or palpiform lobe or *galea* to the maxillæ divided into two joints; and the coxæ of the hinder legs extended inwards, and becoming transverse on approaching the middle legs. In the males, the basal joints of the front tarsi (i.e. those nearest to the tibiæ) are nearly always widened.

Superficially, the *Geodephaga* may be known by their active habits, slaughtering propensities, thin legs and antennæ, and hard outer covering. They are the highest in development, and may be considered as the *Carnivora* of the beetle race; passing their lives, both in the larval and perfect state, in the pursuit and destruction of their weaker insect brethren. Their chief haunts are wet marshy places, salt and fresh; on the banks of streams and ponds; under stones, bark, and felled trees; in the cracks of mudbanks and chalky cliffs, and on sands and dry heaths.

The greater part, and the larger species, are nocturnal feeders, prowling about on the ground and up the trunks of trees in search of their victims and victual, and concealing themselves by day: some few, however, are pure lovers of sunshine, being most active in the greatest heat. They are usually provided with ample wings, which are readily used by those of diurnal habits; but several of the dark-loving species (especially the true *Carabi*) are apterous, and in that case often have the wing-cases soldered together. It may be remarked that this wingless condition does not always afford an indication of the habits of the members of a genus; since, of two species, closely allied, and found under similar conditions, one will often be apterous and the other winged: as a rule, the former may be known by the sloping shoulders and flattened upper surface of its wing-cases.

Such species as live under bark or in the cracks of dried mud or cliffs are very thin and flat: others frequenting plants (in pursuit of vegetable-feeding insects), have their tarsi widened and adapted for climbing; some, again, whose life is passed in wet sands, are narrow, cylindrical and smooth, with strongly toothed and widened front legs for burrowing; —briefly, nature in all has fitted the instrument for the purpose in a degree more or less evident to our limited perceptions.

Most of the active day-feeding species are metallic, shining and brightly coloured, some also being prettily banded or spotted; a few are clothed with scales or scanty hairs, but the majority have plain suits of armour, more or less polished, and in some cases elegantly sculptured longitudinally: the prevailing tints are, however, black, dark brown, obscure red and dull green, with occasional metallic reflections.

The best monograph of our British species is Dawson's "Geodephaga Britannica" (1854, Van Voorst); this is, however, out of print and rather scarce, and many species have been described since its publication.

The larvæ of the *Geodephaga* are mostly found in the same places as the perfect insects, and are equally carnivorous and active. A singular exception is nevertheless afforded by *Zabrus gibbus*, the larvæ of which have been stated to feed during the night upon young shoots of wheat, burying themselves by day. It is, however, somewhat doubtful whether their normal food may not be the grubs of a species of Cockchafer found at the roots of the wheat.

A Geodephagous larva is usually flat, elongate, parallel-sided, fleshy, with the head and first segment hard; the eyes are rudimentary, usually being compounded of six small ocelli grouped together; the legs are horny, six in number, and situated on the first three segments; there are short jointed antennæ and palpi, and powerful sickle-shaped jaws, and the apex of the body is usually furnished with a cylindrical anal appendage and two jointed tail-like projections called "cerci," which are sometimes much developed.

The pupa is generally (if not always) formed in a cell underground, and is rarely met with.

The *Geodephaga* are divided into two families, the *Cicindelidæ* and *Carabidæ*; the former being represented by one English genus, and the latter separated into two great divisions, which are further subdivided into several groups and tribes.

1. The CICINDELIDÆ (commonly called "Tiger-beetles," on account of their rapacity) are distinguished, among other characters, by having their maxillæ ending in a small movable hook, the ligula very short, hidden beneath the mentum, with the labial palpi free, and the clypeus extending laterally in front of the insertion of the antennæ. The sole English genus, *Cicindela*, may be known by its strongly arched and pointed jaws, prominent eyes, and very slender legs and antennæ. All our species are moderately large, averaging half an inch in length, of rather flattened appearance, and more or less bright in colour, being green or olive-brown with metallic reflections; their elytra are shagreened in texture, with white or cream-coloured spots, or interrupted bands, and their legs long and hairy.

The larva of the common green Tiger-beetle (*C. campestris*) is found during the summer months in the same situation as the perfect insect, viz. hot sandy places. It is a whitish, soft-skinned grub, with a darker, horny, flat, broad head and first segment, the former being armed with strong sickle-shaped mandibles. The eighth segment of its body is larger than—and considerably elevated above—the rest; with two curved, hook-like spines, surrounded by stiff bristles on the top: this gives the entire larva a zig-zag shape, and affords a strong support when it is on the look-out for prey in its cylindrical burrow, which is a foot deep (or more) in the sand, and perpendicular at the entrance. The larva digs with its flat head; and, as the work gets below the surface, scrambles up the shaft, by its hooked segment, to eject the dirt: when the pit is completed, it takes a firm hold with the hooks inside, and fills up the mouth with its broad head and first segment, which are kept level with the surface, the sharp jaws being ready to seize any passing insect. The victim, when captured, is immediately dragged to the bottom of the den and devoured, the larva finally closing the mouth of the burrow, and turning into a pupa.

The *Cicindelæ* frequent hot sandy banks and shores, flying and running alternately with great rapidity.

One species only, *C. germanica*, the smallest and most elongate, is found in marshy places (especially at Black Gang Chine, Isle of Wight); it never takes to the wing, but runs with great rapidity over the wettest places, like an *Elaphrus*. The commonest is the above-mentioned *C. campestris*, plentiful round London, and indeed almost everywhere, in sandy places: it is half an inch long, with the head and thorax much narrower than the wing-cases; bluish-green above, with six round white spots on each elytron. When handled, it often emits a smell of roses. The largest species, *C. sylvatica* (Plate I., Fig. 1) is found on the "Bagshot sand," and at Bournemouth.

2. The CARABIDÆ, distinguished from the Cicindelidæ by the maxillæ not having any articulation at the tip, and by the fact that the clypeus does not extend laterally in front of the insertion of the antennæ, may be divided into two sections, the *Carabinæ* (*tribûs*) and the *Harpalinæ* (*tribûs*); in the former the meso-thoracic epimera reach the middle coxal cavities which are not entirely enclosed by the sterna, and in the latter the same parts do not reach the middle coxal cavities which are entirely closed by the sterna.

The CARABINÆ may be divided again into the following tribes: *Carabina, Nebriina, Elaphrina, Loricerina,* and *Scaritina* (*genera*); the first two of these tribes may be known by having the anterior coxal cavities open behind, whereas in the three latter they are closed behind.

The tribe *Carabina* contains the giants of the section, some of them being very large and convex, and a few small and flat. Two or three of the species of the genus *Carabus*, often called "garden" or "ground" beetles, are well known, being abundant in gardens and cultivated grounds, where they should be encouraged (and not destroyed), as they devour all manner of insect pests, and never touch vegetable produce. On being handled they emit a peculiarly acrid black liquor, which is sometimes squirted for a considerable distance. Perhaps the most often noticed are *C. violaceus*, *monilis*, and *nemoralis*, all of which are about an inch in length, and of a long oval shape. *Violaceus* is nearly smooth, dull blue-black, with the sides of the thorax and elytra bright purple; *monilis*, coppery-green, with three series of slightly elevated and interrupted lines, separated by three elevated striæ, on each wing-case; and *nemoralis* (rather broader and shorter than the other two) has a purplish thorax and coppery or brassy elytra. All three of these may be seen dead on pathways in the suburbs early in the morning, having been trodden upon in the dark, in the course of their nocturnal roamings, seeking what they may devour. Another, and much rarer species, *C. nitens*, found in mossy bogs, and on the Lancashire sands, is brilliant golden-copper on the head and thorax, with silky green wing-cases, each of which has three elevated ridges, and the margins reddish-copper. It is, perhaps, the most brilliant and effectively coloured beetle we possess (Plate I., Fig. 5).

Calosoma sycophanta, the largest Geodephagous insect taken in England, has blue-black or violet head and thorax (the latter with the margins greenish), and very broad, rich metallic green wing-cases, the green changing into gold and orange-red as the position of the beetle is altered. It is found on our shores occasionally, but can scarcely be considered a true British species, though one or two instances have occurred of its being found inland. In Silesia, and elsewhere on the Continent, it frequents pine forests, feeding on the caterpillars of various moths, and being especially attached to colonies of the "processionary" and "gipsy" moths, of which it devours both the larvæ and pupæ in the most gluttonous manner. It has ample wings; and, being a robust insect, is thought to come across the Channel.

Cychrus rostratus is remarkable on account of its elegant shape; having a slender stretched-out head (with the last joints of its palpi very large and hatchet-shaped), delicate antennæ, contracted waist, and convex, oval, finely granulated wing-cases. It is about three-quarters of an inch in length, dull-black in colour, relieved by its polished black legs, suture and margins; and is found under dead leaves, among stones, but not very commonly. It has been observed to make a squeaking noise, caused probably by the friction of the tip of the abdomen against the under side of the elytra.

The *Nebriina* contain the pretty brown and blue *Leisti*, whose mouth organs, if dissected out, form most beautiful microscopic objects; the genus *Nebria* containing the very local *N. livida* and *N. complanata*, of which the former, a black insect with a bright reddish-yellow border and long light legs, has been found abundantly by splitting the clay cliffs at Bridlington; and, lastly, the *Notiophili*, which may be worthy of notice, as some of the species are likely to be seen running over dry hot paths, even in the metropolis; they are the smallest members of the tribe, of obscure copper or bronze colours, with shining flattened bodies, very large eyes, and strongly wrinkled foreheads.

The *Elaphrina* exhibit a likeness in miniature to the *Cicindelæ*, owing to their thin legs, large eyes, and general build; they frequent very wet places, running daintily almost in the water, and are curiously marked with circular depressions.

The *Loricerina* contain the single genus *Loricera*, which is an exceedingly common insect, and is remarkable for its antennæ being adorned with long stiff hairs.

The *Scaritina* (represented in England by a few small species) may be distinguished by their elongate, cylindrical shape; the separation of their thorax from the elytra by a neck; the enlargement and palmation of their front tibiæ, which are often toothed on the outer edge, and are fossorial, or adapted for digging; the non-dilatation of the basal joints of the front tarsi in the male; and the shortness, and comparatively bead-like joints, of their antennæ. We possess only two genera of this family; one, *Clivina* (Plate I., Fig. 4, *C. collaris*), the species of which frequent garden refuse; and the other, *Dyschirius*, consisting of minute, brassy, cylindrical, sand-burrowing beetles. None of these are either conspicuous, likely to be casually observed, or peculiar in habits; except, perhaps, that some of them live in large colonies on the sea-shore, and appear to be often found with *Bledius* (a genus of *Brachelytra*), upon small species of which they are supposed to prey. An exhaustive monograph has been written by Mons. J. Putzeys (Mon. des Clivina, &c., 1846) upon these insects.

The HARPALINÆ may be divided into two divisions, the *Intruncatipennes* and the *Truncatipennes*; in the former of these the elytra are not truncate at apex, whereas in the latter they are more or less truncate. Mr. Bates, who is the chief living authority on the Carabidæ, divides the first of these divisions into five subdivisions, which depend upon the number of joints of the anterior tarsi of the male which are dilated, and upon the clothing of their under surface.

To the first of these, the DIVERSIMANI, which need not here be further discussed, we must refer the two British genera, *Broscus* and *Miscodera*. *Broscus cephalotes* is an opaque black, elongate monster, with large head, and thorax contracted behind: it is found rarely inland, but abundantly on the coast, where it burrows under stones and tidal rubbish, devouring ruthlessly everything that comes in its way, even its own species. *Miscodera arctica*, a near but small relation to the above savage, dwells on our highest moors and mountains, and is but rarely taken. It is very shining and entirely brassy, with its globose thorax and dilated elytra separated by a neck. The two last-mentioned genera have much the appearance of *Dyschirius* in the *Scaritina;* from which the dilatation of the basal joints of the front tarsi in the males, and the want of a tooth on the outer side of their anterior legs, will serve to separate them.

In the PATELLIMANI the male has the first two or three joints of the anterior tarsi dilated, either *square, transverse-oblong,* or *rounded,* the soles being clothed with fine short erect hairs. Many of the species are gaily coloured, being variegated with red and black markings; some are clothed with short silky down, and all are more or less elegant either in shape or structure. The majority live in wet places, under reeds, &c., but a few are to be found under chalk-stones in exposed situations.

The species of the genus *Chlænius* are very beautiful, presenting somewhat the appearance of oxidized metal;

reddish-copper or bluish-green being their prevailing tones about the head and thorax, and their elytra being more or less shagreened or granulated, generally rich green or brown, with thick golden pubescence, which imparts a "shot-silk" like lustre. They are of moderate size, and rather robust in the body. The commonest, *C. vestitus*, has the sides and apex of the elytra, and the legs and antennæ yellow; it is about five lines in length, and may be found abundantly in very wet places, such as reedy spots on canal banks, &c., near London.

The palm of beauty must, however, be conceded to *Callistus*,—as its name implies, "the fairest of the fair." Our single species, *C. lunatus*, is about a quarter of an inch long; its head metallic, bluish or greenish-black; its thorax heart-shaped, orange-red; its elytra oval, orange-yellow (when alive, rose-pink), with a shoulder spot and two transverse bands deep black; its legs are yellow tipped with black, and the entire insect has a delicate velvety appearance (Plate II., Fig. 1). It frequents chalky districts, and may sometimes be found under stones on the downs near Croydon. Under similar circumstances at Box Hill, and on the south-coast downs, the species of *Licinus* may be taken. One of them was, I believe, at first only known to be a British species from a single specimen having been caught in Cheapside, whither it must have had a long flight from its chalky haunts. This insect, *L. silphoides* (Plate I., Fig. 6), superficially resembles certain members of the genus *Silpha* in the *Necrophaga*: from which the beginner may distinguish it by its long slender antennæ,—those organs in *Silpha* being short, with an abrupt knob at the tip. It is about half an inch in length; broad, flat, deep dull-black in hue, and distinctly wrinkled, punctured and striated. The two basal joints of the front tarsi in the male are very strongly and widely dilated.

The *Panagæi* have red elytra, marked with a large black cross; and the species of *Badister*, found usually in the cracks of wet mud or clay banks, are recognizable by the rounded front of their heads.

In the QUADRIPALMATI the males have usually the first four joints (occasionally joints 2–4) of the anterior and middle tarsi (but sometimes only those of the front tarsi) dilated in the male, and densely spinose. Their paraglossæ are free at the apex, the first and second joints of the antennæ quite smooth, and the mentum obsoletely toothed. Several of the species are slightly pubescent; and in the genera *Diachromus*, *Dichirotrichus* (Plate II., Fig. 5; *D. obsoletus*, a saltmarsh insect) and *Anisodactylus* the widened joints are densely hairy beneath, this hair being replaced in the others by slightly elevated transverse ridges, or squamæ as they are called by most authors.

Very few are likely to obtrude themselves upon the notice of the casual observer, on account of their hiding by day, and generally frequenting retired places, viz. bottoms of cliffs, sand-pits, stones on moors and sea-shores, &c. *Harpalus ruficornis*, the most abundant of the tribe, is, however, found commonly in gardens, and may be seen when mould is dug up, &c.; it is rather more than half an inch long, robust, dull black, with reddish legs and antennæ, and its wingcases covered with a very short greyish-yellow down.

Visitors to Hastings should look about for the very rare *Diachromus germanus*, which is occasionally found running on paths in that part of the south coast. It is not quite half an inch long, ovate, with very short downy hairs; its head, legs, and antennæ are reddish-yellow, thorax dark-blue or green, and elytra reddish-yellow, with a large blue or green patch at the apex.

The species of *Bradycellus* are small reddish insects, which are often found under stones, or in moss in winter; *Acupalpus exiguus* is one of the smallest of the British Carabidæ; the rare *Stenolophus elegans* is one of the prettiest of our lesser species: the latter insect has been taken in some numbers by Dr. Power on the banks of the Thames towards Gravesend and Sheerness.

The members of the next division, the TRIPALMATI, are distinguished by the fact that the males have the first three joints of the anterior tarsi dilated, *cordiform* or *emarginate*, and their soles clothed with squamæ much as in *Harpalus;* the division contains four tribes, the *Zabrina, Pterostichina, Amarina,* and *Anchomenina*.

A large number of species are contained in this division, the most often seen (and the most puzzling to the young student) being the "Sunshiners," which are members of the genera *Pterostichus* (sub-gen. *Pœcilus*) and *Amara* (Plate II., Fig. 4; *A. fulva*, found in sandy places).

These insects may often be seen running rapidly over hot paths in the early summer, and are frequently to be met with on the wing, and even darting about the pavement in London, on the first really warm spring day; when the sun's rays tempt them from their winter quarters, and incite them to search for food and their mates. The species of *Amara* (to kill one of which, according to childish superstitions, is to call into operation the drum and cone of the late Admiral Fitzroy) exude a peculiar acrid fluid when handled; a strong-smelling habit, common (though in a less disagreeable degree) to most of the *Geodephaga,* and intended doubtless to be a weapon both of defence and offence: the secretion is probably owing, also, to the constantly carnivorous propensities of the beetles in question.

To the tribe *Anchomenina* belong the "Cellar-beetles,"—not the lazy, foul-smelling *Blaps,* which will be mentioned in the section *Heteromera,*—active, black insects of the genera *Sphodrus* and *Pristonychus;* the former having its hind trochanters prolonged in the male into a spike.

The *Anchomeni*—mostly gregarious, small, and of elegant shape—frequent very wet spots, abounding at the roots of old willows, &c., near watercourses. One of them, *A. sexpunctatus,* is found in boggy places on heaths, sometimes being plentiful on Wimbledon Common; it is about a quarter of an inch long, with its head and thorax very bright green, and wing-cases coppery-red with green margins (Plate II., Fig. 2). It is a most brilliant creature, and darts about in the hot sunshine over the wet peat, looking like a live coal.

A great contrast to this elegant insect is afforded by the heavy hippopotamoïd *Zabrus gibbus,* whose broad, convex, black carcase may sometimes (especially near Brighton and Croydon) be found trodden on, in the paths of cornfields. It has been accused of devouring wheat, owing in all probability to its having been seen on or near that plant, where its instinct leads it to pursue vegetable-feeding insects.

The species of *Pterostichus* are for the most part

black, uniformly coloured insects, but *P. cupreus* and one or two others are brilliantly metallic; they are very variable in size; *P. madidus* is one of the commonest of all our insects, and may be met with in almost every garden or back-yard; *P. picimanus* (Plate II., Fig. 3) is found in cracks of tanks, and under stones, near water.

In the BIPALMATI the males have the first two joints of the anterior tarsi dilated (or, in some instances, quite simple), and the soles almost always clothed with squamæ; in *Tachypus* alone they are pilose; the division may be naturally subdivided into two tribes, the *Bembidiina* and the *Trechina*.

The Bembidiina, which have, until comparatively recently, been usually regarded as the last of the *Geodephaga*, may readily be known by the end joint of their palpi being acute, needle-shaped, and extremely small, the preceding joint being large and club-shaped. The two first joints of the front tarsi are sometimes widened in the male; but often the front tarsi are simple in both sexes.

The members of this tribe are all very small, the largest not being a quarter of an inch in length, and one of them, *Tachys bistriatus*, three-quarters of a line long, is the smallest British Geodephagous insect. They occur generally in very wet places, such as the sea-shore, banks of ponds, rivers and streams; in reedy marshes, and under stones in bogs, &c. Their prevailing colour is brassy-green or bronze, many being black; and there is a tendency in the majority to assume a pattern of four white or yellow spots on the wing-cases. Several species emit an acrid, nasty-smelling, milky fluid, on being captured.

B. flammulatum, found commonly in marshes, is one of the prettiest in marking, being greenish-bronze, with variegated yellow transverse zigzag bands; and *B. pallidipenne* (Plate II., Fig. 6), which occurs in great numbers on the Lancashire coast, though not met with often elsewhere, is also worthy of observation; having a metallic head and thorax, and straw-coloured wing-cases, with a transverse indented darker fascia, which varies in intensity of colour and extent in different specimens. The curious species, *B. paludosum,* and *Tachypus flavipes* and *pallipes,* present a considerable likeness to the *Elaphri* and *Cicindelæ,* at the beginning of the section; their large eyes, slender legs, elegant shape, and semi-aquatic habits, encouraging the notion of their relationship, which is, however, prevented by their structural differences, the needle-pointed apical joint of the palpi in *Bembidium* being sufficient for a diagnostic character.

The *Trechina* have the last joint of the palpi, as a rule, long and tapering, but in one or two genera it is short, although always considerably longer than in the *Bembidiina;* the tribe has usually been regarded as containing only three British genera of small species; one, *Trechus,* not in any way remarkable; the next, *Æpys,* being composed of two very minute flat, yellowish insects, found absolutely under the tide-mark at mouths of rivers, under stones, and in salt-marshes, in Scotland, Ireland, Devon, Isle of Wight, &c.; and the third, *Perileptus,* represented by a single species, *areolatus,* another very small pitchy-black beetle, which is found rarely on sands at the mouths of rivers, in Wales, &c.

Patrobus and *Pogonus* are, however, now regarded

as belonging to the tribe; the members of the latter genus delight in salt or semi-saline marshes; one of them, *P. luridipennis,* is remarkable for its brilliant green head and thorax and testaceous elytra; the *Patrobi* are moderate-sized usually dark insects which occur under stones, more especially in hilly or mountainous districts.

The TRUNCATIPENNES have a constant character in their wing-cases not reaching to the end of their abdomen, and being cut straight off at the apex. Their front tibiæ are notched on the inner-side. In most of them the ligula and paraglossæ are united, and the basal joints of the front tarsi are not widened in the male; and in some the first joint of the antennæ is very elongate. The body is never very convex, but usually more or less depressed; none are very large, and most of them small. Their chief habitats are in and under reeds, &c., in clay and mud-cracks, under bark, and beneath stones and shingle. The type, and most elegant of the family, *Lebia crux-minor,* is very rare; only occasional specimens having been found, in different parts of the country, until some numbers were taken in moss at Holme Bush, near the Devil's Dyke, Brighton. It is about a quarter of an inch long, with the thorax, legs, base of antennæ and the elytra (which are broad) orange-red, and the head and a broad cruciform mark on the wing-cases black (Plate I., Fig. 2).

Another allied species, *L. chlorocephala,* is not uncommon about the broom-plant at times; it is rather smaller than *crux-minor,* and has brilliant blue or green elytra and head, the thorax and legs being red.

The *Dromii*, small, elongate, flattened beetles, often ornamented with four whitish spots, are found mostly under—or in the chinks of—bark, where they subsist upon other subcortical insects.

Odacantha melanura, a narrow, cylindrical species, with head and thorax bluish-green, and reddish elytra and legs (the apex of the former, and joints and feet of the latter, being blue-black), is found in the stems of reeds in the Cambridgeshire fens and elsewhere; *Drypta dentata*, occasionally taken in some numbers out of clay-banks at Alverstoke, Hants, is conspicuous for its lovely, silky, azure clothing, and the very long basal joint of its antennæ; and *Lionychus quadrillum*, an obscure little bronze-black insect, with two dull lighter-coloured spots on each wing-case, is noteworthy from its haunting wet shingle and stones on the coast, in Devonshire and at Southend.

The species most likely to have been seen by casual observers is the tiny *Blechrus maurus*, which may be noticed darting rapidly over sun-dried pathways, reminding one of an animated grain of gunpowder; and the one which has made most noise in the world is the 'Bombardier,' *Brachinus crepitans*, a moderately small rusty-red fellow, with dull blue-black wing-cases, and a narrow head and thorax (Plate I., Fig. 3). It is abundant on the south coast, especially under chalk, on the banks of the Thames below Gravesend; where, in the month of August, a dozen may be found under one stone, the explosion of whose 'stern-chase' guns sounds like a Lilliputian battery. The noise is caused by a peculiar fluid secreted by the insect, which, being emitted from its lower extremity, volatilizes on coming into contact with the atmosphere. On being irritated, the Bombardiers will repeat their rear-volleys for some few times, but with diminishing noise; the substance emitted by some of the exotic species belonging to the tribe is of a very corrosive nature.

CHAPTER X.

THE HYDRADEPHAGA, OR AQUATIC CARNIVOROUS BEETLES.

Sub-section 2. HYDRADEPHAGA, *M'Leay*.

THE members of this sub-section, the predaceous Water-beetles, are the aquatic representatives of the *Geodephaga*, exhibiting, in many respects, a similarity of structure, with modifications adapted to the change of element. Their body is nearly always smooth, depressed or ovate, with a continuous outline; the parts not being conspicuously separate, but for the most part fitting into each other closely. The eyes do not project; the antennæ are mostly slender, and, with the front and middle legs (which are close to each other), pack securely against the body. The hinder legs are removed from the middle pair, so as to allow of an extended "fore and aft" movement in rowing; they are, in nearly all, strong, broad, and shallow—their width being in a transverse direction, —and strongly fringed with hairs on the inner side. The hinder coxæ are much enlarged, and soldered to the metasternum, thus allowing a greater internal surface for the attachment of the propelling muscles (Fig. 10, *dd*; p. 35).

The mentum is emarginate, and, in nearly all the species, strongly toothed in the middle; the ligula horny, quadrate, with the paraglossæ soldered to its sides; the palpi are mostly thread-like; the maxillæ are fringed on the inner side; the scutellum is either very small, or not visible: the basal joints of the front tarsi are widened in the males, and all the species have stout and large wings.

Their larvæ are also aquatic, and very predaceous; they are mostly elongate, somewhat cylindrical, and tapering to the tail, and with a broad head armed with two strong, pointed jaws. They generally construct hollow cells in banks of ponds, &c., and turn into pupæ underground, near their native element.

Our species may be divided into four families, the *Haliplidæ, Pelobiidæ, Dytiscidæ,* and *Gyrinidæ.*

Of these, the HALIPLIDÆ form a good connecting link with the *Bembidiina* in the *Geodephaga,* their legs not being widened, and formed for swimming, as in the other *Hydradephaga,* but thin, slender, and adapted for walking; indeed, the species—though of aquatic habits—swim but feebly, frequenting woods, &c., and running readily, with an *alternate* motion of the legs. The basal joints of their front tarsi, also, are not dilated in the males, a character found in some of the *Bembidiina,* and very rare in the *Hydradephaga,* some members of which afford, perhaps, the greatest known development of this structure. Their head is not so sunk in the thorax as in the majority of their allies; and, lastly, in the genus *Haliplus,* the apical joint of the palpi is very small and needle-pointed, as in *Bembidium.*

Their antennæ are ten-jointed, and the coxæ of the hinder legs not enlarged in front, but produced behind into a semicircular flat plate, which in *Haliplus* covers three (and in *Cnemidotus* six) segments of the abdomen.

They are all small, ovate, and convex; mostly light yellow in colour, varied with obscure darker patches. One species, *Brychius elevatus*, is more elongate and flatter than the rest, and is also more distinctly marked; it has strong longitudinal ridges on its elytra, and long straggling legs, and may be found in running streams, clinging to stones and weeds. Another, *Haliplus obliquus* (Plate III., Fig. 4), is prettily spotted; it occurs in stagnant water.

The PELOBIIDÆ, represented by one species, *Pelobius tardus* (*Hermanni*) (Plate III., Fig. 5), have the antennæ eleven-jointed, the hinder coxæ not produced into a plate, but enlarged in front, the scutellum distinct, tarsi all five-jointed, the head stretched out, and the legs adapted more for walking than swimming. This insect, commonly known as "the Squeaker" (about half an inch long, convex, dull black and red in colour), is found somewhat plentifully in stagnant ponds near London, clinging to weeds, and grovelling in mud; it makes a sharp noise by rubbing the hard reflected margin of the last segment of its abdomen in a groove under each wing-case.

The DYTISCIDÆ have the antennæ eleven-jointed, glabrous and shining, the maxillæ with two lobes, the inner or *lacinia* being curved at the extremity and acuminate, and the hind coxæ very large, soldered with, and appearing part of the metasternum, reaching the margin of the elytra when closed; the posterior legs are modified for swimming by the tibiæ and tarsi being furnished with swimming hairs, and being broadened and flattened; the posterior tarsi are always five-jointed, and the anterior and middle pairs either four or five-jointed.

Dr. Sharp, in his most valuable monograph of the Dytiscidæ (published in the Transactions of the Royal Dublin Society, 1880-2), divides the family into two great divisions, the *Dytisci fragmentati* and the *Dytisci complicati*.

In the former of these divisions the episterna of the metathorax do not reach the middle coxal cavity; it contains two British genera, *Laccophilus* and *Noterus*, which have no visible scutellum, and in some points appear to bear a relation towards the Gyrinidæ, their hind legs being much thickened. *Noterus*, also, has the antennæ short, and much thickened; being, moreover, of a somewhat similar build to *Gyrinus*, and having similar "jerky" habits. Species of both genera, also, occur in brackish water, a habitat of some of the *Gyrini*.

The second division, the *Dytisci complicati*, is by far the largest and most important; it is characterized by the fact that the episterna of the metathorax reach the middle coxal cavity; in the tribe *Hydroporina* all our species have the anterior and intermediate tarsi four-jointed, whereas in all the other members of the division they are five-jointed.

The HYDROPORINA are all small, with no visible scutellum, only four joints to the front and middle tarsi (often much widened) and the posterior coxæ enlarged in front. Some gaily-spotted species (*Hydroporus rivalis*, Plate III., Fig. 3) are found in running waters, but the majority frequent ponds and lakes. Many have pubescent elytra; and the surface is usually bright in the males and dull in the females, a character also found in many *Geodephaga*.

Hyphydrus ovatus, common near London, affords a good link to *Pelobius*, on account of its globose form, and the basal joints of its tarsi being very long, as well as wider than the apical joints. Fresh specimens of this insect have been noticed to have a smell something like that of honey.

The characters of the other tribes need not here be discussed; they are closely related, and have by many authors been classed together. In the genera *Dytiscus*, *Cybister*, *Hydaticus*, and *Acilius*, the three basal joints of the front tarsi in the males assume the form of a round sucker, fringed with hairs, with little cups on the under side; and in the first and last, also, the females have the wing-cases deeply furrowed longitudinally, the furrows reaching in *Dytiscus* halfway down, and in *Acilius* to the apex of the elytra. These two peculiarities of structure are evidently to assist the sexes in pairing. The females of *Dytiscus* are, however, sometimes found without these dorsal furrows; and somewhat analogous instances of what is termed "sexual di-morphism" occur rather frequently in the genus *Hydroporus*, &c.

The true *Dytisci* are well known, being "*the* Water-beetles" of the aquarium. They are large, olive-brown, with a yellowish side-band, and very rapacious, attacking all that comes in their way. They swim rapidly, diving with great quickness, and may be often seen at the surface of the water, with their tail upwards, taking in air, which thus reaches the spiracles. *D. punctulatus* (Plate III., Fig. 1) is entirely black beneath.

When ponds, &c., are dried up in the summer, the *Dytiscides* take to the wing, flying by night or at the evening in search of fresh waters; it is astonishing, however, with what a small supply of damp they will exist, and the greatest "hauls" of specimens are often made out of the merest cupful of muddy water, the residue of some large pond, in which all the beetle occupants are congregated. They have been known, in flight, to dash against glass or lights, possibly mistaking them for water.

Water-beetles, as a rule, are fond of gathering round reeds and water-plants in the middle of ponds; and, in dragging for them, the net should be scraped along banks, round any projecting wood or stones, and through and under weeds. After doing so, it is a good plan to go over the same water again, in a reverse direction, as many specimens get dislodged, but not captured, by the first operation. In running streams, the beetles often congregate in little pools caused by eddies and backwaters, and shelter themselves on the quiet sides of arches. To show how readily they fly, it may be remarked that holes in gravel pits, when converted into pools by heavy rain, are soon tenanted by the large *Dytisci*.

The species of *Dytiscus* exhibit a great family likeness, but are separated chiefly through the greater or less width, length, and sharpness of the forked processes of the coxæ at the base of the two hinder legs. They are mostly found in stagnant waters, but many of their allies delight in running streams, and these latter are usually more metallic and variegated with light spots (*Agabus maculatus*, Plate III., Fig. 2).

The larva of the common *D. marginalis* (Fig. 1,

p. 17) is, when full-grown, about two inches long, dirty brown in colour, and tapering to the tail, which is provided with two thin appendages fringed with hairs. The larva suspends itself in the water, head upwards, with these appendages at the surface, and thus obtains air; for the ordinary breathing-holes on the sides are closed up, and the air-vessels are reached by means of two spiracles at the apex of the eleventh segment near the fringed extremity. Its head is large and oval, with composite eyes (Fig. 1 *a*, p. 17), rudimentary antennæ, and very long, sickle-shaped, pointed jaws, which are channelled so as to allow the larva to extract the juices of its prey, there being no opening at the mouth. It is very rapacious, and is often called the " Fresh-water Shrimp."

Cybister, reputed British, has its wing-cases widened behind, and not furrowed in the female. *Acilius sulcatus*, a moderately large, common, flat, grey species, has been observed to make a considerable humming noise, apparently produced by the action of the air upon the *alulæ* or winglets, two small circular membranous plates at the base of the elytra (Fig. 8 *h*, p. 33).

The GYRINIDÆ differ vastly in structure from all the above. They have four eyes; two on each side, one above and one below (Plate III., Fig. 6ᵃ); the ordinary single eye being divided by the cup formed for the articulation of the antennæ: the palpiform outer lobe of their maxillæ is wanting, except in the genus *Gyrinus*, where it is extremely small, slender, and rudimentary; their antennæ are short, robust, and stiff, the second joint being very large and ear-like, with the third and remaining joints jammed together

G

and inserted in its middle (Plate III., Fig. 6ᵇ). The anterior legs are long and slender, and the intermediate and hinder pair close together, removed from the front, and extremely compressed, with the femora, tibiæ, and basal joint of the tarsi very broad and triangular (Plate III., Fig. 6ᶜ). The *Gyrini*, commonly known as "water-fleas," "whirlwigs," or "whirligigs," may be seen in fine weather forming endless "figures of 8" on the surface of both running and still waters. They are small, metallic, shining black, elongate beetles, exceedingly wary and quick in their movements, and with a power of exuding a very nasty-smelling acrid milky fluid, from nearly all parts of the body apparently, when handled. This fluid is analogous to that secreted by some *Geodephaga*, which it resembles in evil odour. The female lays small cylindrical eggs, end to end, in level rows, on water-plants, the larvæ proceeding from which are very peculiar, being narrow and flattened, with a long slender filament rising out of each side of all the segments except those bearing the legs. These filaments act as air-conductors, and give the animal the look of a Centipede. When full-grown, it ascends water-plants, and forms a small oval cocoon, of a substance like grey paper, in which it assumes the pupa state.

Gyrinus bicolor (Plate III., Fig. 6), the narrowest and most elongate of our "whirlwigs," is found plentifully in brackish water at Southend, and elsewhere on the coast.

Orectochilus villosus, one of this family, differs from the others in being hairy: it is supposed to be less gregarious than the true *Gyrini*, though instances occur when it is found in great numbers. Unlike the light-loving whirlwigs, it hides itself in banks by day, and mostly performs its evolutions on the water by dark. Its larva forms a white silky cocoon, which has been found under willow-bark, and in a fresh-water shell.

By far the best work on the *Dytiscidæ* is Dr. Sharp's monograph above alluded to (on Aquatic Carnivorous Coleoptera, Trans. Royal Dublin Society, 1880-2). M. Regimbart's monograph of the Gyrinidæ (published in the French Annales for 1883) will also be found of the greatest service to the student of the group.

CHAPTER XI.

THE PALPICORNIA OR HYDROPHILIDÆ.

THE members of this group really form a division of the large section CLAVICORNIA; they may be divided into two sub-families, the *Hydrophilinæ* and the *Sphæridiinæ*.

In the HYDROPHILINÆ (often called *Philhydrida*),—which, with the next family, constitute the *Palpicornes* of the French entomologists,—the palpi are as long as, or longer than, the antennæ, which have from six to nine joints, the basal one being elongate and the apical (usually three) forming a club; the mentum is large and unnotched, the maxillæ terminate in two untoothed lobes, and the mandibles are very short. The tarsi are always five-jointed, and the hinder legs formed for swimming in some species: in short, the members of this family, which are all found either in or about water, and are not carnivorous in the perfect state, are the aquatic representatives of the *Lamellicornia*, and probably of other families. They are fully described by Mulsant, Hist. Nat. des Col. de France; Palpicornes: Paris, 1844.

In *Spercheus emarginatus*, the antennæ are six-jointed; the thorax is narrower than the elytra, and the hind legs are not natatorial. The female makes a small bag containing eggs, which she carries attached to her abdomen, and from which, in about ten days, the larvæ are disclosed; in a few hours another sac being formed. This insect formerly occurred at Whittlesea Mere, but was supposed to have become extinct in England, until it was found in some numbers in 1878, in a ditch adjoining some marshy ground at West Ham, Essex, by Mr. T. R. Billups. It appears to be rare on the Continent, in spite of the fertility of the female. It lives in stagnant water, at the roots of aquatic plants. The larvæ are very voracious, and are cannibals.

In *Helophorus* and its allies the tarsi are not natatorial, and have the first joint very short and often scarcely distinct from the second. Some of them are slightly metallic, and most of the species live either in or close to the water, among stones, &c.; one or two, however, often occur in dry places (*H. rugosus*, Plate VII., Fig. 4). The *Hydrænæ* and their allies, in which the last joint of the maxillary palpi is shorter than the penultimate, frequent stones half immersed in the water or the water-line of muddy banks; the species of the remaining genera living absolutely in the water. One of these, *Hydrophilus piceus*, often seen in aquaria, and known as the "harmless water-beetle," is perhaps the largest British beetle; the female makes a paper-like, pear-shaped sac, containing eggs, which is fixed on some aquatic plants at the surface of the water. The larva is, when full-grown, extremely long and stout, of a leathery texture, wrinkled transversely, and dirty-brown in colour; the head is horny, flat on the upper side, and with strong projecting sharp mandibles; the legs are short, and the body contracts behind, having two openings at the extremity of the last segment, being the terminations of two great lateral tracheal tubes, through which the insect breathes. These larvæ are very voracious, feeding on other insects, &c.; they swim well, bending themselves into an arch, and often placing the head backwards on to the body: when handled, they become flaccid, and emit a fetid black fluid from the end of the abdomen. The pupa is formed in a cell in the wet earth of the banks of ponds.

A smaller species, *Hydrobius fuscipes* (Plate VII., Fig. 5), is very common in stagnant waters.

There is perhaps no group of Coleoptera in which the members vary so much in size: thus *Hydrophilus piceus* is sometimes nearly two inches long, whereas the tiny *Limnebius picinus*, which almost resembles the last-named species in miniature, does not measure one line; the species of *Hydrochus* are distinguished by their elongate form and prominent eyes; one or two of them have the interstices of the elytra rather strongly raised; the *Berosi* are dirty-brown or testaceous insects with the disc of the thorax metallic; they are better swimmers than most of their allies, and by the movement of their abdomen are able to produce a rather strong stridulation; their larvæ are very peculiar, by reason of the very long branchial appendages borne by the first seven abdominal segments: the little shining-black globular *Chætarthria seminulum* is perhaps the only other member of the section worth mention; it is found in damp moss, and is remarkable for having the first and second ventral segments of the abdomen covered by two plates meeting in the middle.

The SPHÆRIDIINÆ are mostly terrestrial in their

habits, though many frequent damp situations; the majority, however, are found in the dung of cattle.

Their tarsi are not natatorial, and have the first joint of the posterior pair much longer than the others; their antennæ have either eight or nine joints, and the second joint of their maxillary palpi is more or less inflated. The species are nearly all very small, black, and convex, being, as a rule, at most variegated with dull red spots. *Cyclonotum*, the largest, is aquatic and very globose; the species of *Sphæridium* and *Cercyon* abound in cow-droppings, &c. The allied *Megasternum* and *Cryptopleurum* are distinguished by their very large prosternum and metasternum; and the former may be known from *Cercyon* by the notch at the apex of the outer edge of its front tibiæ.

CHAPTER XII.

THE STAPHYLINIDÆ, OR "ROVE-BEETLES."

THE *Staphylinidæ*, or "Rove-Beetles" (of which perhaps only one species, the "Devil's Coach-horse," *Ocypus olens*, is known to casual observers), constitute a very large group, and are readily distinguished by their elongate abdomen,—of which usually six or seven entirely horny segments are exposed,—and their extremely short and straightly sutured wing-cases, beneath which the many folds of their ample wings are hidden. The least typical forms have, however, the wing-cases somewhat elongate, and present a considerable likeness to certain of the smaller *Geodephaga*; from which, apart from other characters, the absence of a palpiform lobe to their maxillæ will separate them.

Many of them, especially the larger species, are eminently predatorial; and must on no account be placed in the collecting-bottle with other insects. A great number also (including some of those which attack living insects) are carrion feeders, abounding in the dead bodies of small animals, &c.; very many habitually frequent the dung of our domestic quadrupeds; others swarm in fungi, especially when rotten; and the remainder may be briefly described as living in decaying vegetable matter, or haunting very wet places. Among the exceptions to these habitats, it may be remarked that a few species live under bark, in flowers, in sand or shingle, sometimes beneath the tide-mark, or as parasites upon insects of the order *Hymenoptera*.

Many authors have placed this section at the extreme end of the *Coleoptera*,—either with the idea of a circular system, coming back to the *Geodephaga* at the beginning through *Dromius* and *Homalium*, or wishing to establish a link with the *Dermaptera*, or Earwigs. Such a position, however, if only by removing it from its close ally, the section of *Necrophaga*, seems directly opposed to the natural affinities of its members.

The *Staphylinidæ* (by many authors called *Brachelytra*) are nearly always of an elongate, linear, and flattened shape; rarely convex; moderate in size, the majority being very small, and some exceedingly minute; dull, or slightly metallic in colour, occasionally ornamented with red or yellow spots on the elytra, and but rarely exhibiting bright tints. Some are very polished and destitute of hairs, but the greater part are clothed with a fine short pubescence, which is in a few instances long and thick.

Among the points to be noticed in discriminating between closely allied forms, the following will be found most worthy of attention:—the relative length and width of the joints of the antennæ and tarsi, the degree of punctuation and pubescence, the length of the elytra, the markings (if any) on the thorax, and the sexual characters afforded by the sculpture, &c., of the under side of the terminal segments of the abdomen in the males of very many species.

This sculpture, &c., usually takes the form of a

more or less angulated or deeply impressed notch in the hinder margin of the last segment but one, which notch is in some families much increased, and armed with lateral teeth, &c., on the ante-penultimate segment; the greater part of the lower surface of the abdomen being sometimes affected by somewhat similar alterations of structure, and in a few cases adorned with curls of hairs.

In some of the smaller species the penultimate segment of the male exhibits a notch, or one or more tubercles or ridges (or both) on its *upper* side.

The tarsi of the *Brachelytra* are for the most part five-jointed, though there are many of them in which the Heteromerous character is reproduced and reversed, the posterior and intermediate tarsi having five joints, and the anterior only four; some also are entirely *four-*, and a few *three-*jointed.

The coxæ, especially of the anterior legs, are much increased in size, and capable of extension from the body; thus allowing considerable freedom of action to those limbs.

Their antennæ are nearly always composed of eleven joints, and filiform, sometimes a little thickened towards the tip, or even slightly clavate; and in one genus, *Micropeplus* (a very aberrant form, which is now often placed near the *Nitidulidæ*), decidedly abruptly knobbed. The basal joint is occasionally elongate, the antennæ then somewhat resembling those of the *Rhynchophora*.

The remark before made, as to the development of the eyes in such species of *Geodephaga* as frequent very wet places, applies also to *Brachelytra* of similar habits; and in the *Homaliidæ*, besides the ordinary compound lateral eyes, there are two small simple eyes, or ocelli, on the back of the head (as in the *Hymenoptera*); *Phlœobium* also has a single ocellus in the same position.

The parts of the mouth are well developed, though not quite so highly as in the *Adephaga*; the labrum very often has a membranous margin, and is sometimes furnished with appendages, or fringed or clothed with hairs; the mandibles vary according to the habits of their possessors, but are often strong, curved, and sharp; the maxillæ have no *galea* or palpiform lobe, and are not toothed at the apex, their palpi being four-jointed, with the apical joint often very small and subulate; the labium is well defined; the ligula being distinct, narrow, and linear, often bifid at the extremity, and with its paraglossæ frequently conspicuous.

The abdomen is often furnished at the apex with two fleshy papillæ, from which a disagreeable odour is emitted when the insect is handled. It is, in nearly all, so long as to be capable of being bent forward and used in arranging the folds of the wings under the elytra. There are usually seven segments distinctly visible on the lower surface, but there is also another, by which it is articulated to the metathorax, and which is only visible on the upper side, when the elytra and wings are removed. In Erichson's descriptions the sixth segment means the last but one, which is termed the seventh by Dr. Kraatz; the latter being in reality correct, though the former *seems* to be right.

The larvæ of the *Brachelytra* somewhat resemble the perfect insects, being of elongate, narrow shape; and are found under similar circumstances. They differ but little in general structure among the different species, and may be distinguished from those of the *Geodephaga* by their mandibles not being toothed on the inner side, their closed-up mouth, the *single* claw at the apex of their tarsi, and their two double-jointed anal forks or "cerci," which are beset with stiff hairs. The extremity of the body is produced into a fleshy tubular support, which often serves as a pro-leg. They are very active and voracious, using their sharp jaws with great effect, and sucking the juices of their prey through them, after the same fashion as the larvæ of the *Hydradephaga*.

Descriptions of the European species of *Brachelytra* are to be found in the works above alluded to (pp. 37, &c.); and an indispensable help to the student of this group is afforded by the "*Genera et Species Staphylinorum*" of Dr. G. F. Erichson (1839-1840). This book contains descriptions, entirely in Latin, of all the then known *Brachelytra*; and is conspicuous for the way in which its lamented author seizes, as if by intuition, upon those characters most useful in comparison, and for the exact application of his varied terms for differences of structure and colour.

The beginner will find the insects of this group difficult both to determine and to set out properly. Care must be taken in mounting them, not to rub off the pubescence, gum the upper side, or distort the parts, as a specimen thus maltreated is additionally hard to make out. They are best set out soon after being killed; and must not be left in laurel, or else their limbs come to pieces very readily on being manipulated. It is necessary to have the abdomen displayed in its proper proportions; and this is no easy matter, as the rings usually contract within each other at the instant of death: the best way to counteract this, is to gum only the head, thorax, and breast on the card at first, and, when these are securely dried (which may be in about a quarter of an hour, or less), to damp the abdomen slightly on its upper and under sides; the setting needle may then be inserted into the opening at the extremity of the body, and the segments gradually and gently pulled out by its slightly hooked point. Another, and less secure way is to drag out all the segments by piercing the last one through its under surface after inserting the point of the needle; but this is apt to destroy or distort the end of the abdomen. In either case the abdomen must not be left with the articulating surfaces of the segments exposed, or unduly elongated; and a good supply of thick gum on each side, after the first gum is dried, is necessary to retain it in its place. Sometimes even a small card brace is required to prevent it from again contracting, or losing its hold on the card.

A level position of the head and thorax is best obtained by placing the two front legs rather backwards than forwards, otherwise the great development of the anterior trochanters often gives trouble in setting.

A specimen of each sex should be mounted on its back, to show the abdominal characters beneath.

The British species of *Staphylinidæ* (upwards of 800 in number) may be considered as divided into sixteen sub-families, viz. the *Aleocharinæ, Tachyporinæ, Habrocerinæ, Trichophyinæ, Staphylininæ, Xantholininæ, Pæderinæ, Evæsthetinæ, Steninæ, Oxyporinæ, Oxytelinæ, Homaliinæ, Proteininæ, Phlœobiinæ, Phlœocarinæ,* and *Piestinæ;* to these may be added with reserve the *Micropeplinæ,* which in many respects bears a closer relation to the Nitidulidæ than to the Staphylinidæ. These families, the members of which (except perhaps in the *Aleocharinæ*) preserve a certain family likeness amongst themselves, are chiefly separated by the place of insertion of their antennæ, by the shape of the coxæ, and by the hidden or conspicuous position of their first (or prothoracic) pair of stigmata or spiracles, which are situated on the under side of the "thorax," behind the coxæ of the front pair of legs.

The ALEOCHARIDÆ, extensive in numbers and puzzling to determine, have the antennæ inserted upon the front, close to the inner anterior margin of the eyes, and the prothoracic spiracles conspicuous. The apical joint of their maxillary palpi is very small and needle-pointed, and the labial palpi have mostly 3, though in some (*Aleochara*) 4, in others (*Autalia, Gyrophæna*, &c.) but 2, and in a few (*Myllæna*, &c.) *no* evident joints.

Their front coxæ are conic and prominent, being only joined to the prosternum at their upper extremity, and the posterior trochanters are somewhat elongate, running along the base of the femur.

Their tarsi vary in the number of joints, having either 5 or 4 or 3 joints to all the feet, or 4 to the front pair and 5 to the intermediate and hinder; and the anterior tarsi are never dilated in the male, which may be known from the other sex generally by the penultimate segment of the abdomen on the upper side having a tubercle or ridge, or an assemblage of tubercles, or a thickened or notched hinder margin. There is, sometimes, in the male a tubercle on the anterior part of the abdomen, and the penultimate segment beneath is often produced in the middle: the antennæ, also, are frequently more elongate and robust.

In habits they are very varied, mostly, however, frequenting decayed vegetable matter. Some species (*Autalia, Bolitochara, Gyrophæna*, &c.) are found in fungi; others (*Ocyusa, Tachyusa, Myllæna*, &c.) haunt very wet places; many (*Ischnoglossa, Phlœopora*, &c.) occur under bark, and some in sandy localities; members of the great genus *Homalota* are found in all these habitats. The true *Aleocharæ* feed in animal matter (hence their name), or in the dung of animals or putrefying seaweed; but perhaps the most curious habit of any of the family is that of parasitism; *Thiasophila, Homœusa, Dinarda, Atemeles, Myrmedonia*, and some *Oxypodæ* and *Homalotæ*, being constantly found in the nests of certain species of ants, and *Haploglossa* in those of the sand-martin.

These Myrmecophilous (or ant-loving) species occur not only in the "runs" and purlieus of the nests, but also in the most inner sanctuaries, where they appear perfectly at home, and are never molested by their multitudinous hosts. The terms of the agreement between these landlords and tenants have never yet been satisfactorily determined; nevertheless, it is certain that the ants must be much attached to the beetles. I have seen *Atemeles emarginatus* (not uncommon in nests of *Formica fusca*) being carried about tenderly in the mouth of an ant much less than itself. This curious species (Plate IV., Fig. 1), like others of its allies, coils itself up almost into a ball; and one is much astonished to see the length of leg and antenna which it unfolds on endeavouring to escape. *Myrmedonia funesta*, abundant in nests of

F. fuliginosa, is strikingly like that ant in appearance; and, with others of its genus, acquires a very pungent odour, from constantly living in an atmosphere impregnated with formic acid. It is possibly from this cause that these species so often stain with purple the card on which they are mounted.

The species of *Ilyobates*, *Callicerus*, &c., are especially remarkable for the development of their antennæ, of which the terminal joint is often of great length in the male. They occur rarely in sand-pits, &c.

Tachyusa constricta, a slender, graceful insect, found in wet shingle on the banks of rivers (especially the Mole, near Leatherhead), has a peculiar appearance, owing to its very "pinched-in" waist; when alive, like the greater part of this family, it curls its abdomen upwards and forwards, and runs with great quickness. Perhaps, however, the most curious instance of this curling propensity is afforded by *Encephalus complicans*, a small black species found in rotten fungi, &c., and about as unlike the insect last mentioned as possible, being extremely "squab" and flat: it is not very common, and may be easily passed over by a novice, on account of its turning its abdomen entirely over its back, and thus (when not in motion) looking more like a small black seed than a beetle. The species of *Gyrophæna*, minute bright-coloured insects, also occurring (gregariously) in fungi, and very closely allied to *Encephalus*, have a similar habit, though in a rather less degree: they are difficult to determine, but may generally be distinguished *inter se* by the rows of punctures on the thorax. Full English descriptions of our species, by Mr. G. R. Waterhouse, are to be found in the Transactions of the Entomological Society of London, 3rd series, vol. i. (1861).

The genera *Oxypoda* and *Homalota*, comprising many small species, and very troublesome to beginners, exhibit a considerable likeness to each other: the former may, however, be known by all its tarsi being five-jointed (the front tarsi in *Homalota* having only four joints); the more elongate basal joint of its hind tarsi (except in the instance of *Homalota gregaria*, which has a similar formation in that respect); its usually more convex form and stouter antennæ; and the greater sinuation of the hinder margin of its elytra.

Diglossa and *Oligota* have only four joints to all the tarsi; the former genus is remarkable for its very long maxillary palpi; it is found among shingle, often below high-water mark, like the very curious little *Actocharis Readingii;* in *Deinopsis* the tarsi are all three-jointed; the last-mentioned genus, together with *Myllæna* and *Gymnusa*, are much contracted behind, and clothed with a short, more or less dense, silky pubescence; in *Myllæna* the labial palpi are long and slender, and apparently without joints.

Full descriptions of the British *Homalotæ* will be found in Dr. Sharp's revision of the British species, published in the Entomological Society's Transactions for 1869: the *Myllænæ* are the subject of an essay by the Rev. A. Matthews, which will be found in the " Cistula Entomologica" (September, 1883, Part xxvii.).

The TACHYPORINÆ (so named on account of their rapid movements) are composed of usually bright-

H

coloured species, found principally in fungi, moss, or dung, and considerably contracted at both extremities, especially behind, the front being more obtuse. The abdomen is usually elongate and pointed; but, when the insects are dead, the segments run up frequently, as in a telescope, so that it is by no means easy to preserve the correct facies of the insect in a dried specimen. The best way in mounting them is to put gum arabic (with which a little white sugar has been melted) *under* the tail; and, as soon as that is dry, gum the entire last segment over with tragacanth, keeping the abdomen from contracting (if you can) with a card brace. They should *not* be dried quickly.

Their antennæ are inserted towards the hinder part of the side margin of the forehead, before the eyes, and the prothoracic spiracles are conspicuous on removing the front coxæ. Their maxillary palpi have the apical joint subulate in some species; and the antennæ are filiform and eleven-jointed in most, but ten-jointed and thickened in one genus, *Hypocyptus*, comprised of very small shining globular insects, which have somewhat the appearance of the *Agathidia*, in the next section. The legs are usually spiny, and the tarsi have five joints in all except *Hypocyptus*, which has but four. The anterior tarsi are widened at the base in the male, and both sexes often exhibit very striking characters at the apex of the abdomen, both on the upper and under sides.

The *Tachini*, moderately large, flat, and stout-looking (but fragile), abound in rotten fungi and dung, being also often taken at the fermenting sap of cut-down trees.

They present admirable characters for specific diagnosis in the very pronounced teeth and notchings of the upper and under sides of the sub-apical segment of the abdomen, which is different in the two sexes. In order to obtain a clear outline of this structure, it is as well to remove the extreme apical segment of specimens showing the upper and under surface of each sex.

The species of *Tachyporus*, small, shining, flattish, and more or less yellow marked with black, exhibit somewhat similar sexual characters. They are difficult to determine, owing to their want of punctuation, and are generally abundant in moss and wet places. The *Bolitobii*, gaily coloured (Plate IV., Fig. 2, *Bolitobius atricapillus*) and very active species, occur in profusion in fungi in the autumn. English descriptions of all our species will be found in the first volume of the "Entomologist's Monthly Magazine," by the present writer. Lastly, the members of the genus *Mycetoporus*, smaller and narrower than the *Bolitobii*, are found sometimes in moss, but more usually in sand-pits, &c., during the early spring. The position and number of certain deep punctures on the elytra and sides and front of the thorax will assist in determining the species of this genus.

The TRICHOPHYINÆ and HABROCERINÆ (containing respectively the genera *Trichophya* and *Habrocerus*) are conspicuous from their hair-like antennæ, which are adorned with slender rings of hairs, resembling microscopic *Equisetum* : *Trichophya pilicornis* is found plentifully in the corridors of the Crystal Palace at Sydenham, whither it flies from its haunts among the fir-trees at Shirley, &c.

A useful monograph of the group has been published by M. Pandellé in the French Annales (1869, p. 261).

In the STAPHYLININÆ the antennæ are situated at the anterior margin of the forehead, but differ somewhat in position in the two tribes into which the subfamily may naturally be divided, viz. the *Quediina* and the *Staphylinina;* the anterior coxæ are large and conical; the trochanters of the hind legs are prominent; the tibiæ, at least the intermediate and posterior pairs, are spinose; the antennæ are eleven-jointed, and the tarsi five-jointed; and the hind body is more or less strongly margined, and is, as a rule, capable of being raised by the insect into a perpendicular position, or even curled over towards the head.

The *Quediina* are distinguished by having the prosternum connected with the sides of the thorax behind the anterior angles which are consequently free; the antennæ are inserted at the front of the side margin of the head; the eyes are very often large and prominent, and the thorax is smooth and glabrous, and has very few dorsal punctures, those that exist being situated for the most part on the anterior portion: the latter character will separate them from the majority of the *Philonthi*, to which they present a certain resemblance, and they may further be distinguished by having the sides of the thorax simple (with no marginal line) and more rounded. *Euryporus* has the third joint of the labial palpi hatchet-shaped (the enlargement being more evident in the male), and the head small and somewhat ovate; it is very rare, and occurs occasionally in moss, often in and near waterfalls; the palpi of *Astrapæus* resemble those of *Euryporus*; this species was formerly reputed as British, but is now omitted from our lists.

Acylophorus, taken under cut reeds, &c., at Merton, Surrey, by Dr. Power, is conspicuous as well from its rarity as the band of orange-red colour near the apex of its abdomen, the elongate basal joint of its antennæ, and its cylindrical anterior tarsi, of which the apical joint is as long as the four preceding, and armed with strong claws; the posterior tarsi having the basal joint the longest, and the apical with small claws.

The species of *Heterothops* closely resemble the smaller *Quedii*, from which they may be known by the subulate apical joint of their palpi. They are found at the bottoms of haystacks, under seaweed, &c.

Quedius comprises several species, of varied habits and sizes, and is by many authors divided into two sections; the first having the part of the prosternum behind the anterior coxæ horny, and the second having the same part membranous. The size and position of the eyes presents, however, a better character for the separation of the genus; the number of punctures in the dorsal rows of the thorax (never exceeding three in each) also assists in separating these insects. *Q. dilatatus*, a very large, broad, black species, with slightly iridescent abdomen and serrated antennæ, is found occasionally in hornets' nests, and also in the burrows of the larva of the goat-moth, being evidently parasitic in its habits. Another (and much smaller) species, *Q. brevis*, with red elytra, tail, antennæ, and legs, is of similar social propensities, being found in ants' nests. *Q. lateralis*, next in size to *Q. dilatatus*, found in rotten fungi and dung in the autumn, is shining-black, with the reflexed side-margins of its elytra yellowish. *Q. truncicola, cruentus* (Plate IV., Fig. 3), *scitus*, and *lævigatus*, are all subcortical species; the latter, a flattened, polished insect, occurs under pine-bark in Scotland; it has lately been referred by Dr. Sharp to a new genus, *Quedionuchus*.

The remaining species (with the exception of the little *Q. auricomus*, conspicuous from its abdomen being striped with rows of fine golden or silvery pubescence, and which is found in wet moss, &c., near or *in* waterfalls) offer no peculiarity of structure or habit: they are mostly dull in colour, though sometimes having red elytra, and occur in moss, haystacks, dead leaves, dung, &c.

The *Staphylinina* have the prosternum connected with the sides of the thorax at the anterior angles which are not free; the antennæ distant at the base and inserted in front, within the base of the mandibles; and the thorax with a lateral marginal line, both on the upper and under side. Their mandibles are generally large, the maxillary palpi filiform, the ligula small and rounded, entire in *Philonthus*, but emarginate in the other genera, and with the paraglossæ always long. The males are usually known by their larger heads and dilated anterior tarsi, and by the penultimate segment of their abdomen being slightly notched on the under side. The different species are found under stones, in dung, carrion, or decaying vegetable matter, or flying in the hot sunshine.

Creophilus maxillosus, a common large carnivorous insect, may often be seen in dead animals. It runs rapidly and flies strongly, and is elegantly mottled with short grey pubescence; the head and mandibles sometimes attaining a very large size in the males (Plate IV., Fig. 4). A variety (*ciliaris*, Leach) with golden-brown hairs is found sometimes in Scotland.

The very rare *Emus hirtus*, so thickly clothed with long yellow hairs as to look somewhat like a humble-bee on the wing, flies in the hot sunshine, and has been captured in cow-droppings, where it is supposed to feed on dung-loving beetles; it has been found chiefly in the New Forest.

The true *Staphylini* are (with the exception of *S. cæsareus*, which may often be seen settling on hot pathways in the spring) of rare occurrence, and have mostly red wing-cases, their abdomen being often adorned with golden spots. *S. erythropterus*, found in the north of England, closely resembles the above-mentioned *S. cæsareus*, from which it may be known by its golden-haired scutellum. *S. fulvipes* is a cyaneous insect, with conspicuous bands of silvery-yellow pubescence at the base of the sixth and seventh segments of the hind body. *Ocypus* contains several large (and mostly black) species, one of which, *O. olens*, is well known, being *the* " Devil's Coach-horse" *par excellence*. This rapacious monster, of fetid smell, with extended jaws, elevated head, and turned-up tail (from which two yellowish vesicles protrude), may often be seen in pathways or gardens; its larva seems to be equally savage, having somewhat similar habits to that of *Cicindela*, and not sparing even its own species. The perfect insect is quite fearless, and will seize upon anything, however large, that is placed in its path. The pupa appears to have a fringe of long hairs on the front of its thorax. *O. cyaneus* is of a beautiful cyaneous-blue colour; it is extremely rare, but a few specimens have been taken in Sherwood Forest, near Newark-on-Trent, Colchester, and other places.

Two species of this genus, *morio* and *compressus*, are distinguished by the want of any inner tooth to their mandibles, which are simply sickle-shaped.

The great number of *Philonthi*, black or brassy insects, with the elytra sometimes spotted or suffused with red, are divided into sections, characterized by the longitudinal row of punctures on each side of the middle of the thorax; those of the first section having the disk smooth, and the others increasing from two rows of three punctures each, until the thorax is entirely thickly punctured, with the exception of a smooth middle line. Some little caution, however, is required in separating specimens by this character, as there are sometimes irregular punctures, interfering with the proper dorsal rows, and often not alike on both sides.

The XANTHOLININÆ have the prothoracic spiracles as in the *Staphylinidæ*; but their antennæ are inserted before the base of the mandibles, and are not more distant from each other than they are from the eyes. The species are mostly very long and narrow, with the basal joint of the antennæ elongate (whereby the antennæ become elbowed, as in the *Rhyncophora*), the middle legs rather longer than the others, and the elytra uneven and rather lapped over at the suture; the genus *Othius*, however, has the antennæ of the usual structure and the suture straight.

The members of this family are found in moss,

decaying vegetable matter, sand-pits, &c.,—one species, *Leptacinus formicetorum*, occurring in ants' nests; and they are not conspicuous for variety of colour, being at most black, slightly relieved by yellow or red.

The species of *Xantholinus* have a peculiar habit of curling (or rather "doubling") themselves up in reposo, their linear shape and free joints allowing numerous angular bends; their head is very elongate, not contracted at the base, with small eyes placed near the front, which is deeply furrowed and connected with the thorax by a small cylindrical neck, and they may generally be separated by the dorsal punctuation of the thorax, which varies considerably in amount and degree. A variety (with the thorax entirely reddish) of the prettiest species, *X. tricolor*, occurs not rarely at the seaside in the south; and the type-form,—which is rufo-testaceous, with the head, base of the thorax, and the abdomen pitchy,—has been taken under refuse in Scotland, where (and, indeed, all over the country, also) *Baptolinus alternans*, a flat, broad-headed, gaily-coloured insect, is found under bark.

Xantholinus fulgidus (Plate IV., Fig. 5), a shining-black species, with bright red elytra, lives in hotbeds, vegetable refuse, dead wood, &c.

Nudobius lentus, a somewhat depressed species, with bright testaceous-red elytra, is found very rarely in Scotland under bark of Scotch fir.

The PÆDERINÆ have the prothoracic spiracles hidden, and the antennæ inserted under the apex of the lateral margin of the forehead; the space behind the anterior coxæ is membranous, and the posterior coxæ are conic.

Their maxillary palpi are more or less elongate, with the apical joint subulate or pointed and very small; the labrum and ligula both bilobed (the apex of the latter being tridentate in *Scopæus*), the apical joint of the labial palpi small and pointed, and the paraglossæ linear and ciliated on the inner side. The mandibles are slender, sharp, and long; the head either attached to the thorax by a slender neck, or distinctly pedunculated; and the tarsi, which are all five-jointed, have the fourth joint simple, except in *Pæderus* and *Sunius*, where it is bilobed.

The species of *Pæderus* are all very brightly coloured;—red, bluish- or greenish-black, and yellow, in sudden contrast, being their usual tints; and they are especially noteworthy for the very deep notching of the penultimate segment of the abdomen beneath in the male.

P. caligatus (Plate IV., Fig. 6), hitherto exceedingly rare, has recently been found in profusion in very wet mossy places on Wimbledon Common.

Lathrobium comprises certain elongate, flattish, marsh-loving insects (some, also, occurring in sand-pits), of which the most gaily coloured have merely half the elytra stained with red, and which afford no subject of remark, except that good characters for their specific discrimination are to be found in the notching, &c., of the under surface of the penultimate abdominal segment in the males.

Achenium, found in the cracks of mud-banks and under stones, has a wide, but very thin body, eminently adapted to its habitat; and a departure from the normal form of antenna, in this family, is afforded by the light-footed *Cryptobium fracticorne* (in which the basal joint is much elongated), found in thick wet moss.

The species of *Stilicus*, living in dead leaves and moss, present a considerable family-likeness to each other, on account of their slender long legs, and dull head and thorax, the former of which is wide and orbiculate, and separated by a neck from the latter, which is narrowed in front. The males in this genus exhibit strong differences, as in *Lathrobium*; and the coloration of the apex of the elytra and legs assists materially in making out the species, one of which only, the "red neck" (*S. fragilis*), departs from a level obscurity of tone.

The EVÆSTHETINÆ have usually been associated with the *Steninæ*; they are, however, distinct by reason of the posterior coxæ being contiguous, and by having the antennæ inserted under the sides of the front; the tarsi, also, are four-jointed; the species of our single genus *Evæsthetus* are exceedingly small dark-red or reddish-black insects, which are found in marshy places, at roots of grass, in flood refuse, haystack refuse, &c.

The STENINÆ have the antennæ inserted between the eyes or at the anterior margin of the forehead; the anterior coxæ minute, and the posterior conic and widely separated; the basal joint of the maxillary palpi elongate, and the apical joint so small as to be scarcely perceptible; the paraglossæ membranous, soldered to the ligula in *Dianoüs*, and free, with rounded ends in *Stenus*; and the tarsi five-jointed.

They live in wet places for the most part, sometimes occurring in the water itself; *Dianoüs cœrulescens*

(Plate V., Fig. 1) being taken under stones and in moss in waterfalls, &c.

The quadrate mentum, longer antennæ, smaller eyes, and finer punctuation of this species, added to the long styles at the extremity of its abdomen, at once distinguish it from any of the *Steni*, to some of which it bears considerable resemblance.

Stenus (in which the ligula with the paraglossæ and labial palpi are so slightly articulated to the mentum, which is triangular, that, when suddenly killed, they are often thrust out adhering to the end of the gullet, and form a kind of proboscis) comprises a great number of species, of great family-likeness, owing to their cylindrical shape, strong punctuation, dull colour, and prominent eyes; in the latter point affording another instance of the remark before made as to a similar development in water-frequenting *Coleoptera*. They are divided into two sections, in which the fourth joint of the tarsi is respectively simple or bilobed; and these are again formed into subdivisions, having the abdomen (seven segments of which are distinctly exposed) either with or without a lateral marginal ridge. Some of the species in both sections are also spotted on the elytra, and the males exhibit good distinctive characters in the notching, &c., of the terminal segments beneath;—*S. providus*, var. *Rogeri*, having a strong row of curled yellow hairs turned inwards, on each side of the middle of the lower surface of the abdomen, besides certain notches and elevations at the apex.

Those with bilobed tarsi are often found crawling slowly on plants, whilst many of the other section run quickly in dry places; *S. Guynemeri*, found in the north and west of England, lives almost (if not entirely) in the water, especially in mountain streams.

English descriptions (by the author of this work) of all our species will be found in the first volume of "The Entomologist's Monthly Magazine."

The OXYPORINÆ, containing the single genus *Oxyporus*, are remarkable for the great development of the last joint of the labial palpi, which is very much dilated and crescent-shaped, giving the palpus the appearance of a stalked cup-moss or fungus; the anterior coxæ are prominent and conical, and the intermediate pair are very widely separated; the tarsi are all five-jointed.

Oxyporus rufus (Plate V., Fig. 2) is conspicuous for its robust build, bright colours, sharp elongate jaws, and the large size of the head in the male; it is found in fungi, eating transverse galleries through the "gills" on the lower side, and runs with great swiftness.

The OXYTELINÆ have the prothoracic spiracles difficult to perceive on account of the prominence of the sides of the thorax; the antennæ (which are more or less elbowed, on account of the elongation of the basal joint) inserted under the elevated lateral margin of the forehead; the thorax beneath membranous behind the anterior coxæ, which are elongate, subconic, and prominent, the posterior pair being transverse; the posterior trochanters small; the ligula membranous, with the paraglossæ either soldered to it or entirely absent (*Oxyporus* and *Bledius*); the apical joint of the maxillary and labial palpi generally subulate; the anterior and intermediate tibiæ spinoso in all except *Trogophlæus*; and the tarsi with only three joints (of which the apical one is much the longest), except in *Coprophilus, Acrognathus, Syntomium,* and *Deleaster,* in which they have five.

The species of *Bledius* are mostly gregarious, frequenting the sea-sands, banks of rivers, sand-pits, &c. They are elongate and cylindrical in shape, as might be expected from their burrowing habits, and have the front tibiæ thickened and strongly spined. In the males of some, the head bears two orect horns, and the thorax also has one in the middle, pointing forwards: these horns are much developed in the large males; but, in the smaller specimens, are of more feeble build. The *Bledii* pass all the stages of their existence in the sand, and are often preyed upon by some of the *Dyschirii (Geodephaga)*; they fly readily towards the evening, and have been observed to remain in their burrows beneath the tide for some time; their presence may easily be detected by the casts which they throw up in making their excavations.

Platystethus has the apical joint of the labial palpi not subulate, and its members (all of which are small, black, and shining) live in dung or the cracks of mud-banks.

The true *Oxyteli* abound in dung, at the fermenting sap of felled trees, under rotten seaweed, &c.; they are all more or less flat, dull-black, with the parts of the body somewhat loosely articulated; the thorax with three longitudinal furrows, and the abdomen shining; the males have the apical segments of the abdomen beneath sinuated, notched, and tuberculated;

the females, also, exhibiting a tendency to similar irregularities.

The species of *Trogophlœus*,—diminutive, cylindrical, dull-black, pubescent insects, with very short tarsi,—occur in mud-banks and wet places, and have usually a deep impression at the back of the thorax. *Syntomium æneum*, a small, metallic, "stumpy" beetle, very strongly punctured and slow of foot, and with three apical joints of its antennæ suddenly thickened, may be found under dead leaves in sand-pits, and also in moss in woods. Lastly, the rare *Acrognathus* and *Deleaster*, larger, rufo-testaceous species, live in very wet places, in rotting leaves at the edges of ponds; the former is very sluggish, and seems swollen with the water in which it soaks, but the latter flies readily, and runs with great swiftness.

The HOMALIINÆ have five-jointed tarsi; the prothoracic spiracles hidden; the thorax membranous beneath, behind the anterior coxæ; the antennæ inserted under the lateral margin of the forehead, which margin is not elevated; the anterior coxæ almost conic and exserted, and the posterior transverse; the maxillæ armed with a horny hook at the apex; the elytra reaching beyond the metathorax, and rounded at the outer hinder corners; and two ocelli on the middle of the head. They are mostly somewhat depressed, with long, slender antennæ; and live in wet places, under seaweed, stones, and bark, and in flowers.

The species of *Anthophagus*, *Geodromicus*, and *Lestera*, on account of their long slender legs, long elytra, and somewhat heart-shaped thorax, present considerable resemblance to certain of the smaller

Lebiina in the *Geodephaga;* and one of the former genus, *A. alpinus*, has the head of the male (which sex is very rare) enlarged, with a spine on each side in front, and strong, curved, prominent mandibles.

Acidota, found under pine-bark and in moss, has very stoutly built legs, and spiny tibiæ; the species, also, are somewhat larger, linear and shining. *Olophrum* and *Lathrimæum*, on the contrary, are convex and short; and the little black *Micralymma brevipenne*, with very short elytra, is noteworthy from living far below high-water mark on the coast in all its stages. *Eupshalerum* and *Anthobium* sometimes abound in flowers, the latter occurring on *Umbelliferæ* in woods, and the former in primroses.

The species of *Homalium*, in which the four basal joints of the tarsi are equal, and scarcely so long as the apical joint alone, are varied in habits; many are found under bark, others in flowers, some at sap, or in marshy places, and one or two in profusion under decaying seaweed. *H. planum* (Plate V., Fig. 3) is, perhaps, as good a type of a subcortical insect as could be seen.

The PROTEININÆ are closely allied to the *Homaliinæ*, but differ in having no ocelli on the vertex of the head; the anterior coxæ are transverse, sublinear, and scarcely prominent (somewhat like those of the Nitidulidæ), and the posterior are large and transverse; the antennæ are eleven-jointed, and all the tarsi five-jointed; the paraglossæ are distinct, and in *Megarthrus* longer than the ligula.

The species of *Proteinus*, which are very small, flattish-oval, and black, are found in rotten fungi, &c., often in great numbers; they may be distinguished *inter se* by their antennæ, of which the basal portion varies in the number of its light-coloured joints.

The *Megarthri*, living in fungi, under bark, and in vegetable refuse, have the thorax deeply channelled and notched at the sides and hinder angles; the hinder and intermediate femora and tibiæ are also more or less curved, thickened or toothed in the males.

The PHLŒOBIINÆ are very closely allied to the preceding sub-family, but differ in having a single ocellus on the vertex of the head. *Phlœobium clypeatum* (Plate IV., Fig. 4) is a reddish-testaceous insect, found in tufts of grass, &c.; it has similar sexual differences to those found in *Proteinus*.

The PHLŒOCHARINÆ have the prothoracic spiracles hidden; the antennæ inserted under the lateral margin of the forehead; no ocelli; the anterior coxæ conic and prominent, the posterior transverse and the tarsi five-jointed; the thorax membranous beneath, behind the anterior coxæ; and the abdomen widely margined. This sub-family is closely allied to the *Oxytelinæ*, and chiefly differs in the more strongly developed posterior trochanters.

We possess but two genera, each containing a single species: *Phlœocharis subtilissima*, a very small dark-brown, dull-looking insect, with the maxillary palpi subulate, found in dry dead sticks and wood; and *Pseudopsis sulcatus*, occurring rarely in haystacks and vegetable refuse near London, and conspicuous on account of its elongate shape, dull black colour, and very strong longitudinal furrows and elevations.

The PIESTINÆ, represented in England by one genus and species, *Prognatha quadricornis*, have the prothoracic spiracles hidden; the thorax entirely horny below; the anterior coxæ globose, not prominent, and the posterior transverse; the tarsi five-jointed (in our species); and the apical segment of the abdomen inconspicuous.

P. quadricornis (Plate V., Fig. 5) is found under bark, sometimes in considerable numbers; it is elongate, flat, and narrow, pitchy-black and shining, with the elytra, antennæ, legs, and apex of abdomen reddish. In the male the head is much enlarged, the forehead hollowed, with a horn on each side stretching forwards, and the mandibles also armed each with another horn, larger than itself.

Occasionally specimens of the male occur in which these characters are developed to an inordinate extent.

Lastly, if we leave them in this position, the MICRO-PEPLINÆ, also represented by a single genus, have the spiracles hidden and thorax horny, as in the last family; the anterior coxæ not prominent, and the posterior globose; the front and hind legs distant at the base; the tarsi three-jointed; and the antennæ nine-jointed, knobbed, and fitting into grooves.

Their sculpture is very remarkable, the entire upper surface being strongly costated or divided by longitudinal ridges; on account of which, added to their knobbed antennæ and short compact form, they have often been classed among the *Nitidulidæ*, somewhat resembling also certain species of *Onthophilus*.

Micropeplus margaritæ (Plate V., Fig. 6), found—like its congeners—in vegetable refuse, is not uncommon; and *M. tesserula*, the rarest species, may be known by its polished appearance.

CHAPTER XIII.

THE NECROPHAGA, OR CARRION AND BURYING BEETLES AND THEIR ALLIES.

This section must be regarded as more or less artificial, and as adopted for the sake of convenience, rather than as being scientifically accurate; it comprises groups of very different appearance and habits; its members (which feed principally upon decaying animal or vegetable matter) have the antennæ clubbed or incrassate at the apex, sometimes elbowed or with a longer basal joint, and inserted near the mandibles, which are usually strong; the inner lobe of the maxilla is not palpiform; the tarsi are variable; the scutellum large, and the elytra nearly always covering the sides of the abdomen (the apical segments of which are often exposed), and occasionally truncate. It may be regarded as divided into twenty-eight families, the *Leptinidæ, Silphidæ, Scydmænidæ, Clavigeridæ, Pselaphidæ, Trichopterygidæ, Corylophidæ, Sphæriidæ, Phalacridæ, Coccinellidæ, Endomychidæ, Erotylidæ, Colydiidæ, Histeridæ, Nitidulidæ, Trogositidæ, Monotomidæ, Lathridiidæ, Cucujidæ, Byturidæ, Cryptophagidæ, Scaphidiidæ, Mycetophagidæ, Dermestidæ, Byrrhidæ, Georyssidæ, Parnidæ,* and *Heteroceridæ;* but it must be admitted that there is considerable difference of opinion as to the affinities of these insects.

The LEPTINIDÆ are closely allied to the *Silphidæ*, but differ in their long filiform antennæ, small anterior coxæ, and very short metasternum; the eyes are entirely wanting, or are represented by translucent eye-spots. *L. testaceus* is a small, oval, much depressed, dull-testaceous insect, which occurs rarely in dead leaves, rotten wood mould, birds' nests, on small rodents, &c.; it has been found very rarely in nests of the black ant, *Formica fuliginosa*, and in numbers in a humble-bee's nest near Burton-on-Trent.

The SILPHIDÆ exhibit a considerable affinity to the *Staphylinidæ*; having the elytra more or less truncate, with the apex of the abdomen exposed and the coxæ free, the anterior pair being exserted. Their larvæ, also, are much alike, differing principally in the possession of a labrum by those of the *Silphidæ*. They are divided into five tribes, the *Clambina, Anisotomina, Cholevina, Sphæritina,* and *Silphina.*

The *Clambina* have the posterior coxæ very large and laminated, and the tarsi all four-jointed in both sexes; the head is large and transverse, and the edges of the wings are fringed with long hairs, a point which brings the tribe into relation with the *Trichopterygidæ*; it is also closely related to *Agathidium*, as most of the species have the power of rolling their body up into a ball; its members are very minute insects, and are found in hotbeds, at the bottoms of haystacks, &c.; in *Calyptomerus* (*Comazus*) the antennæ are ten-jointed, and the abdomen has six segments, whereas in *Clambus* the former are nine-jointed, and the latter has five segments.

The *Anisotomina* differ from the *Silphina* in having the anterior coxal cavities closed behind, and from both the *Silphina* and *Cholevina* in having the posterior trochanters small and not projecting from the femora; they are also more convex (some, indeed, being quite globular), with short legs and antennæ, the posterior coxæ close together, the tarsi variable in number of joints, and the mandibles with a blunt tooth at the base. They are never found in animal matter, but chiefly in fungi and dead leaves and under rotten bark, being mostly commoner towards the north, and more readily found in the evening about autumn, especially near fir-trees. The males frequently have the hinder femora dilated and toothed, the hinder tibiæ elongated and curved, the basal joints of the front tarsi widened, or the left mandible elongated, hooked, or even bearing a horn; in all these cases, however, individuals of smaller development often exhibit intermediate conditions, sometimes not even differing from the females in these particulars.

The number of joints in the tarsi is very variable: thus, in *Hydnobius* all the tarsi are five-jointed; in *Anisotoma* and *Cyrtusa* the two front pairs have each five joints, and the posterior only four; *Colenis* has the two hinder pairs four-jointed and the anterior five-jointed; and in *Agaricophagus* the front pair are four-jointed, whilst the two hinder pairs have only three joints. All the above genera have the same number of joints in both sexes, but in *Liodes*, *Amphicyllis*, and *Agathidium*, the males have five joints to the two front pairs and four to the hinder pair; the females of *Liodes* and *Agathidium* having either four joints to all the tarsi, or five to the front pair and four to the two hinder pairs,—and of *Amphicyllis*, four joints to all the tarsi. The club of the antennæ, also, varies from five to three joints.

Anisotoma cinnamomea (Plate VI., Fig. 3, male), the largest of the family, is found in truffles, and by sweeping under trees among dead leaves; the species of *Liodes* are not uncommon in the black dust of old fungoid growth on trunks of trees, &c., in the north of England; and the *Agathidia* are conspicuous from their habit of rolling themselves up into black shining balls.

The *Cholevina* are rather small, dull, and finely pubescent insects, occurring gregariously in decaying animal and vegetable matter; they differ from the *Silphina* in having the anterior coxal cavities closed behind; their tibiæ are not armed with spines on the outer side, and their head is short and sunk in the thorax. Our species of *Choleva* (having the antennæ but little clubbed, and with the eighth joint very small) are described in Murray's monograph of the genus *Catops* (Annals and Magazine of Nat. Hist., July, 1856), and the members of the rarer, smaller, and closely allied genus *Colon* (in which the antennæ have the eighth joint nearly as large as the ninth, and the hinder femora of the males are often very strongly and sharply toothed on the lower side) are described by Dr. Kraatz, in the Stettin Ent. Zeit., 1850, and also by M. Tournier in the French Annales, 1863: in this genus the front tarsi are not always widened in the male. The little *Adelops* is conspicuous from its want of eyes; it has but four joints to the anterior tarsi; it lives in rotten vegetable matter, and has been found abundantly in the old moist husks of seed potatoes, when the new crop has been dug in the summer.

The *Sphæritina* have only five free ventral segments to the abdomen; the metallic, *Hister*-like *Sphærites* has the basal joint of the antennæ long, and is found in the north of Scotland, in dead animals, &c.

In the *Silphina* the anterior coxal cavities are open behind, and the abdomen has six free ventral segments. They comprise the well-known "Sexton" or "Burying" beetles, found in dead animals; which, if not too large, they contrive to drag beneath the ground, several individuals of both sexes often uniting in the work, and the females laying their eggs in the buried carcase. Some of them are also occasionally found in fungi, or in decaying fish on the sea-shore. They belong to the genus *Necrophorus*, the largest in size of all the section, and have strongly-clubbed ten-jointed antennæ, being sometimes black, but often adorned with orange-coloured bands (Plate VI., Fig. 1, *N. mortuorum*). They fly strongly, smell somewhat of musk, and exude a fetid black fluid from the mouth. Their larvæ, also carrion-feeders, have cylindrical fleshy bodies and weak legs.

The *Silphæ* are smaller, flat, with less strongly-clubbed eleven-jointed antennæ, and broad, flat, horny, active, strong-legged larvæ.

The SCYDMÆNIDÆ are all extremely small, and more or less pubescent, living in vegetable refuse and muck-heaps: the largest, *Eumicrus tarsatus* (Plate VI., Fig. 2) is common in cucumber frames, &c. They are apterous, with the elytra covering the abdomen (which has six segments); the tarsi five-jointed; the coxæ

conic; the hinder legs widely separated; the maxillary palpi long, and the eyes strongly granulated. Descriptions and figures of most of our species are to be found in Denny's "Monographia Psolaphidarum et Seydmænidarum Britanniæ," 1825, Norwich.

Of the CLAVIGERIDÆ we possess one genus and species, *Claviger foveolatus* (Plate XVI., Fig. 6), found in chalky districts on the south coast and Surrey hills, associated with small yellow ants, whose nests are formed under large stones. It is very small, entirely yellow, shining, eyeless, wingless, sluggish, with short stiff antennæ, and a deep depression in the middle of the abdomen; the tarsi are three-jointed, the first and second joints being very short, and the third long and terminated by a single claw; the ants, with which these insects live, by caressing the tufts of hair which grow on their abdomen, cause the exudation of a fluid; this they swallow greedily, and in return appear to support the Clavigers, which seem to have lost the natural instinct of feeding themselves.

The PSELAPHIDÆ are often considered as belonging to the *Brachelytra*, apparently for the sole reason of their elytra being short. They constitute a very well-defined and most interesting group of small species, especially distinguished by their abbreviated elytra, acute mandibles, prominent granulated eyes, more or less abruptly clubbed antennæ (of which the last joint is very large), elongated and highly-developed maxillary palpi, margined abdomen (nearly all of which is exposed), clavate femora, obsoletely-spurred tibiæ, and usually single-clawed tarsi. They are shining, hard, light-yellow, brown or red in colour, and with a distinct neck to the head. The *Pselaphidæ* have been monographed by Leach, Reichenbach, and Aubé; also by Donny, Norwich, 1825 (with coloured plates).

They are mostly found in moss, damp marshy places, refuse heaps, or ants' nests, and are supposed to feed on *Acari*.

Many curious forms are found in this country; the type genus *Pselaphus* affording two, one of which, *P. Heisii* (Plate XVI., Fig. 4), is of frequent occurrence in moss, and may be known from its allies by its depressed body (which is broadest behind), entire sutural striæ, very long and thin palpi and legs, and long and stout antennæ. Its ally, *P. dresdensis*, is darker, and has a semicircular impressed line at the base of the thorax.

Our species of *Bryaxis* are found in wet marshy places, among moss and reeds, at the sides of rivers, or on the sea-shore under heaps of vegetable matter or stones. They have long antennæ, and are mostly black or dark-brown, having often red elytra, and being sometimes entirely pale; their shape is more convex than that of *Pselaphus*, their dorsal stria abbreviated, and their thorax (which is convex and contracted behind) usually has three large punctuations behind and at the sides. The largest, *B. sanguinea*, has the antennæ very long in the male.

The *Bythini* are much smaller, convex, and with short antennæ, of which the basal joint is much dilated. In the males (which are by far the rarest) the second joint also is subject to a still more considerable increase in volume, assuming in some species an irregular and toothed appearance. The palpi are nearly equal in bulk to the antennæ, the apical joint being strongly hatchet-shaped and more or less elongate. The elytra are always more or less distinctly punctured in this genus, which, with *Bryaxis*, is apterous.

In *Tychus*, the fifth joint of the antennæ is much enlarged in the male.

The species of *Trichonyx* are of considerable rarity, and of (comparatively) large size; they are light testaceous in colour, of more elongate shape, and with the antennæ widely distant at the base instead of approximated, as in the preceding. They have been taken under bark, among black ants in a tree, with yellow ants under stones, and (in greater quantity) from moss.

The *Euplecti* resemble *Trichonyx* in miniature, having the antennæ distant at the base, but they are more linear and less convex, and occur in rotten wood, refuse heaps, cut grass, &c., being, moreover, often taken on the wing.

Three species, *E. nanus* (Plate XVI., Fig. 5), *signatus*, and *Karstenii*, are not uncommonly found together in decaying vegetable matter; and the collector, who has the means of doing so, should not fail to keep a heap of dead leaves, compost, twigs, and cut grass in his garden, as it will be found a constant trap for these and many other species.

The TRICHOPTERYGIDÆ (by far the most minute of all *Coleoptera*, most of them being less than the sixth of a line long) have eleven-jointed antennæ, which are long, very slender, beset with hairs, with a very large basal joint, and an abrupt three-jointed club; their elytra are either truncate behind or cover the abdomen entirely; their wings (which are sometimes rudimentary) are usually twice as long as the body, very narrow, composed of a thin neck and broader plate, fringed with very long closely-planted hairs; their metathorax is very large; their abdomen composed of six or seven segments, of which the first or the last is usually the largest; and their tarsi are composed of three joints, the apical being very long, and having a long hair between its claws. The labrum is usually large and transverse; the mandibles short, arched, sharp at the point, and milled on their outer edge; and the maxillæ have their stem much developed and terminated in two lobes. In some of the genera the posterior coxæ are very much enlarged.

This family has been elaborately monographed by the Rev. A. Matthews (London, 1872), and also, but far less completely, by Dr. Gillmeister (Nuremburg, 1845); the drawings of the minute species, in both these works, are models of what drawings of insects *should* be.

Our species occur under bark, in wet leaves, marshy places, refuse heaps, &c.; and *Trichopteryx atomaria* (one of the largest), a black, flattened, square little insect, may be seen running actively if garden stuff be shaken over brown paper, being often accompanied by the smaller, narrower, more convex, and shining *Ptenidium apicale* (Plate XVI., Fig. 2).

Nossidium pilosellum, the largest of the family, convex, and set with evident hairs, is rare, but occurs in profusion when found, on the surface of decomposing wood; and the species of *Ptinella*, elongate, yellow, flat, with their black folded wings often showing through their elytra, live under bark.

The CORYLOPHIDÆ comprise several minute insects,

which are not conspicuous, except for their small size.

Their head is small and retractile; their antennæ clavate at the apex; their thorax margined at the sides; their elytra wide, generally obtuse at the apex, and not covering the sides of the abdomen; their intermediate coxæ rather—and the posterior very—widely separated; and the first segment of their abdomen large. They approach the *Trichopterygidæ* in having their wings fringed with long hairs, but differ in having the maxillæ unilobed and the tarsi four-jointed.

The species occur in refuse heaps, cut grass, &c., and are difficult to preserve in good condition on account of their small size and feeble structure.

Corylophus cassidioides (Plate XVI., Fig. 1), often abundant on the coast, has its thorax red, and more or less dark in the middle.

The family SPHÆRIIDÆ, consisting of one genus and species, *Sphærius acaroides* (taken in the Cambridge fens), appears also to have certain characters in common with the *Trichopterygidæ*, viz., a large projecting labrum, the antennæ with a suddenly enlarged and ciliated club, and very large triangular posterior coxæ. It differs, however, from the latter in having the abdomen composed of only three segments, and the parts of the mouth (except the labrum) not similarly formed.

S. acaroides is of extremely small size, globose above, black and shining, with its anterior femora strongly toothed; and, as its name imports, resembles certain of the *Acari*, or mites.

The PHALACRIDÆ have their coxæ approximated;

the anterior being globose instead of nearly oval and transverse, and the posterior transverse, semicylindric, and close together, instead of being separated by an elongation of the first ventral segment of the abdomen. Their tarsi, also, have the three basal joints velvety beneath; their palpi are filiform, instead of short; they have two lobes to the maxillæ (as in the *Brachypterina*); and the elytra are convex, covering the whole of the abdomen. Our species are all small, shining, and found chiefly on flowers.

The COCCINELLIDÆ (*Aphidiphagi* of Latreille, and *Securipalpes* of Mulsant) are hemispherical and convex above and flat beneath, with elytra covering the abdomen, and never truncate or punctate-striate; a short transverse thorax, short antennæ, in which the club is three-jointed and flat; the last joint of the maxillary palpi hatchet-shaped; the mandibles bifid at the tip; the labrum broad and laterally rounded; the legs short with contractile tibiæ, and the second joint of the tarsi large and deeply bilobed.

To *Coccinella*,—the principal genus in this family,—belong the numerous insects known generally as "lady-birds" or "lady-cows," so abundant all over the kingdom, but especially in hop-counties and on the coast, and such good friends to us on account of their "blight"-destroying habits, for it is upon *Aphides*, or plant-lice, that these beetles exist, both in their larval and perfect states.

They have been observed in the southern counties to follow the *Aphis* in swarms, unexpectedly making their appearance by thousands, and settling upon every available resting-place; indeed, I have known them to occur in such numbers that it has been necessary to sweep them away from paths and windows. They fly strongly, but are not rapid or strong walkers, and have, both in the condition of larva and perfect insect, a habit of distilling a peculiar and pungent yellow oily fluid, similar to that of certain of the *Chrysomelidæ*, and which, also, has been stated to be a specific for toothache.

Their patches of small yellow eggs can often be seen deposited by the parent insect on plants infested by *Aphides;* and the slaty-blue larvæ, which are tuberculated and spotted, contracted behind, and with six conspicuous legs in front, may be observed crawling about shrubs in gardens or on walls preparatory to the change to pupa, which is fastened by the tail, and does not get rid of the skin of the larva.

The large seven-spot and smaller two-spot ladybirds are well known to all observers; the latter insect is exceedingly variable, specimens of it occurring of every intermediate gradation between red with a rudimentary dot on each elytron to entirely black. Oddly enough, it is extremely difficult to obtain a variety of the first-mentioned beetle.

Some of the species, such as 13-*punctata* and 19-*punctata*, frequent reedy or marshy places; these are more elongate than the rest, and, when alive, of a pinkish tone, with many spots. Others, *obliterata* (bearing an M-like mark on its thorax), *hieroglyphica* (varying to deep black), 18-*guttata*, *oblongo-guttata*, and *ocellata* (the largest, and conspicuous for the yellow rim surrounding each of its spots during life), are peculiar to fir-trees; and a few, especially the delicately-dotted lemon-coloured 22-*punctata* (Plate

XVI., Fig. 5), and the little, convex *Micraspis* 16-*punctata*, frequent the seaside.

Chilocorus and *Exochomus*, both usually found on fir-trees, present much the appearance of the *Cassididæ*, their legs being short and retractile, their head hidden, and their elytra very convex, though they are quite flat beneath. In the former genus the tibiæ are armed with a tooth in the middle. In them, and in all the preceding species, the elytra are entirely glabrous, but in the remainder of the family they are more or less clothed with a short pubescence: this is especially evident in *Lasia globosa*,—a small, round, convex, reddish-brown insect, variegated with many small irregular black spots and streaks, though sometimes immaculate,—common on the coast.

The *Scymni* are found about fir-trees and in marshy places; they are very small and inconspicuous, dark in colour, and having at most a red spot or stain on the elytra. The larva of one of this genus has been observed to feed upon small *Aphides*, and to be entirely clothed with a white cottony secretion.

Lastly, the reddish species of *Coccidula* (one of which, *scutellata*, has its elytra spotted with black) frequent wet places, reeds, &c., and may be known by their comparatively narrow shape and posteriorly right-angled thorax, which is narrower than the elytra.

The ENDOMYCHIDÆ (termed also *Sulcicolles*) have comparatively long antennæ; the thorax impressed behind; the last joint of the maxillary palpi slightly thickened, and never hatchet-shaped; and the posterior coxæ wide apart.

Two of our genera, *Endomychus* and *Lycoperdina*,

have been generally associated; but the others, *Mycetæa*, *Symbiotes*, and *Alexia*, have been usually separated and placed in other families; in the three latter the tarsi are plainly four-jointed, whereas in the two former only three joints are visible.

Endomychus contains one species, *coccineus*, beautifully coloured and marked (Plate XV., Fig. 6); it occurs not uncommonly under bark, in fungoid growth, and presents a certain superficial likeness to some of the ladybirds, from which its long, gradually-thickened antennæ, more elongate shape, and palpi of lesser development will distinguish it. In some specimens the thorax is entirely red, whilst in others it has a broad black stripe down the entire middle. Its larva has been found under fir and willow bark, and seems to depart entirely from the type of its present allies, being much like that of the *Silphidæ*, flat, with comparatively long antennæ; the three first segments large, and the remainder lobed at the sides.

Lycoperdina bovistæ, a little flattish black insect, found in puff-balls, of rare occurrence, but plentiful when found, is not unlike certain of the *Heteromera* (*Blaps* or *Heliopathes*) in miniature. Its thorax has a very deep longitudinal impression on each side.

Mycetæa hirta (a very small, coarsely-punctured, hairy, brownish, ovate insect, contracted behind, and abundant in old cellars) and *Symbiotes latus* (larger, wider, rarer, and found in rotten wood),—both gregarious,—have been by some authors placed in the *Lathridiidæ*, and by others in the *Cryptophagidæ*; and *Alexia pilifera*,—small, round, globose, set with delicate but distinct hairs, strongly punctured, but with no lateral impressions to its thorax,—commonly found in moss, is sometimes associated with the *Coccinellidæ*, and at others eliminated from all companionship, as an insect whose true position cannot be ascertained.

The EROTYLIDÆ have the tarsi either distinctly five-jointed, or apparently four-jointed (the fourth joint being very small and connate with the fifth); their antennæ have a large three-jointed flattened club, and their maxillary palpi terminate in a very large clavate joint, from which latter structure they were termed *Clavipalpi* by Latreille.

We possess three genera, *Engis*, *Triplax*, and *Tritoma*; all the species of which feed in fungi. These, with *Endomychus* and *Lycoperdina*, are placed by Thomson between the *Cryptophagidæ* and *Mycetophagidæ* in the *Necrophaga*.

Our species of *Engis* are found in profusion in fungi on trees; they are shining, somewhat quadrate-elongate and convex, polished, dark, and (*humeralis*) with either the thorax and shoulders of the elytra reddish-yellow, or (*rufifrons*) with only the shoulders of that colour. Individuals are often found entirely testaceous or brown.

Triplax,—the largest species of which (*russicus*) is not uncommon,—is very like *Tetratoma*, having a red thorax and blue-black elytra, being of the same build, and occurring in similar places: the three-jointed club to its antennæ will, however, readily distinguish it.

Tritoma bipustulata (Plate XV., Fig. 4), not uncommon in fungoid growth under bark, or on the rotten stumps of felled trees, is more rounded and convex than its allies.

The COLYDIIDÆ are composed of a somewhat heterogeneous alliance of species, with the parts of the mouth but little developed: their antennæ have either ten or eleven joints, and are not elbowed, being either clavate or knobbed; the front and middle coxæ are globose, and the hinder transverse and semicylindric; the tarsi four-jointed and simple, and the abdomen composed of five segments, of which only the last, or the last two, are free. They principally affect wood, but also occur in vegetable refuse, ants' nests, and sandy places. *Cicones variegatus* (Plate VI., Fig. 6) is found under bark of beech, but is very rare: it has been taken at Bromley, Mickleham, and elsewhere. *Sarrotrium* has strong spindle-shaped antennæ; *Colydium*, found in burrows of *Platypus* in the New Forest, and *Teredus*, which occurs in decaying stumps in Sherwood Forest, are very elongate; *Cerylon* very much resembles a small *Hister*, and has the penultimate joint of the palpi large, and the apical joint needle-pointed; *Myrmecoxenus vaporariorum*, which is now referred to this family, is very like a small *Cryptophagus*; it is a very rare, or rather local, small, testaceous, flat, parallel insect, and is usually found in hot-beds, or crawling on walls near hot-beds or dungheaps; and lastly, *Langelandia anophthalma*, which has comparatively recently been discovered in Britain, must not be passed over; it is an elongate, parallel, dull-ferruginous insect, and may easily be recognized by having the thorax and elytra ribbed with raised lines or keels.

The HISTERIDÆ are hard, polished insects, usually square and stout in build, thick, but flat, or at most slightly convex; never pubescent; generally black, though sometimes spotted with red; and having the head retractile, and the antennæ and legs capable of being closely packed to the body. The antennæ have the basal joint very long, and are strongly clubbed; the mandibles are very strong, and, with the labrum above, and mentum below, nearly close up the mouth; the paraglossæ are long and divergent; the elytra truncate at the apex, leaving two segments of the abdomen exposed; and the legs wide and flat, the separate parts packing one upon another, and the tibiæ being strongly dentate or spinose externally; the middle and hinder pair, moreover, are widely apart, and the tarsi in all (except *Acritus*, which has four-jointed posterior tarsi) are five-jointed. The abdomen has five segments, of which the first is usually much the widest, and the wings are ample. The true Histers, from *Platysoma* to *Paromalus* inclusive, have the prosternum produced into a chin-piece, for the protection and reception of the head, which is wanting in *Saprinus* and the rest of the family.

They are found chiefly in dung or decaying vegetable matter; some species, however, preferring dead animals, others frequenting ants' nests, and a few living under bark or in wood. They fly strongly, and, when handled, often simulate death, from which habit their name *Hister* (*histrio*, a mimic) is derived.

One of the prettiest species, *Hister bimaculatus* (Plate VI., Fig. 4), is not uncommon in cow-dung, under stones, &c.; and with it the rounded, deeply sculptured *Onthophilus striatus* may be found.

The larvæ appear to be found in similar situations to the perfect insects; they are linear, depressed, nearly smooth, soft, and dirty white in colour, except the head and first segment, which are harder and darker; the legs, antennæ, and palpi are short, and the mandibles sickle-shaped and prominent; there appear, also, to be various impressions and transverse rows of hairs on the ventral segments, with a fleshy tubercle on the under side of the apex.

M. de Marseul has published an admirable monograph of this family in the Annales of the French Ent. Soc. (sér. 3, i. p. 131 *et seq.*), and Herr Schmidt has tabulated and described the European species in the Bestimmungs-Tabellen der Europäischen Coleopteren XIV. (Berlin, 1885).

The NITIDULIDÆ have the head (except in *Rhizophagus*) much sunk in the thorax; the antennæ not elbowed; composed of eleven (in *Rhizophagus* apparently ten) joints, of which the two or three last form a knob; the tarsi, with five joints (rarely with only four to the posterior in the male), of which the last but one is very small; the elytra usually truncate behind, and the abdomen with five or six segments free. The species are mostly small, flat, and rather wide, a few being convex, and one genus (*Rhizophagus*) linear. They chiefly frequent flowers, but dead animals, sap of trees, fungi, decaying vegetable matter, and ants' nests are also haunted by many species. They may be divided into six sub-families,—the *Brachypterina, Carpophilina, Nitidulina, Cychramina, Ipina,* and *Rhizophagina.*

The *Brachypterina* have the two or three apical segments of the abdomen exposed, and two lobes to the maxillæ. Our species occur in the flowers of *Antirrhinum, Spiræa,* &c., and are in no way remarkable, except that the male of *Cercus pedicu-*

larius has the two basal joints of the antennæ much enlarged.

The *Carpophilina* have the abdomen exposed, as in the last sub-family, but possess only one lobe to the maxillæ. One genus, *Carpophilus*, is found in Europe; and we possess but three species; one of which, *hemipterus*, an oblong, depressed insect, with very short elytra, which are spotted with yellow at the apex, is probably imported, being cosmopolitan, and mostly occurring in houses; and the others rest on very slender grounds, as indigenous.

The *Nitidulina* have the pygidium (or apical segment) alone exposed, and that sometimes only in part; a single lobe to the maxillæ; and the base of the elytra not covered by the thorax. The genera from *Epuræa* to *Omosita* (inclusive) have no elongation of the prosternum between the anterior coxæ, which prolongation is found in the remainder of this subfamily; the furrows for reception of the antennæ are also different in certain of the genera. The species of *Epuræa*, mostly yellowish in colour, chiefly frequent flowers and the exuding sap of trees, and also live under bark: whilst the *Meligethes* are exclusively to be found in flowers. The latter are very puzzling to determine, owing to their uniformity of size and build, and want of difference of colour and sculpture; they may, however, be separated by the variation in pattern and degree of the toothing on the outer edge of the front tibiæ, especially near the apex. *Soronia punctatissima* (Plate VI., Fig. 5) is found in and about the burrows of the larva of the goat-moth in willow-trees, feeding on the frass and exuding sap caused by the ravages of the latter in the solid wood. The larva of S. *grisea*, a commoner willow-bark species, is dirty white, nearly oval, narrowed behind and rather flat, with a small horny head, bearing three simple eyes on each side, two large horny prothoracic plates, and a transverse row of small plates on each of the remaining segments, which have also a lateral projection terminating in a bristle; the last segment has two pairs of horny hooks on the upper side, and a cylindrical anal tube.

The (British) *Cychramina* have the prothorax covering the base of the elytra, the club of the antennæ more or less loose, and the elytra covering nearly the whole of the abdomen, at most part of the pygidium being exposed; the three basal joints of all the tarsi are widened. We possess one genus only, *Cychramus*; the species of which,—brown, broad, and very pubescent,—abound in May blossom and fungi.

The *Ipina* have a single lobe to the maxillæ; the front of the head produced so as to cover the labrum; and the fourth joint of the tarsi very small; the elytra (except in *Cryptarcha*) not entirely covering the abdomen; the antennæ eleven-jointed, and the tarsi five-jointed; they are usually elongate and narrow, but in some cases oval or subhemispherical.

Cryptarcha (which very much resembles certain of the *Nitidulina*, and is found at the sap of trees, especially if *Cossus*-infected) has its mesosternum covered by an elongation of the prosternum; which elongation is not so evident in other genera; the body is oval, and the upper surface more or less pubescent. *Ips*, flat, elongate, shining, and mostly black with red spots, frequents freshly-cut pine-trees, &c., beneath the bark of which its larvæ are found. M. Perris ("Annales," sér. 3, i. p. 598 *et seq.*) states that *I. fer-*

rugineus enters into the holes made in the wood of fir-trees by certain species of *Xylophaga*, and lays eggs in their galleries; its larvæ feeding on those of the latter insects, and, being of slower development, taking more than a year to transform.

The females in this genus, as in *Cryptarcha*, have the elytra rather pointed at the apex.

The *Rhizophagina* have the antennæ apparently ten-jointed, with the club solid, the eleventh joint being merged in the tenth, and the tarsi dissimilar in the sexes, heteromerous in the males, and all five-jointed in the females; the species of our single British genus, *Rhizophagus*, have the anterior coxal cavities completely closed behind, and the males have a small additional segment to the abdomen. They are small, linear insects; chiefly found under bark, though some occur in ants' nests, and others in bones, &c. The larva appears to be like that of *Soronia grisea* above described, in miniature. M. Perris states that he has observed the larvæ of *R. depressus* to have similar habits to those of *Ips ferrugineus*; and that more than once he has seen two or three of the larvæ with half their bodies plunged into the larvæ or pupæ of *Hylesinus* or *Hylastes*, devouring them. He has also taken home the larvæ of both *Rhizophagus* and *Hylesinus*, and often not one of the latter escaped being eaten.

The *Rhizophagus* appeared to turn to pupa in the ground, and not under the bark.

The TROGOSITIDÆ have two lobes to the maxillæ; the tarsi five-jointed, simple, and with the first joint very small; and the elytra covering the abdomen. The apical joint of the tarsi is also very long, and has between its claws a small and slender styliform lobe, terminated by two diverging bristles. The tibiæ are unspined on the outer side, but have a more or less hooked spur at the apex of the anterior pair. *Nemosoma elongata*, a linear narrow species (with ten joints to the antennæ), very rare in England, is found on the Continent, under bark, with *Hylesinus varius* and *vittatus*; which, with their larvæ, it appears to destroy. *Tenebrioides* (*Trogosita*) *mauritanica*, a flat, black insect, has evidently been imported in merchandise; and *Thymalus limbatus*, almost a *Cassida* in shape, found under bark in the New Forest, has a horny hook at the apex of its maxillæ, and all its tibiæ armed at the tip with very small simple spines.

The MONOTOMIDÆ have by many authors been regarded as belonging to the Colydiidæ, Cucujidæ, or Lathridiidæ; in the formation of the antennæ, however, as well as in other characters, they present considerable points of difference from either of these families; the antennæ are inserted under the sides of the front; they are stout and apparently ten-jointed, the last joint being obsoletely two-jointed, and forming a club; the head is large, and the mandibles short and robust, and the anterior coxal cavities are broadly closed behind; the tarsi are three-jointed; the species are elongate, more or less depressed, usually dull and rough-looking, with the thorax crenulate at the sides, and the elytra not covering the pygidium; they are mostly gregarious, and especially abound at the wet bottoms of haystacks, and in hot-beds and grass-heaps; two species occur in ants' nests.

The LATHRIDIIDÆ have clavate antennæ inserted a

little before the eyes, the club being three-jointed in *Lathridius* and *Corticaria*, and two-jointed in *Holoparamecus*; the latter is also noteworthy on account of the variation of the number of joints—from nine to eleven—in the antennæ of certain of its species, of which we possess two, which are very rare, and probably introduced from abroad.

Their femora are clavate, and tibiæ slender and wiry, with obsolete apical spurs; their mentum more or less hexagonal, their labial palpi apparently biarticulate, the third joint being soldered to the second, which is inflated; their mandibles bifid at the apex (sometimes very minutely so), and their maxillæ bilobed, but with the outer lobe obsolete; the tarsi are three-jointed.

Our species of *Lathridius* are found in refuse heaps, dry wood, &c., the largest, *L. lardarius* (Plate XVI., Fig. 3), occurring plentifully in grassy places in some of the midland counties. It received its unsuggestive specific name on account of having been reared by its discoverer from larvæ found in a dry pig's bladder; and many similar instances of inappropriate naming occur, through insects having been observed for the first time under accidental circumstances.

Another species, *L. nodifer*, much smaller, dull black, with little humps on its elytra, is now very common in cut grass, rubbish heaps, &c., all over the south and midland parts of the country, though unknown some few years ago. When quite fresh it has a thin white membrane on each side of its thorax, somewhat like the pellicle filling up the marginal notch in the same part of *Ochthebius*.

In this genus the body is never pubescent, or the

sides of the thorax cronulated, as in its ally *Corticaria*, the species of which are more convex and cylindrical, and have the front coxæ more approximated.

The CUCUJIDÆ have five ventral segments to the abdomen, all of which are free; the tarsi either all five-jointed in both sexes, or with four joints to the posterior in the male, and their antennæ filiform or with a club at the apex. They mostly live under bark, and are generally rare; the little spotted *Psammæchus*, however, occurs commonly in marshy places; and *Silvanus* and *Nausibius* (both very like *Monotoma*) comprise species for the greater part introduced here from abroad. The diminutive *Læmophlæi* (in which the maxillæ are hooked) are found (often gregariously) in small twigs, and under bark.

The family BYTURIDÆ comprises the puzzling genus *Byturus*, which has been shifted about to a considerable extent by authors: it was originally placed by Latreille among the *Nitidulidæ*; then in the *Melyridæ* by Erichson; subsequently, by Redtenbacher and Lacordaire in the *Dermestidæ*; and, lastly, by Thomson, again returned to the *Nitidulidæ*, but associated with such heterogeneous neighbours as *Thymalus* and *Micropeplus*; many writers associate it with *Telmatophilus*, to which it appears to bear a close relation, and regard it as belonging to the *Malacodermata*.

Byturus has the tarsi five-jointed and velvety beneath; the second and third joints produced into long side lappets, the first and fourth being very small (the latter hidden between the lobes of the third), and the fifth as long as all the rest together, with the apical hooks much curved, and furnished with a strong tooth at the base. The front coxæ are ovate and not exserted, and the posterior approximated. The abdomen is composed of five equal free segments; the mandibles have a stout tooth at the base, and are slightly toothed before the apex; the eyes are large, round, and prominent; the antennæ eleven-jointed with a graduated three-jointed club; and the body is rather convex and pubescent.

The perfect insects are found in the flowers of the white-thorn, strawberry, &c.; and are entirely unlike any *Dermestes* (to which genus they have been considered closely allied by many authors) in their habits. The larvæ, also, do not present the hairs so characteristic of the larvæ of the latter.

The CRYPTOPHAGIDÆ have the antennæ eleven-jointed and clubbed; the legs far apart, with the anterior coxæ globose, and the posterior cylindric; the tarsi either five-jointed in both sexes, or with those of the hinder legs four-jointed in the male; the elytra entire; and the abdomen composed of five segments, all of which are free, the first being rather longer than the others.

The species are all small, mostly oblong or elliptic, and generally pubescent.

Diphyllus, placed usually among the *Mycetophagidæ*, differs from the members of that family in its tarsi, which have five joints, the fourth being extremely small, and in the club of its antennæ, which is composed of two joints. Our single species, *lunatus*, found in fungi on bark in Norfolk, Somersetshire, Isle of Wight, &c., is small and dull black, with striated elytra, bearing a white crescent-shaped spot in the middle.

The *Telmatophili* have been alternately placed in the

Melyridæ and *Cryptophagidæ;* they are, also, associated by Redtenbacher with *Lyctus* and *Alexia,* and included by Thomson with *Tritoma* and *Mycetæa* in the *Fungicola.*

The species are found upon plants, especially near water: their tarsi are pentamerous, with the fourth joint almost obsolete; the second and third being bilobed (the latter very strongly so), and the two first densely pilose beneath.

The *Cryptophagi* (Plate VI., Fig. 1, *Cryptophagus scanicus*) are found in vegetable refuse, fungi, and flowers; they are difficult to determine, but good characters are to be found in the anterior angles of the thorax, and in the position and development of a tooth on the side between that angle and the base. The species of *Atomaria* are very small: they also occur in vegetable refuse, often harbouring in dry dung, and have been described by Mr. T. V. Wollaston in the Transactions of the Entomological Society of London (vol. iv. n. s., part iii. 1857).

The Scaphidiidæ are represented in England by three species of two genera, *Scaphidium* and *Scaphisoma;* the former, found under logs of wood, in fungoid growth, and the latter in agarics and decomposing wood. Both are very agile, convex on the upper and under sides; rather boat-shaped; hard, shining, with very long and slender legs, the intermediate and hinder pairs of which are far apart; the antennæ, also, are exceedingly delicate in the latter genus, the members of which are very small and black; *Scaphidium* being larger, with four red spots.

The parts of the mouth are not conspicuously developed, the palpi (especially the labial pair), mandibles, and labrum being small; both lobes of the maxillæ are membranous; the head is small and deflexed; the thorax fitting close to the elytra, and in *Scaphisoma* enlarged behind in the middle so as to cover the scutellum ; the elytra truncated obliquely at the tip, leaving the apex of the abdomen exposed, having a sutural and lateral stria, and being covered with irregular scratches ; the anterior coxæ exserted and approximated, the tarsi five-jointed, and the first segment of the abdomen very large.

The MYCETOPHAGIDÆ are either oblong or oblong-oval, moderately convex, and clothed with a depressed pubescence, being also mostly gaily coloured or prettily variegated. Their anterior coxæ are subglobose and free, the posterior being subcylindric and transverse; they have no paraglossæ to the ligula ; the segments of the abdomen (5) are all free, and the tarsi are four-jointed, the anterior pair in the males having only three joints.

The species are all found in fungi or fungoid growth, and are generally abundant when discovered. *Mycetophagus multipunctatus* (Plate VII., Fig. 2) is one of the prettiest, occurring in fungi on rotten oak, &c. The irregularly-punctured genus *Triphyllus* has the club of the antennæ distinctly formed of three joints, and the little yellow delicately-striated *Typhæa* is found in profusion at the bottoms of haystacks.

The DERMESTIDÆ have straight, short, clubbed antennæ, inserted in front and sometimes fitting (in repose) into grooves in the sides of the prothorax ; the head small and retractile, and often received into a prolongation of the prosternum ; the parts of the mouth little prominent ; the anterior coxæ conic and exserted; the tarsi five-jointed, and the elytra covering the abdomen. All of them, except *Dermestes*, have a smooth eye-like spot on the forehead.

They are found in dry dead animals and skins for the most part, the "bacon beetle," *Dermestes lardarius*, being well known as a ravager; some, however, occur in flowers. They partially retract the legs, and counterfeit death on being frightened. The larva of *Dermestes* is long, with leathery plates on the upper side, which is clothed with long scattered hairs; and there is a pair of short spines on the last segment, which has also a fleshy protuberance on the under side. The dry cast skins of this larva may often be seen.

The BYRRHIDÆ are conspicuous from their faculty of packing up their limbs; the head (except in *Nosodendron*, which is exceedingly doubtful as British) being retractile, and immersed in the thorax, against the sides of which the antennæ are placed; the tarsi are usually received into the tibiæ, which, again, pack tight to the femora, the entire legs fitting into excavations on the lower side of the body. The antennæ have eleven joints, except in *Limnichus* and *Aspidiphorus*, which have only ten; the parts of the mouth are not prominent, the ligula having no paraglossæ, and the maxillæ not being toothed. The species are usually oval and very convex, clothed with short silky pubescence, and sometimes apterous. The *Byrrhi* (*B. fasciatus*, Plate VII., Fig. 3) are not uncommon in sandy places, &c., in the spring: the other genera are principally found in moss, and under stones on sandy banks. They simulate death readily, and are hard to set, owing to their retractile limbs.

Aspidiphorus (*Conipora*, Thoms.),—left with doubt

by Redtoubacher and Lacordaire among the *Byrrhidæ*, assigned by Erichson to the *Ptinidæ*, and by Latreille to the *Dermestidæ*, and latterly erected by Thomson into a family, the *Coniporidæ*, and placed by him in the *Xylophagi*, between *Dorcatoma* and *Sphindus* (the last a genus of somewhat uncertain position),—is now, as a rule, classed with the present family. Its tarsi are slender and heteromerous (the first joint of the hinder pair being obsolete), with the apical joint almost as long as all the rest; the legs are not retractile; the antennæ ten-jointed, the two first joints being swollen, and the club elongate; the clypeus large, and with a distinct suture; the maxillæ with a horny tooth; the prosternum with no projection behind the anterior coxæ, but applied against the sloping mesosternum; the middle and hinder coxæ widely distant; and the abdomen with five segments, of which the first is much the largest. The only known species, *A. orbiculatus*, is very small, convex, delicately pubescent, black, with the legs and antennæ (except the club) ferruginous, and the elytra punctate striate. It is rare, and found in sandy places, on low plants.

The GEORYSSIDÆ (comprising one genus and species, which is very small, apterous, and almost globular) have the antennæ of nine joints, of which the three last form a club; the prosternum membranous; the front and middle legs close to each other; the anterior coxæ projecting and approximated, the intermediate oval, and the posterior transverse, the two latter pairs being widely separated between themselves; and the tarsi slender and four-jointed.

Georyssus pygmæus is found in wet places, especially on the sea-coast; it often burrows in the ground, and nearly always bears a little heap of dry mud or caked sand upon its back. When cleaned, the elytra exhibit very coarse punctuation for so small an insect.

The PARNIDÆ are aquatic or sub-aquatic in their habits, and are divided into two sub-families, the *Parnina* and *Elmina*, both having the head received into a prolongation of the prosternum, and the anterior segments of the abdomen soldered together; differing, however, in their anterior coxæ, which are cylindrical and transverse in the first, and almost globular in the latter. In the *Parnina* the body is clothed thickly with short hairs, and the second joint of the antennæ assumes a widened, ear-like form: the species are found near or in running water, on stones or water plants.

The *Elmina* (which are much smaller) have the antennæ very little thickened at the apex, no tooth to the mandibles (which are, however, bifid); scarcely any pubescence on the body, which is often metallic and frequently caked with dirt; and the last joint of the tarsi very long, with exceedingly strong claws. They cling to the rough undersides of large stones in strongly-running waters, especially delighting in such as are under or close to a fall of any kind; and may be found at a considerable depth from the surface. They are gregarious in habit, many examples of different species (or even genera) being sometimes found together.

The HETEROCERIDÆ, comprising a single genus, *Heterocerus*, have the antennæ short, the last seven joints forming a flattened club; the parts of the mouth not hidden, the ligula being very projecting; the legs adapted for digging, with four simple joints to the tarsi; and the elytra covering the abdomen, which has five segments, the apical one only being free. The species are all depressed, broad, and clothed with short thick silky pubescence, which probably keeps the water near which they live away from their body. Their head is very robust, and the prothorax capable of considerable freedom of motion. They live in mud-banks, &c., at the sides of rivers and ponds, and will frequently come up out of the damp mud in great numbers on the collector treading about; and if the sun be shining, will fly readily. Some species form galleries under stones, &c., near semi-saline waters, and most of them appear to be gregarious.

All those found in Britain have been described by Mr. G. R. Waterhouse, in the Trans. Ent. Soc., vol. v. n. s., part 4, 1859.

CHAPTER XIV.

THE LAMELLICORNIA, OR "CHAFERS."

The *Lamellicornia*, which (with the exception of the *Trogidæ*) are exclusively vegetable or dung-feeders, are divided into two great families—the *Lucanidæ* and the *Scarabæidæ*.

They are chiefly distinguished by the club of their antennæ, which is composed of transverse lamellated joints, varying from three to seven in number; and, except in the *Lucanidæ*, moveable like the leaves of a book. Their antennæ are short, usually nine or ten-jointed (the *Geotrupina* alone having eleven joints), with the basal joint enlarged or lengthened, and always inserted in front of and near the eyes, under a reflexed margin of the head.

Their legs, and especially the anterior pair, are formed for digging; with all the tarsi five-jointed, the posterior coxæ moveable, and the front acetabula (or pits for the reception or articulation of the anterior coxæ) enclosed by a rim on every side.

Internally, they appear to be distinguished by the peculiar disposition of their central nervous system; which, as far as has been yet observed, consists of a large ganglion (or depôt) situated in the thorax, without any trace of abdominal ganglia; the *Lucanidæ*, however, possess these latter, as well as, and distinct from, the thoracic mass.

They exhibit, also, a difference in their respiratory organs from the other *Coleoptera*, in the possession of a multitude of vascular tracheæ annexed to the main canals of the ordinary tracheal tubes. It is (as M. Lacordaire remarks) doubtless owing to these reserves of air that these insects, in spite of their heavy build, take so easily to the wing.

Their larvæ,—which are found in dung, at the roots of plants, in decaying vegetable matter, or rotten mould in old trees,—are fleshy, cylindrical, recurved behind in an arch, with the last segment much enlarged; so that, except when very young, they cannot extend themselves into a straight line, but lie on their sides. They are usually yellowish or bluish-white, with a transparent skin, through which the dark intestinal canal can often be seen, especially at the apex; and the segments exhibit very evident transverse folds, and have the anal orifice also transverse, except in the *Lucanidæ*, wherein these folds are almost entirely absent, and the orifice is longitudinal.

Their head is brownish or yellow, horny, rounded, with the forehead directed forwards, and the mouth on the lower surface; the mandibles are robust and arched; the antennæ five-jointed; and the eyes entirely wanting, except in the instance of *Trichius fasciatus*, which (according to the observations of M. Perris, a distinguished French entomologist) possesses a smooth, spherical, reddish eye a little behind each antenna. The legs are rather long, and composed normally of five joints, of which the coxa is much developed, and the apical joint, or tarsus, is sometimes wanting; the hooks which it bears in that case being transferred to the fourth joint, though sometimes entirely wanting.

The pupæ are formed in cocoons or cells, constructed (usually underground) of portions of the food of the larva, often mixed with particles of dirt; and in which the perfect insect, after its exclusion, remains for some time until its integuments are hardened.

The LUCANIDÆ have the club of the antennæ composed of lamellæ or plates, which assume a pectinated form, and are not capable of being closed up together, or widely separated, as in the other families.

For this reason, added to the above-mentioned differences of the nervous system and structure of the larvæ, and the strong sexual characters afforded by the development of the head and its appendages in most of its members, this family has been raised by M. Lacordaire to the rank of a section, equal in value to the *Lamellicornes*, under the name of *Pectinicornes*. It must remain, however, for future observers to determine whether this elevation be warranted; for, until all the known *Lamellicornia* are dissected, it cannot be considered proved that there exists no species of them with a nervous system as in the *Lucanidæ*; it is moreover known that there is a genus of the latter family (*Passalus*) wherein the appendages of the head are not developed as in the other *Lucanidæ*, and whose nervous system is intermediate between the two above-mentioned conditions; there being also some of their larvæ, which, whilst they have no transverse folds, still have the anal orifice transverse; thus uniting the two forms of difference. In *Lucanus cervus*, moreover, the larva exhibits traces of these folds on the front of its body. There is, also, another genus (*Sinodendron*) of the *Lucanidæ*, which has an excess of development in the *thorax* of the male, as in many of the species of *Lamellicornia*.

The LUCANIDÆ have ten-jointed antennæ, with a long basal joint; the ligula membranous or leathery, bilobed, ciliated, and situated on the inner side of the mentum, except in *Sinodendron*, where it is situated at the apex; the mandibles exposed, and often attaining an enormous size in the male; the outer lobe of the maxillæ not toothed, and ending in a pencil of hair; the sides of the elytra covering the abdominal epipleura; the prosternum large; the intermediate coxæ transverse; and the abdomen composed of five ventral segments, with an extra segment in the male.

Lucanus cervus, the "stag-beetle," is well known to most inhabitants of our southern counties; the male, with branching antlers or jaws, being often seen sailing in a ponderous way round oak-trees in its search for the female, or blundering in flight along country lanes about July, especially towards evening. The males have been noticed fighting for the possession of the other sex, whose mandibles are very small, and which may be sometimes observed upon pathways, on her back, sprawling out her legs in empty air, having dropped from her leafy perch. This species is not peculiar to the oak, but is found sometimes on willow; the specimens reared from the latter tree being smaller than the oak-fed examples. It is, however, a well-known fact, that great differences in size are always found in species of which the larvæ feed on wood; owing to the many variations to which they are subject, from the good or bad quality, or too great or too little moisture, of their food, and the long period during which they remain in the larval state.

Some of the males of this species are very large, and have the head very square and massive, with mandibles of great length and thickness and bearing strong teeth; others, however, are smaller than the general run of the female, and possess narrow heads, with comparatively slight, simple jaws. It is supposed that the insect uses its powerful mandibles, for abrading young twigs, &c.,—applying its tufted ligula afterwards to the juice flowing from the bruise. I possess an old male who has evidently worn down the apex of his jaws evenly and gradually by some such habit. Instances have been recorded, nevertheless, of members of this family attacking other beetles, and also caterpillars. Mr. G. R. Waterhouse (Ent. Mag., vol. ii. 59) has recorded the fact of his having kept a stag-beetle alive for some time, which became comparatively tame, and nipped raspberries, &c., with its mandibles, sucking the juice afterwards with its tongue. It also frequently cleaned the club of its antennæ, by drawing it between the patch of yellow silky pubescence at the upper side of the base of the anterior femora and the fringe of similar hairs on the lower side of the coxæ of the same legs. In Germany there is (or used to be) a superstition that this beetle carries hot coals in its jaws from place to place.

The eyes in *Lucanus* are considerably encroached upon, both in front and behind, by the lateral margin of the head; and have their greatest bulk on the lower side.

The larva of the stag-beetle takes about four years before it assumes the pupa state; it is very large and fleshy, of a semi-transparent yellowish white colour, with a large reddish head. It is peculiar on account of the anterior part of its body exhibiting certain slight transverse folds, a character at variance with its allies. When mature, it forms a cocoon of chips, in which it undergoes its final metamorphoses; the pupa exhibiting the parts of the future perfect insect, —which, when disclosed, appears to remain quiet for some time before coming into outer air. The larva feeds in the solid wood, usually near the bark, and reduces it to a sort of tan: it has been considered to be the "Cossus" of the Romans.

An allied but much smaller species, *Dorcus parallelopipedus* (Plate VIII., Fig. 4), has each eye almost divided into two by a similar structure. It is flat, parallel, and very stoutly built, looking as if a broad-wheeled waggon had gone over it without inflicting any particular damage beyond a slight compression. Its male and female have been observed in company, digging holes in dead trees wherein the latter might deposit her eggs.

Sinodendron, found in the rotten mould of old ash and birch trees, is more elongate and cylindrical, with its eyes entire. In the fully developed male there is a stout horn on the head, bent backwards, and hairy behind; the thorax, also, is semicircularly truncated in front, with a rounded tooth in the middle, and the margin of the truncation denticulated. In the female the head bears a tubercle, and the thorax, which is very coarsely punctured, has a slight depression in front.

The SCARABÆIDÆ are divided into two sub-sections, founded on the position of the abdominal spiracles, which are always seven in number on each side; the first being at times easily seen (as in *Copris* and *Geotrupes*), and at times hidden between the metathorax and abdomen, and the remainder varying as follows:—
In the *Scarabæidæ Laparosticti* (including the *Coprina*, *Aphodiina*, *Geotrupina*, and *Trogina*) they are all placed in the membrane connecting the dorsal and ventral corneous plates of the abdomen, and consequently covered entirely by the closed elytra; and in the *Scarabæidæ Pleurosticti* (including the *Melolonthina*, *Sericina*, *Hopliina*, *Rutelina*, and *Cetoniina*) some of them are placed in the membrane connecting the dorsal and ventral plates of the abdomen, but the greater number are situated on the upper side of the ventral segments themselves, with the last spiracle at least uncovered when the elytra are closed. There is this further difference, that in the *Pleurosticti* (with the exception of certain of the exotic *Hopliina*) the ligula is horny, and soldered to the mentum; and in the larva the two lobes of the maxillæ are soldered together; whilst in the *Laparosticti* the ligula is leathery or membranous, and distinct from the mentum, and the lobes of the maxillæ are not soldered in the larva. In the *Pleurosticti*, also, the *Cetoniina* and *Rutelina* have the three last pairs of abdominal spiracles diverging strongly outwards; whilst in the *Melolonthina*, *Sericina*, and *Hopliina* the divergence outwards is very slight; the last three tribes are by some authors formed into a third division, intermediate between the other two, called the *Scarabæidæ Melolonthini*.

The *Coprina* (to which family the "sacred beetle" of the Egyptians belongs) have the organs of the mouth invisible from above, being concealed by the clypeus, which is semicircular, enlarged, and notched. Their intermediate coxæ are widely separated, those of the posterior legs (which are near the apex of the body) being approximated; the four hinder legs have the tibiæ dilated at the tip, and the posterior pair are armed with only one long terminal spur; the tarsi usually diminish gradually in width from the base to the apex, the basal joint being always very long; the eyes are half divided by the side of the head; the scutellum is hidden, and the pygidium exposed.

They are of squarer outline and more "squab" shape than the *Geotrupina;* the thorax being convex and wide, —and, as usual in fossorial species, capable of great freedom of motion,—and the front tibiæ widened and strongly toothed on the outer side.

In *Copris* the basal joints of the labial palpi are dilated with the third joint distinct; and the metasternum is large, flat, and in the shape of a parallelogram. *C. lunaris*, a large, shining, deep-black species, clothed with scanty reddish-brown hairs beneath and on the sides, has a long erect horn on the head in the male; the thorax, also, in this sex is somewhat squarely truncated in front, and excavated and toothed externally on each side. The female exhibits a very slight tendency to a somewhat similar structure; having, also, the thorax more closely punctured: and it is needless to repeat that the small males are intermediate between the two extremes of development.

This insect burrows a foot or more down into the hard ground beneath cow-dung, two specimens being often found at the bottom of the burrow. It flies but seldom, and produces a considerable noise by rubbing the abdomen against the hinder margin of elytra. It occurs near Greenwich Park, at Bath, &c.

The species of *Onthophagus* have nine-jointed antennæ, some of the joints of the club being concave; the last joint of the labial palpi scarcely visible; and slender tarsi. They are mostly small and flattened; with the thorax greenish-black, and the elytra luridbrown chequered with black; and are found gregariously in dung, especially in sandy places and near the coast, but they never dig burrows deep below the surface. At times certain of them have been observed in dead animals.

The back of the head in the male is often armed with a broad thin horn, bent backwards; of which there are, as usual, modifications in size.

The *Aphodiina* are all small, oblong, and cylindrical; with the organs of the mouth (except the apex of the palpi) hidden by the clypeus; the antennæ nine-jointed; the abdomen with six free ventral segments; the scutellum visible; the metasternum of ordinary size; the intermediate coxæ oblique, and approximated behind; two spurs to the apex of the tibiæ; and the club of the antennæ flat. Their eyes are only slightly divided by the side of the head, and their elytra almost always entirely cover the apex of the body.

The males differ from the females in the greater development of certain tubercles on the clypeus; in the greater bulk and lesser amount of punctuation of the thorax; in the longer spine at the apex of the front tibiæ; or in the presence of a more decided channel in the middle of the metasternum.

The species of *Aphodius* are very abundant, especially in spring and autumn; flying readily, and occurring in profusion in the droppings of our domestic animals. They are usually black and shining, but sometimes livid yellow or red, or spotted. *A. inquinatus* (Plate VIII., Fig. 3), one of the prettiest, is found in profusion on the Lancashire sandhills. In this genus the anterior margin of the eyes is visible, when viewed from above, and the lobes of the maxillæ are leathery or membranous, and unarmed; in *Ammœcius* (more globose behind) no part of the eye is to be seen from above in repose; in *Psammobius* (of which the thorax is strongly transversely furrowed) the outer lobe of the maxillæ is horny and hooked; and in *Ægialia* (found in sandy places) the mandibles and labrum project slightly beyond the clypeus. Several genera have been founded by French entomologists at the expense of *Aphodius;* but most of them are generally abandoned, as being dependent more upon facies than any structural differences.

The *Geotrupina* have the antennæ eleven-jointed (the club having three joints); the eyes entirely divided into two by the side margin of the head; the abdomen short, with six free ventral segments; the mandibles and labrum not hidden by the clypeus; the body convex, the thorax being very large; the intermediate coxæ oblique and the anterior transverse; and the pygidium not quite covered by the elytra.

Geotrupes stercorarius, the well-known "shard-born beetle," "Clock," or "Dumble-dor" (the last possibly an inflection of the American "Tumble-dung," a name given on account of certain of these insects rolling pellets of the excrement of cattle, in which they deposit the eggs), is common all over the country; flying strongly, though in a blundering sort of way, towards evening; and often simulating death, by keeping motionless and stretching out its legs like pieces of wire, when handled. Sometimes it is observed on the wing in the hot sunshine, suggesting the idea of an owl under similar circumstances. This insect is sometimes called "Lousy Watchman" among the vulgar; the qualifying epithet being deserved from its being frequently infested on the lower surface by several of a species of *Gamasus;* though it is not easy to comprehend how so delicately constructed a parasite can extract a meal through the stout armour of the beetle in question.

The strength of the *Geotrupes* is very great, so much so, that it is scarcely possible to retain one in the hand: this is caused by the great devolopment of the thorax, containing the muscles of the anterior spinose digging legs. The female, usually in the autumn, digs a burrow, about a foot deep, into the earth beneath patches of cow-dung, a portion of which is carried down as food for the larva to be hatched from the egg she deposits at the bottom.

The larvæ afterwards ascend to the surface, having eaten the contents of the burrow.

Typhæus vulgaris (Plate VIII., Fig. 2), an allied insect, found in dung, or crawling about pathways, on sandy commons in early spring and autumn, has the thorax in the male armed with three strong horns, of which the outer pair are the longest; the female having a rudimentary sketch of a similar structure, and small or feebly developed males exhibiting but a weak edition of the normal projections.

All these insects hum considerably in flight, and possess the power of making a stridulating noise, which is caused by the friction of a transversely striated elevation on the posterior border of the hinder coxa against the hinder margin of the acetabulum into which it fits.

Although naturally feeders on animal excrement, some species (e.g. *Geotrupes vernalis*) are often found in rotten fungi.

The *Trogina* have five ventral segments to the abdomen (except in some species of *Trox*, where there is an indication of a sixth), but slightly moveable; the anterior legs are not fossorial, the tibiæ not being enlarged, or strongly toothed; the antennæ ten-jointed; scutellum small; the coxæ contiguous, those of the front and intermediate legs being very short (the latter almost globose, and scarcely at all oblique); the elytra entirely cover the abdomen; and the mandibles and labrum are uncovered by the clypeus.

We possess but one genus, *Trox;* of which the species are rather rare. They are dull black, moderately large, oblong, of strong integuments, and usually with interrupted rows of short pencils of bristles on the elytra. When seized they make a squeaking noise by rubbing the abdomen against the elytra, and contract their limbs. They are found in sandy places, in half-dry carcases, of which they consume the harder portions; in rams' horns, &c. Some of them have imperfectly developed wings, the others appearing to fly only in the evening; and certain exotic species possess the faculty of contracting themselves into a ball, after the manner of *Agathidium*.

The *Melolonthina* have the outer lobe of the maxillæ strongly toothed; the mandibles robust, with no inner membranous border; the labrum very prominent, and deeply notched; the anterior coxæ transverse; the scutellum rounded; the body cylindrical, and the ventral segments of the abdomen soldered together, with the points of junction effaced in the middle.

In *Melolontha* (the common "cockchafer") the abdomen is produced behind into a strong point (this structure being, however, not constant in the genus); and the club of the antennæ is composed of seven joints in the male, and six in the female. The habits of this species and its larvæ are, unfortunately, too well known. The smaller *Rhizotrogus solstitialis* (belonging to the section of the genus which has but nine joints to its antennæ, for which Latreille founded the now abandoned genus *Amphimallus*), the "summer-chafer," has a three-jointed club: it is conspicuous for the long hairs in the front of its body, and for its habit of wheeling in flight towards evening round any solitary tree.

The *Sericina* have the labrum entirely confused with the clypeus; the outer lobe of the maxillæ toothed; the scutellum triangular; the posterior coxæ very large and much widened outwards; the metasternum obliquely truncated on each side behind; the segments of the abdomen not soldered together; and the tarsi long and slender.

In *Serica* the antennæ are nine-jointed, but the club varies in number; our British species, *S. brunnea*, having three joints, which are very long and conspicuous in the male. This insect, clylindrical in shape, with long and slender (but stiff) legs, of a light testaceous-red colour with opaline or silky reflections, is nocturnal in its habits; and may be found in spiders' webs, sand-pits, water-troughs, &c., frequently "coming to grief" on account of its delicate structure. I have seen a red ant dragging a disabled but living specimen along the bottom of a sand-pit.

The little *Homaloplia*, shorter and darker in colour, is diurnal in its habits, and may be found (but rarely) settled in flowers near woods. It has shorter front tarsi, and is clothed with more decided pubescence.

The *Hopliina* are here represented by a single genus and species, *Hoplia philanthus*, a small, robust, dark-coloured insect, with scanty bluish-silvery scales, remarkable for its habit of flying for only a short time in the hottest part of the day, and then hiding in flowers, &c. This family is subject to considerable variations in form and structure, but has the labrum indistinct; the club of the antennæ three-jointed; the anterior coxæ projecting; the hooks of the tarsi unequal; and the ventral segments soldered together, the sixth being generally indistinct. The genus *Hoplia* has the hooks of the posterior tarsi simple; and the males are generally narrower than the females, with one tooth less in the anterior tibiæ, which are more slender, and the hinder legs stronger, with more robust hooks to the tarsi. *H. philanthus* has ten joints to the antennæ.

The *Rutelina*, apart from the greater divergence of the last abdominal spiracles, differ chiefly from the *Melolonthina* (to which they are allied) in always having the ligula horny and soldered to the mentum; the mandibles horny; the labrum distinct, and free from the clypeus; and the club of the antenna three-jointed, and alike in both sexes. Their tarsi are robust, rigid, prehensile, with the terminal hooks unequal, the outer one being often forked at the apex; and the metathoracic epimera always visible. In our species the antennae are nine-jointed; the mesothoracic epimera do not ascend to the anterior part of the clytra; the clypeus has no projection in front, and the prosternum no elongation behind the coxæ; the elytra, also, are lined with membrane, which projects behind in the form of a thin rim.

Phyllopertha horticola, the small "June-bug" (Plate VIII., Fig. 1), is often very destructive to plants.

Anomala Frischi, a moderate-sized species, with green thorax and reddish-brown elytra, is common on sandhills near the coast in many localities.

The *Cetoniina*, of which the exotic species are numerous, large, and beautiful, are here represented by a very few (but not inconspicuous) insects. Their mandibles and labrum are hidden under the clypeus, the former being composed of an outer horny and inner membranous plate; the antennæ are short, with ten joints, the club being composed of three; the elytra are somewhat depressed, not reflexed at the sides, and leaving the pygidium exposed; the anterior coxæ are ovate-conic and projecting; and the hooks of the tarsi equal and simple.

In *Gnorimus* and *Trichius* the elytra are not sinuated near the shoulder, at the sides, and the mesothoracic epimera are not visible from the upper side. The species of the former occur in all their stages in the rotten mould of oak and cherry trees; and one of the latter (*T. fasciatus*, Plate VII., Fig. 6), found in Perthshire, where it is called "bee-beetle," is conspicuous for its banded body, and long, bright-yellow hairs: it flies round thistle-tops, in the hot sunshine, like a *Bombus*.

In *Cetonia* the mesosternum is produced forwards into a rounded knob; the elytra are deeply sinuated externally, below the shoulder; the mesothoracic epimera are enlarged, carried upwards, and conspicuous between the hinder angles of the thorax and shoulders of the elytra: the metathoracic epimera, also, are enlarged, visible from above, and joined to the outer margin of the laminated hinder coxæ (of which the posterior angles are acute), which form a strong tooth about the middle of the sides of the elytra, and slightly turned outwards, when viewed from the upper side. This development of the mesothoracic opimera acts as a "skid" or "break" upon the base of the elytra, and is accompanied by a departure from the ordinary method of flight; for, in *Cetonia*, the elytra are scarcely separated, and only elevated a little, so as to give room for the wings to expand: in flight, also, a humming noise is made. In *Gnorimus* and *Trichius* the elytra are, as usual in *Coleoptera*, widely separated, and much elevated.

Cetonia aurata, the common "Rose-beetle," is too well known to require description: besides being found in roses it occurs on elder-flowers and thistles, and at sap, or on rotten pear blossom; another species (*C. ænea*), duller in colour, is found in Perthshire, where its larva has been found in ants' nests, feeding on the eggs; the perfect insect, also, has been seen burying itself in the nests.

CHAPTER XV.

THE STERNOXI, OR "SKIPJACKS" AND THEIR ALLIES.

This section is divided into four families,—the *Buprestidæ, Throscidæ, Eucnemidæ,* and *Elateridæ;* in which the tarsi have five, and the antennæ eleven (except in certain of the latter, where there are twelve) joints; and the prosternum is elongated into a projection behind, fitting into a cavity between the middle legs.

In the three first families the prothorax fits tightly against the base of the elytra, and there is no power of jumping when the insect is placed on its back: whilst in the last the prothorax is not applied closely to the mesothorax, but loosely articulated, and there is nearly always great saltatorial power.

They are all wood or vegetable feeders, with serrated, flabellated, or filiform antennæ; mostly elongate and cylindrical, or a little depressed; metallic in colour, and of hard integuments. They have no paraglossæ to the ligula; their posterior coxæ are immoveable, and transverse, receiving in repose the upper part of the hinder femora for their whole length; the anterior coxæ are globose; the tibiæ have no rows of spines; the penultimate joint of the tarsi is often bilobed; and the abdomen is five-jointed.

The BUPRESTIDÆ have the antennæ short, serrated, and inserted in cavities; the head buried in the thorax up to the eyes, which are large, and vertically oblong; the mouth on the lower side of the head; the labrum small: the ligula often hidden behind the mentum; two fringed, lamelliform, toothless lobes to the maxillæ; the mandibles short and strong; the thorax not produced into spines at the hinder angles; the front and middle coxæ globose, forming conspicuous cups for the trochanters, and the posterior coxæ lamelliform, with small trochanters; the tibiæ always armed with short spurs at the apex; the four first joints of the tarsi with membranous plates on the under side; the two first ventral segments of the abdomen soldered together; and the prosternum ending in a flat projection, received and fixed into a sternal cavity, which in *Anthaxia* and its allies is formed by the *meso-* and *meta-sternum*, and in *Agrilus* and *Trachys* almost entirely by the latter.

In certain species there are one or two more or less retractile additional segments to the abdomen, attached to the generative organs.

They are remarkable for their hard integuments, metallic colour, and rigidity of body; and are usually cylindrical, elongate and somewhat depressed,— *Trachys* only being short and " dumpy."

The parts of the mouth are small, and present but little assistance in classification; but the conspicuous development of certain pores in their antennæ (first pointed out by Erichson, and considered by him as olfactory channels) has been made use of by Lacordaire in separating the different tribes and groups of this (exotically) extensive family. These pores, which are not found on all the joints, appear to be invisible in the majority of *Coleoptera*, being hidden by very fine velvety pubescence: but here they are perfectly distinct, and are diffused over the upper and lower surface of the joints on which they are situated, or concentrated in a little depression situated either on the inner side, or on the anterior part of the lower side, or on the front edge of the joints.

In the *Buprestidæ* the scutellum is often absent or very small; the elytra seldom cover more than the back, and often leave the sides of the abdomen projecting; and the antennæ, which vary considerably as to their point of insertion, fit into cavities in the prosternum.

In tropical regions, and even in Southern Europe, they occur in great numbers, often of large size and splendid colours; but in England we possess not a dozen really indigenous species (all of small stature), although several have been from time to time introduced into our lists, on account of their frequently being captured alive in this country. This arises through their larvæ being easily imported in foreign timber, &c.; and through the long period during which they remain without changing to the perfect state, so that the beetle often makes its appearance at a considerable interval both of time and space from its introduction.

The larvæ are usually smooth, slender, elongate, cylindrical or depressed, and very suddenly enlarged in front; the head sunk in the thorax, distinctly divided into two portions, with two short hard mandibles and small antennæ, but no eyes; and the legs entirely wanting, the end of the body being furnished with a projection, which in *Agrilus* is prolonged into two horny toothed lateral pieces. In the larva of *Trachys*, however, the head is not sunk in the thorax, and has a kidney-shaped eye on each side; there are six widely separated two-jointed legs; and the body rapidly contracts behind, each of its segments being moreover separated from its neighbours by deep incisions, and furnished with an upper and lower horny shield, and two lateral fringed tubercles.

They feed either in solid wood (especially of dead or decaying trees), or under or in the bark. *Agrilus biguttatus*, our largest indigenous species (Plate VIII., Fig. 5), may be taken in all its stages at Darenth Wood at the end of June: its larvæ work sinuous galleries in the damp bark of large oak stumps in open cuttings, that have been left for about two years in the ground, and turn to pupæ in cells between the outer and inner layers; the perfect insect remaining quiescent therein for some time. This species, in common with all the *Buprestidæ*, flies during the hot sunshine; and, on the least alarm, packs its limbs tight to its body, simulates death, and rolls to the ground. The very rare and lovely emerald *Anthaxia* has a similar provoking habit of vanishing from its resting-place in the flowers of *Hieracium* and *Ranunculus ficaria* in the New Forest, when approached by the collector.

The species of *Trachys* found on sallows, in moss, &c., are very small, triangular, thick, and wiry-legged.

The family THROSCIDÆ has been by several authors classed with the *Eucnemidæ*, but appears to be distinct by reason of the formation of the anterior coxal cavities which are formed by the pro- and mosostern um, whereas these parts in the *Eucnemidæ* and the *Elateridæ* are entirely prosternal; it contains the puzzling genus *Throscus*, which has by some authors been placed, as above stated, with the *Eucnemidæ*, whereas by others it is, as here, separated, and placed (together with the exotic *Lissomus*) in a separate family; it further differs from the *Eucnemidæ* in the fixity of its prosternal projection in the sternal cavity; the existence of an anterior projection to the prosternum (as in *Hister*); and the strong flat three-jointed club of its antennæ, which are inserted near the eyes, and (excepting the club) received into furrows in the prosternum. The common little *T. dermestoides* is found in sand-pits and crawling on old palings; it has been said to possess the power of jumping, as in the *Elateridæ*, but its structure appears to be opposed to such a habit: it certainly contracts its legs (of which the front pair are received into cavities) and falls in a jerky fashion when approached.

This is a most irritating insect to mount, and may be considered as a test object for proficiency in setting, owing to its tightly-packed legs and lop-sided proclivities.

The EUCNEMIDÆ possess many of the characters of the *Buprestidæ*, but have the eyes small and round; the antennæ inserted on the forehead, at the inner margin of the eyes, and in the British species usually strongly flabellated; the apical joint of the palpi clubbed; the labrum obsolete; the outer lobe of the maxillæ sometimes (in certain foreign genera) absent; the spurs of the tibiæ very small, or wanting; the hinder angles of the thorax produced; and the projection of the prosternum more or less received into a cavity of the mesosternum, which admits of free motion.

The most important addition to the British beetles that has been made for a long period is that of the type species of this family, *Eucnemis capucina*, which was taken in an old beech-tree near Brockenhurst, New Forest, in some numbers, by Dr. Sharp, Mr. Champion, and Mr. Gorham, on June 13th, 1886 : it is an elongate-oval, subcylindrical, shining-black insect, from two to three lines in length, and is clothed with silky greyish pubescence; the legs are strongly retractile, and render the insect extremely difficult to mount ; the larva is fully described by Dr. Sharp in the Transactions of the Entomological Society, 1886 (Part iii., pp. 297—302).

Melasis and *Microrrhagus*, our other undoubted species in this family, are of considerable rarity. The latter, a small black elongate insect, with long antennæ, which are strongly flabellated in the male, and received in repose into slight furrows on the sides, is occasionally taken in the New Forest; and the former, which is larger, more cylindrical and robust (Plate VIII., Fig. 6; *Melasis buprestoides*, male), occurs sometimes close to London, on palings, and in old trees. The males have flabellated antennæ, and are usually smaller than the females; and the larva closely resembles those of the *Buprestidæ*, from which it chiefly differs in the structure of the organs of its mouth, and in not having its head divided into two portions: it eats galleries in recently dead wood, and forms a cell in which to undergo its metamorphosis ;

the perfect insect (and especially the female) being frequently to be seen lurking at the mouth of the burrow.

The structure of the larva, the insertion and different cavities of the antennæ, absence of a labrum, and more closely fitting prothorax, accompanied by the lesser development of saltatorial power, distinguish this family from the next, to which in many respects it is closely allied.

The ELATERIDÆ have long antennæ, which are either serrated, pectinated, or filiform, inserted immediately in front of the eyes, and (except in the first sub-family) not received into prosternal grooves in repose; the eyes large and round; the head (except in *Campylus*) sunk in the thorax, with the mouth very rarely on the lower side; the labrum always distinct; the mandibles normally short and somewhat semicircular, often bifid at the apex; the apical joint of the palpi more or less securiform (except as above); the thorax produced into spines at the hinder angles, and sloped at the base towards the elytra, which are also sloped forwards; the scutellum mostly situated in a depression; the prosternum usually produced into a chin-piece in front, and always with a dagger-like elongation behind, which moves very freely in the mesosternal cavity; and the tarsi often furnished with lamellæ beneath.

They are nearly always of narrow, elongate, cylindrical shape, though sometimes flattened; and are conspicuous for their power of jumping when placed on the back, from which their common names of "Skipjacks," or "Click-beetles," are derived.

An *Elater*, before jumping, arches its body strongly,

depressing the head and thorax, and elevating the middle, so as both to free the dagger-like projection of the prothorax from the sternal groove, and obtain a purchase for its rapid re-insertion, which is accompanied by a sharp clicking sound: the effect of this is to make the end of the abdomen and elytra act as a lever, whereby the insect is elevated to a considerable distance in the air, nearly always coming on its legs, which are too short, and too closely articulated to the body, to enable it to reach the ground in any other way. If unsuccessful in its first endeavour, it persists in skipping until it lands itself right side up.

The wings in this family are ample, and the flight strong; many of its members flying in the hot sunshine, and basking in warm places; though others are nocturnal, or at least crepuscular, in their habits.

The British species may be divided directly into seventeen genera, or into three tribes, the *Agrypnina*, *Elaterina*, and *Campylina*; of which the first is distinguished by its antennæ being received into the furrows of the prosternum in repose. Our sole undoubted species, *Lacon murinus*, a broad, somewhat convex, and mottled-grey insect, is found in garden heaps and grassy places. The prosternal furrows are not open behind, and there are no lamellæ to its tarsi beneath.

The *Elaterina* present no decided character beyond having the antennæ free in repose: they comprise a great number both of genera and species, all possessing a certain family likeness, but whose divisions are comparatively artificial. The typical genus *Elater* comprises some flattish shining-black insects with blood-red elytra, and one species, *E. sanguinolentus*

(Plate IX., Fig. 1), having also a black mark on the suture; it occurs at the roots of heath on Wimbledon Common, where it has also been taken copiously on the blossom of the nettle.

They frequent grassy places, flowers, and the leaves of trees; some also being found in rotten wood, or under stones on river banks.

Their larvæ are very like the common "mealworm," being horny, slender, and elongate; usually almost cylindrical, but sometimes more or less depressed. They have no eyes or labrum; the maxillæ and mentum are elongate and soldered together, with palpi which have respectively three and two joints; the antennæ are four-jointed and short; the legs very short, robust, close together, and three-jointed; and the apical segment usually larger and more horny than the rest, frequently with toothed projections, and possessing an anal prolongation. They are found at the roots of plants (the common "wire-worm" being only too well known), or in the black rotten wood-mould of old trees, under bark, &c.; and have frequently been known to destroy other subcortical larvæ, not even sparing those of their own species.

One of our most abundant "skipjacks" is *Athoüs hæmorrhoidalis*, a long chestnut-brown beetle with a lighter-coloured abdomen, found in profusion on fern and young hazel in the spring. *Ludius ferrugineus*, a very rare, broad, rather flat, dull-red species (called "the rusty gun-barrel" by one of our best working collectors), is the largest we possess; the little *Cryptohypni*, found under stones on banks, being the smallest. The members of the latter genus appear to be gregarious: I have seen a dozen of *C. dermestoides* (which is not superficially unlike the *Throscus* with a similar trivial appellation) skipping about, on removing a stone on the shore of Loch Rannoch.

The north of England seems to be more productive of the larger species than the south; where, indeed, but few of the *Elateridæ* can be said to abound. The males of some of the metallic species (*Corymbites cupreus* and *pectinicornis*) have the antennæ very strongly flabellated; and in *Synaptus, Agriotes* (the larvæ of certain common species of which are known as the "wire-worm" above alluded to), *Sericosomus, Dolopius,* and *Adrastus,* the head is almost vertical instead of transverse.

The *Campylina* have the head exsorted, with the eyes very prominent and freed from the thorax; the labrum deflexed; no chin-piece to the prosternum; the metasternum sharply narrowed in front, with the intermediate coxæ approximated; the mandibles projecting, straight at the base and curved at the apex; the last joint of the maxillary palpi often oval or subcylindric; and the tarsi not lamellated beneath.

Our solitary species, *Campylus linearis,* is chiefly noticeable from the great variation in colour often seen in the female.

Through this sub-family the passage is easy to the next section, by means of the *Cebrionidæ,* and other families not found in Britain.

M. E. Candèze has monographed the *Elateridæ* of the world in four vols. (Liége, 1857-63); and his work is indispensable to the student of the family.

CHAPTER XVI.

THE MALACODERMATA.

THIS section, as here employed, is of an essentially artificial nature, comprising insects of very varied appearance and structure, which may be considered as divided into fourteen families: the *Dascillidæ*, *Lycidæ*, *Lampyridæ*, *Drilidæ*, *Telephoridæ*, *Melyridæ*, *Cleridæ*, *Limexylonidæ*, *Cissidæ*, *Sphindidæ*, *Lyctidæ*, *Bostrichidæ*, *Ptinidæ*, and *Anobiidæ*; of these only the first six (and perhaps not all of them) can be considered as strictly *Malacodermata*, wherein the integuments of the body are not horny, but soft and flexible, and usually clothed with short pubescence; the antennæ long, filiform or serrate, with generally eleven joints, though sometimes this number varies to ten or twelve (the latter occurring in certain exotic *Lampyridæ*); the parts of the mouth nearly membranous, the mentum being often indistinct, and the ligula with no paraglossæ; the front coxæ conic, exserted, and sometimes almost cylindrical, and the hinder pair transverse, often approximated, and reaching to the edge of the elytra; the tibiæ seldom spurred at the apex; the tarsi five-jointed, though with only four joints to those of the front legs in the males of certain species; the abdomen composed of six or seven free ventral segments; and the elytra very seldom punctate-striate, and usually not covering the sides of the abdomen.

In the remainder there is great variation in the antennæ, hardness of the body, &c.; so that it is impossible to couple them with the true *Malacodermata;* and yet they differ so much *inter se* as to require the formation of many other sections for their reception if separated from that group, although none of their associations are equivalent in extent or distinctness to it.

The DASCILLIDÆ may be divided into two tribes, the *Dascillina* and the *Cyphonina;* in the former of these the mandibles are prominent, and the anterior coxæ have a distinct trochantin, while in the latter the mandibles are hidden, and the anterior coxæ have no trochantin.

The *Dascillina* are here represented by one genus and species, *Dascillus cervinus*, a large, oblong-oval, convex, hard, dull-grey, downy insect, not uncommon in flowers, especially in chalky districts. It has prominent mandibles, straight and spurred tibiæ, and each of the second, third, and fourth joints of the tarsi furnished with a bilobed lamella. Its short, flat, eyeless larva is set with rows of long hairs, and has four-jointed antennæ, rather long legs, horny plates on the upper segments, and no anal prolongation: it lives in the earth at the roots of plants.

The *Cyphonina* are all much smaller and less oblong, with softer integuments, and very fragile. They have sharp mandibles, which are not prominent; the prosternum linear and transverse; the mesothoracic epimera elongate, and those of the metathorax not conspicuous; the femora hollowed on the under side; the tibiæ angulated; and no bilobed lamellæ to the tarsi.

Their larvæ, which feed on water-plants, differ considerably from those of the *Dascillina* (which somewhat resemble the Lamellicorn type), being more like those of the genus *Silpha*.

The perfect insects are obtained by sweeping in marshy places, beating sallows, &c.; and are extremely difficult to obtain in good condition, on account of their slender and slightly articulated limbs, which often come to pieces on being touched with even a camel's-hair brush in mounting. They are mostly yellowish-brown in colour, with no sculpture, and short silky pubescence. The rare *Prionocyphon* has on two or three occasions been found in ants' nests; though it is a mystery how or why it got there. *Scirtes* is conspicuous for the great development of its hinder femora, and the large curved outer spur at the apex of the tibiæ of the same legs; the inner spur being shorter. *S. hemisphæricus*, a flat, black insect, is abundant in marshy places at Weybridge and elsewhere; and jumps strongly, after the manner of the *Halticina*, for a member of which tribe it might readily be mistaken by a novice who failed to notice its five-jointed tarsi. It has a pleasing habit of dropping its hind legs entirely when handled; and shares the fragility of its allies. *Eubria palustris*, a small black insect with rather deeply furrowed elytra, differs from the rest of the *Cyphonina* chiefly in having the mesosternum level and square instead of concave, and the prosternal projection not narrow but wide and flat, gradually lessened behind, and uniting with the mesosternum. The front and intermediate coxæ are transverse and sunken, with no trochantins; and the hinder pair are but very slightly enlarged on the inner side; it is a very rare species, and has been taken on small sticks submerged in a narrow water-course.

The LYCIDÆ have the antennæ inserted on the upper side between or before the eyes, and very close together; the mandibles very small, slender, and not toothed at the apex; the trochanters placed in the axis of the femora; and the head produced into the form of a rostrum, and covered by the prothorax.

They are conspicuous for their flattened appearance; long and ample clytra, with diminished head and thorax; bright colours, and peculiar reticulated sculpture.

Eros Aurora (Plate IX., Fig. 2) is found, at Rannoch, in Perthshire, on the under sides of felled pine-trees, or among the half-rotten heaps of chips left by the woodman. It is a sluggish species, and is readily captured, not attempting to escape, though it flies heavily towards the evening: the sexes remain coupled for some time, the male being the smaller of the two, with longer antennæ, and having a deep semicircular notch on the hinder margin of the last abdominal segment. The larva of an allied species has been found under bark of dead trees, where it feeds on other insects, &c.: it is black, with a red tail; elongate, very flattened, leathery, with slender mandibles which are placed very close together, and having two recurved hooks and a retractile prolongation at the apex of the body.

The LAMPYRIDÆ are closely allied to the last family, from which they differ, however, considerably in outward appearance; in the mostly apterous state of the female; and in the presence of the power of emitting phosphorescent light. Their palpi, also, are of different structure; the eyes more developed; the head more entirely hidden by the rounded prothorax; and the intermediate coxæ more approximated. The "Glow-worm," *Lampyris noctiluca*, and the curious *Phosphænus hemipterus*, which has only been found at Lewes, are the sole British exponents of this family. The males of the glow-worm are sometimes very slightly luminous, and are considerably rarer than the female; they may, however, be taken by sweeping at night in grassy places where the other sex is found,—sometimes having been observed to fly to a lamp, after the fashion of moths. They are dingy in colour, with a rounded thorax hiding the head, ample wings under their elytra, and very large eyes, resembling those of certain dipterous insects. The female, on the contrary, has smaller eyes, and neither elytra nor wings; her body is flat, soft, and broad; and, in short, she considerably resembles the larva from which she sprang, from which she differs in having the ordinary femur, tibia, and five-jointed tarsi to the legs, eleven-jointed antennæ, and a broad flat semicircular thorax: the larva, moreover, has distinct light-coloured corners to each segment. The pupa of the female exhibits but slight differences from the larva; but that of the male shows the ordinary rudiments of the future members. The insect, both as an imago and larva, devours small *Mollusca* (snails, &c.); and, when in the latter condition, uses certain radii, protruded from the anus, for the purpose of freeing the front of the body from the dirt and slime caused by its habits of feeding.

The phosphorescent light has been observed in all the stages and both sexes of this species; but is especially evident in the full-grown female, proceeding from the under side of the abdomen at the apex, where certain of the segments are lighter in colour than the rest. It appears to be subject to the will of the insect, and is brightest when the latter is found in damp places.

The DRILIDÆ have their antennæ distant at the base, and serrated or flabellated; the mandibles bifid, and armed with a sharp tooth in the middle of the inner side; the head not covered by the prothorax, but inserted in it up to the eyes; the clypeus confounded with the head (as in the *Lycidæ*, *Lampyridæ*, and *Telephoridæ*); the prothorax strongly transverse, and the claws of the tarsi toothed beneath; in some of the exotic genera the palpi are often very extraordinary, and on this account it has recently been proposed to place the family near the *Limexylonidæ*.

Our solitary representative, *Drilus flavescens* (Plate IX., Fig. 3), is found at Dover, near Darenth Wood, &c., by sweeping in grassy places, especially where snails abound. The female, as in *Lampyris*, possesses neither wings nor elytra, and is of the greatest rarity in England.

The larva feeds upon snails (*Helix nemoralis*), closing up the orifice of the shell with its exuviæ whilst preying upon its inhabitant. I once took at the base of Shakespeare's Cliff a full-grown female larva, running rapidly in the hot sunshine among snail shells. It was more than half an inch long; flat, narrow, but rather widening behind; with a flat head, armed with two sharp and rather widely separated mandibles, six moderately long anterior legs, two thin tubercles on each side of the fourth and following segments, gradually getting longer, and clothed with stout brown bristles; and two longer elevated protuberances, also set with long hairs on the upper side, with an anal elongation beneath, on the last segment. It was nearly the colour of raw sienna; and had a widening row of black spots on each side, beginning on the thorax. The figure given in Westwood's Introduction (vol. i., p. 247, f. 26, 18) is not correct; being too broad and not hairy enough.

The female preserves the appearance of the larva to a great extent.

The TELEPHORIDÆ (commonly known as "soldiers" or "sailors") have the head free and contracted behind; the clypeus more or less covering the mandibles; the labrum obsolete, instead of distinct, as in the preceding families; the antennæ filiform; the elytra not rolloxed at the sides, flexible, liable to distortion, and rarely entirely covering the abdomen; the palpi slender; and the fourth joint of the tarsi bilobed.

Although their integuments, compared with those of the families of the preceding section, are as different as the canvas of a sculler's boat from the plates of an ironclad, these insects are "Warriors" *à l'outrance;* and are living disproofs of Scott's well-known lines (Rokeby):—

"Man only mars kind nature's plan,
And turns the fell pursuit on man:"

seeing that they not only prey on other beetles, but also ruthlessly attack those of their own species. Consequently the collector must remember to put them in a bottle containing laurel-leaves, or they will infallibly maim their fellow-captives.

Their larvæ, equally carnivorous, feeding upon earthworms, &c., live underground; but are sometimes found on the surface in great numbers, even upon snow. They are elongate, somewhat parallel, black in colour, with white or reddish spots; and resemble those of the *Lampyridæ* in having a single eye on each side of the head, no labrum, and the clypeus confused with the head: they are, however, softer, and clothed with a fine velvety down; and have the head exposed, and the abdominal segments rounded. Mr. G. R. Waterhouse has described and figured the larva of *Telephorus rufus* in the Transact. of the Ent. Soc. i., p. 31, pl. 3.

The perfect insects, which fly readily in the hot sunshine, and have long loosely-articulated legs, which they use with great effect, are mostly found on flowers (chiefly *Umbelliferæ*), and by sweeping in damp places: it is not easy to obtain a series in good preservation, owing to their liability to distortion in drying; the abdomen, especially in the females, being very large and soft.

Telephorus clypeatus (Plate IX., Fig. 4) is one of the prettiest, owing to its spotted thorax; unlike many of the members of its genus, it does not vary in colour or marking. *Telephorus* is divided into four sub-genera; *Podabrus*, in which the head is constricted at base, forming a neck, and the tibial spurs are obsolete; *Ancystronycha*, wherein the outer claw of the tarsi in the female has a very strong spine-like tooth; *Telephorus* proper, wherein this tooth is less developed; and *Rhagonycha*, in which both the claws are bifid, seeming to be split at the apex. In the latter the tibiæ, also, are straighter, more slender, and with only obsolete spurs.

The species of *Malthinus* and *Malthodes* have very long slender antennæ, and short elytra, scarcely covering two-thirds of the abdomen. They are small, very fragile, and are most easily obtained by sweeping under fir-trees. In the former genus the elytra are longer, and the mandibles have a strong tooth near the apex, which is wanting in the latter.

The MELYRIDÆ have the clypeus separated by a suture from the forehead (a structure, however, not very evident in the British species); the labrum distinct; the abdomen composed of six segments; the spurs of the tibiæ obsolete or absent; and the tarsi not bilobed. In the *Malachiina* (wherein the antennæ, contrary to the prevailing structure of the family, are inserted in the front, instead of at the sides, of the head), containing the genera *Malachius, Axinotarsus,* and *Anthocomus,* there are certain retractile vesicles to the prothorax and abdomen, which in some of the small green metallic species of the former genus assume the appearance of the wattles of a cock. Their larvæ are carnivorous, living under bark, and in dry rotten wood, where they feed upon other larvæ, &c.

The *Dasytina* are mostly slender and elongate hairy insects with antennæ usually plainly serrate, and the *Phlœophilina* are distinguished by having the antennæ moniliform with the three apical joints larger; the latter tribe contains the single genus *Phlœophilus,* which has been by many authors considered as allied to *Mycetophagus* and *Triphyllus.* The single species known, *P. Edwardsi*, was for a long time only found in this country, where it is taken in Nottinghamshire, Leicestershire, Lincolnshire, and Dorset, living in the old lichen-covered boughs of oak-trees. It is an oblong, convex, slightly pubescent, strongly punctured insect, with a dark thorax and grey elytra, more or less variegated with darker lines, and, unlike the *Mycetophagidæ*, is very sluggish.

The CLERIDÆ (which are mostly brightly coloured) have the antennæ often clubbed; the labrum distinct; the tarsi provided with lamellæ beneath and sometimes bilobed; often only five abdominal segments; the posterior coxæ transverse, sunk, not approximated, and covered by the hind femora; the body oblong, usually cylindrical, rather hard, and hairy; the eyes kidney-shaped and notched; and the head and thorax narrower than the elytra. They are remarkable, also, for usually having the labial larger than the maxillary palpi.

In *Tillus*, *Clerus*, *Opilus*, and *Trichodes* there are five joints to the tarsi, and the pronotum is confused with the prothoracic parapleuræ, so that the thorax becomes cylindrical; but in the sub-family *Enopliides*, to which the genus *Corynetes* belongs, there are only four joints (the normal fourth joint being imperfectly developed); and the upper part of the thorax is separated from the sides by a more or less conspicuous ridge.

Tillus elongatus, a narrow black insect with red thorax (the male being rarely entirely black), perforates old wood, and is sometimes found in elder-blossom.

Clerus formicarius (Plate IX., Fig. 5), a regular

Harlequin, occurs beneath bark; where its larva, dark pink and spotted in front (figured by Ratzeburg, Forstins., vol. i., p. 35, pl. 1, f. 7; and by M. Perris, Ann. de la Soc. Ent. de Fr., 1854), preys upon other wood-feeding larvæ. *Opilus* is found in old hedges and posts, its soft, pale pink, hairy larva living under the bark of willows, and feeding on the larvæ of *Anobium*, &c.; and the species of *Trichodes* (of doubtful British origin), large, hairy, blue, red-banded insects, are parasitic in their earlier stages upon honey and mason-bees, whose larvæ they devour. *Corynetes* and *Necrobia*, small, flattish, shining, and blue-black, with the thorax or legs red in some instances, frequent dry skins, dead carcases, &c. (having even been found in an Egyptian mummy); the latter is distinguished by the more elongate apical joint of its palpi, and the larger and flatter club to its antennæ.

The LIMEXYLONIDÆ (*Xylotrogi*, Latr.) are very long, narrow, and cylindrical, with the head free from the prothorax, contracted behind, and having a neck; the front and middle coxæ close together, large, long, cylindrical, and not exserted; the posterior pair being oblique; the prosternum not produced into a point behind; the spurs of the tibiæ imperfectly developed or absent; the legs long and thin, with slender five-jointed tarsi; the labrum small, but distinct; and the palpi considerably developed in the males.

Their larvæ, which bore neat round drills horizontally into solid timber, are elongate, cylindrical, recurved behind, smooth, but with numerous roughnesses on the front of the body, and a projection on the back of the apical segment; their head is retractile into the first thoracic segment, which is enlarged and elevated, and they have no eyes. The pupa is formed near the mouth of the burrow, which is enlarged by the larva; and is thin and cylindrical, as in most wood-feeding insects.

Hylecœtus dermestoides (Plate IX., Fig. 6, male), found at Rannoch, Sherwood, &c., differs considerably in the size and colour of its sexes, and possesses an ocellum on the vertex. The maxillary palpi of the male are of great size, assuming the appearance of a fan, on account of the third joint (which is much developed) having numerous branchial appendages. In this genus there are six segments to the abdomen; but in *Limexylon*, which is of the greatest rarity here, though so common on the Continent as to commit great damage to timber, there are only five.

The CISSIDÆ or CIOIDÆ (described by M. Mellié in the French "Annales," 1848, p. 205, *et seq.*) have four joints to the tarsi, of which the three first are not so long as the apical. Their head is more or less retractile within the thorax, the front of which often projects; the antennæ vary from eight to ten joints in the British genera, but have always a three-jointed club; the organs of the mouth are but little developed, the mandibles only being robust, and the labrum distinct; there are no apical spurs to the tibiæ; and the first joint of the abdomen is longer than any of the others.

They are all small, cylindrical, feebly built insects; varying from yellow to dark brown in colour; generally shining, but sometimes clothed with a very short silky down, which imparts a somewhat metallic reflection. Their punctuation is almost always irregular on the elytra; and they occur gregariously in boleti, and other fungi, especially when the latter are attached to trees. The males are known either by the larger size of their mandibles, or by the presence of certain little horn-like tubercles on the head or anterior margin of the prothorax.

Their elongate, cylindrical, curved, fleshy larvæ are slightly hairy, with two recurved hooks at the apex on the upper side, and appear to resemble those of *Cryptophagus*; and the pupa has two slight spines at its lower extremity.

In *Rhopalodontus* and *Cis* the antennæ have ten joints; the former having the tibiæ dilated at their outer extremity and distinctly toothed, the second joint of the antennæ much longer than the third, the head toothed in the middle, and the last joint of the maxillary palpi more oblong. In *Ennearthron* there are (as its name imports) nine joints to the antennæ, and in the equally suggestive *Octotemnus* but eight: the latter has no tubercles on the head or thorax in the male, and the tibiæ are slightly toothed outside.

The largest and commonest of the family is *Cis boleti*, in which the thorax has several irregular depressions; it is found in damp fungoid wood, or the small greenish laminated boleti on the bark of rotten trees. As in all the rest, individuals of different degrees of maturity are often found associated. They are all difficult to set, owing to their small size, and the shortness, retractile structure, and weak articulation of their limbs, and must not be kept long in laurel, otherwise their members part company.

The position of the SPHINDIDÆ is doubtful, and it is quite possible that they may in time be classed with the *Heteromera*, as the tarsi, in one sex at least, are heteromerous, and the family in some respects bears a relation to certain *Tenebrionidæ*; in the genus *Sphindus* (variously associated with *Anobium, Cis, Tetratoma, Cryptophagus,* and *Lyctus*) the apical joint of the tarsi is as long as the preceding joints together; the head ends in a small quadrangular rostrum, and the antennæ are ten-jointed, with a strong three-jointed club.

S. dubius, very rare in England (where it has occurred at Weybridge and in the New Forest), is a small pitchy-brown insect, more or less variegated with ferruginous; having finely-striated elytra, and clothed with thin depressed reddish pubescence. It lives in Lycoperdons, in which also its larva is found. The latter is whitish, with the head, upper part of thorax, and last segment of the abdomen shining black; and set with rather long hairs on the sides and extremity.

The LYCTIDÆ are sometimes associated with both the next and the preceding family; and have, also, been placed among the *Colydiidæ* and *Cryptophagidæ*, to certain of the former of which they present a considerable external resemblance. Their tarsi have five joints, the first being very small, and the last as long as the four preceding; the first abdominal segment is longer than any of the rest; the club of their antennæ is two-jointed; and their body flat and elongate, with punctate-striate elytra.

This assemblage of characters causes them to fit uneasily with any of their supposed allies; and the difficulty of assigning them to their correct position has been increased by the discovery of the larva of one of the species, which is fleshy, arched, cylindrical, and without eyes or legs;—resembling, in short, those of the tetramerous *Scolytidæ* and *Curculionidæ*; it appears to make straight burrows in the solid wood of felled oaks.

Our common *Lyctus canaliculatus*, which has a depression on the prothorax, is found on fresh oak palings.

The BOSTRICHIDÆ present considerable resemblance to the *Anobiidæ*, from which they differ especially in the structure of their tarsi, wherein the first joint is very small, and the second and apical much enlarged. The spurs to the tibiæ are also more developed, especially in the front legs; the anterior coxæ are very large; the body is harder, and not so pubescent; the head is not retractile, but hidden by the great bulk of the thorax in front; and the elytra are often obliquely truncate at the apex; in which last character (and in general facies) they are exceedingly like certain of the *Scolytidæ*, wherein the number of joints in the tarsi is different.

Their larvæ, also, appear to resemble those of the *Ptinidæ*, but to be less wrinkled transversely; having, moreover, two four-jointed antennæ and no eyes, whilst the latter have exceedingly small two-jointed antennæ and very minute spherical eyes, situated in a depression near the base of the mandibles.

The large and very rare *Bostrichus capucinus* was last taken near Highgate on a felled oak, about the year 1866; and the little *Rhizopertha pusilla*, superficially very like a *Tomicus*, but in which the structure of the tarsi is exactl the same as in the *Cissidæ*, occurs at Glasgow and elsewhere, being probably imported.

The PTINIDÆ and ANOBIIDÆ, which are often associated together, are conspicuous for their habit of retracting their head beneath the prothorax (Plate X., Fig. 1 a), which forms a cowl; their legs, also, are contractile, with no spines on the outer edge of the tibiæ, which have the terminal spurs absent or very small, and short five-jointed tarsi, of which the first and second joints are almost equal in length. They are usually small, of hard integuments, more or less cylindrical, and clothed with short pubescence. Of the two families, the *Ptinidæ* have the antennæ inserted in the front part of the head, and the upper part of the prothorax confused with its sides; whilst the *Anobiidæ* have the antennæ inserted close to the front margin of the eyes, a strong ridge separating the pronotum from the sides of the prothorax, and the anterior coxæ rather more projecting.

Their larvæ, which resemble those of the *Lamellicornia* in miniature, feed chiefly upon dead wood; though sometimes upon living trees, bones, seeds, &c. I have found the cocoons of *Ptinus germanus* in an old post; they were formed of a dirty silken fabric, mixed with pieces of wood; and contained the perfect insects, which (as usual) do not appear to be active immediately after their exclusion from the pupa.

Hedobia imperialis (Plate X., Fig. 1) is the chief species of the *Ptinidæ* that has any pretensions to beauty; it occurs in old white-thorn bushes. The *Ptini* are found in houses and about old palings, often doing considerable damage to Natural History collections; they have the prothorax constricted behind, and the male usually more elongate, and with longer antennæ than the female.

Gibbium and *Mezium*, both house-feeders (and, perhaps, not truly indigenous), have entirely smooth and shining elytra, looking much like certain small *Arachnida*; the former especially so, on account of its thorax also being smooth, its continuous outline, slow gait, and long sprawling legs. The latter has no scutellum; and both contract their legs and antennæ in repose, assuming a globular form, which has been fancifully likened to a drop of blood.

Of the *Anobiidæ*, the cylindrical little *Ptilinus pectinicornis*,—whose neat round drills may often be seen in great numbers in old willow, &c., looking as if a volley of small shot had been discharged very cleanly into the wood,—is noteworthy from the beautiful fan-like structure of its antennæ in the male. The females appear to remain in the galleries made by the larvæ, and the male couples from the outside.

Dorcatoma,—small, round, and convex,—found in old rotten wood or fungi, has the antennæ terminated by a three-jointed, flat, dentated club; and the genus *Anobium*, wherein the three last joints of the antennæ are enlarged or lengthened, comprises the well-known "Death-watch;" an appellation given to certain of its species (*A. tessellatum* especially) found in old furniture, wainscoting, &c., on account of their habit of making an audible clicking with their mandibles against the hard wood, possibly as a call for their mates. This noise, distinct enough in the stillness of the night, and associated by superstition with the advent of death, has doubtless in olden times unstrung the weak nerves of many an invalid. The wood-dust ejected from their burrows in beams, chairs, &c., may frequently be seen in country houses. They retract the limbs and simulate death very readily and pertinaciously.

The members of these two and the four preceding families are associated by Thomson with *Cerylon, Colydium, Myrmecoxenus, Sphindus*, &c., in the *Xylophagi* of Latreille, which he places between the *Lamellicornes* and an equivalent division, *Fungicola*, Latr., immediately preceding the *Sternoxi*.

The *Fungicola* are made to include genera of such different structure as *Monotoma, Lathridius, Cryptophagus, Telmatophilus, Tritoma, Triplax, Endomychus, Tetratoma, Mycetophagus, Diphyllus*, &c.

CHAPTER XVII.

THE LONGICORNIA.

This section belongs to the large group of vegetable-feeders formerly known by the name of *Tetramera*, on account of their apparently possessing only four joints to the tarsi: this name has, however, been modified to that of "*Pseudo-tetramera*," or "*Sub-tetramera*," by Mr. Westwood, who pointed out that they have the normal five joints, although the fourth is so minute as usually to escape notice; being, with the basal portion of the terminal joint, received between the lobes of the third joint, which is always more or less deeply notched at its extremity. The three basal joints are, also, always more or less strongly cushioned beneath. The other sections which have been classed together as possessing these characters are the *Longicornia* and the *Rhynchophora*; the latter, however, are now usually regarded as a group entirely apart from the rest.

The Longicornia present a considerable family likeness to each other, chiefly on account of their long antennæ, which are never clubbed, but at most serrated, being generally filiform or setaceous, and having a long, thickened, basal joint. Their eyes are kidney-shaped, or strongly hollowed out in the middle of their front side, having the antennæ frequently inserted in the excavated portion, and sometimes entirely dividing each eye into two parts; their mandibles stout, sharp at the point, and usually large, the head never being produced into a rostrum in front, as in the *Rhynchophora*. The mentum is transverse and short, and the labium usually membranous and cordate; the palpi being moderately long and filiform, though sometimes short or truncated; the elytra, which are broader than the thorax, do not encase the sides of the abdomen, which is composed of five free ventral segments; the legs are long, having often clavate femora, with the tibiæ not bearing external rows of spines, but distinctly spurred at the apex; and the tarsi have the three basal joints clothed with a dense silky or spongy substance, the first and second joints being widened, the third strongly bilobed, generally being divided into two rounded lappets, the (normal) fourth obsolete, hidden in, or soldered to the centre of the third, and the apical joint long, slender, and strongly clawed.

They are entirely plant-frequenting insects, existing as larvæ and pupæ either in solid timber, or on the surface of felled logs, &c., beneath the bark; and in their perfect state haunting the trunks of trees and bundles of dry twigs, or basking in flowers. Many of the gaily-coloured species delight in the hot sunshine, flying readily, and running with great activity up and down the surface of timber; but some appear to be sluggish in the warmer part of the day, and to fly readily towards evening, often with a humming noise.

The females are less active than the males, being seldom seen on the wing; they are, also, usually larger and heavier, and have shorter antennæ, and a more or less developed ovipositor, partly horny and partly membranous, being a continuation of the end of the abdomen, and capable of considerable elongation, somewhat after the fashion of the tubes of a telescope. With this instrument,—which can be thrust to some distance from the surface into holes in wood or cracks in bark, to the sinuosities of which its substance readily adapts itself,—eggs are placed in positions where the young larva will be both secure and in the midst of suitable food.

The larvæ, which often grow to a large size, and live for a long time before they assume the pupa state, commit much damage to trees; steadily gnawing clean-cut galleries or tubes through solid timber, and filling up their track with their frass of woody fibres. On account of this long duration of their larval condition, and of their habit of boring deeply away from the surface, near which their traces are small, the gallery getting, of course, larger as the larva increases in size,—foreign species have often been introduced into this country in wood; and, as the perfect insects are hardy and fly strongly, they have been caught in places far from their original spot of landing. In this way a large North American Longicorn has occurred near Manchester; and may, indeed, be said to have become naturalized, as specimens of it have been taken at considerable intervals, and always in the same wood, where the original specimen, in all probability, laid her eggs.

The larvæ of the *Longicornia* are soft, dirty white, and fleshy, somewhat flattened, broadest in front, the second segment being large and flat; with the head broad, depressed, hard, retractile, and having strong mandibles, minute retractile antennæ, and rudimentary tubercular eyes on each side. They possess six very small, jointed, horny legs in front; but thrust themselves along their galleries by means of fleshy dorsal elevations, the segments being all more or less retractile.

Our species, very few in number compared with those of most other countries, may be considered as divided into four families:—the *Prionidæ*, *Cerambycidæ*, *Lepturidæ*, and *Lamiidæ*; the three last of which are again separated into sub-families or tribes; by some authors the *Cerambycidæ* and *Lepturidæ* are classed together under one family, *Cerambycidæ*.

The PRIONIDÆ have the labrum obsolete or very small; the mandibles large and robust, especially in the males; the inner lobe of the maxillæ obsolete or small; the palpi moderately long; the labium small; the antennæ inserted close above the base of the mandibles, but with the insertion not surrounded by the emargination of the eyes; the head not narrowed behind into a neck; the thorax subquadrate, spined or toothed at the sides; the prosternum considerably produced in a blunt process behind the anterior coxæ; the elytra spined at the apex; and the anterior coxæ transverse and wide apart.

We possess but one genus and species, *Prionus coriarius*, the largest of the section in England. This insect is by no means common, occurring very rarely near London, though sometimes taken more frequently in woods near the south coast. It is a very large, dull brown, flat, clumsily-built creature, having broad, serrated antennæ, prominent mandibles, strong spines to the sides of its thorax, and wide tarsi; it rests on the trunks of trees during the day, and is usually taken when flying heavily towards evening.

Its larva is a broad, flattish, white grub, narrowed behind, with its head bearing very strong small triangular mandibles, and capable of being considerably retracted into the first segment, which is short, the second being large and flattened: it has six minute legs in front, and also fleshy protuberances on the under side. It feeds in solid timber, and forms a large cocoon with pieces of gnawed wood, &c., taking the precaution (so very prevalent in timber-feeding insects), when nearly full grown, of boring its gallery towards the outer surface of the tree in which it lives, so that the perfect insect has but little work to do in making its escape.

The CERAMBYCIDÆ are divided into four tribes:—the *Cerambycina, Callidiina, Clytina,* and *Obriina;* and are distinguished by their slightly deflexed head, unarmed tibiæ, laterally dilated thorax, and subglobose anterior coxæ, and by having their antennæ (which are generally very long, and never serrated) inserted at some distance from the mandibles.

The *Cerambycina* (which have the head exserted, the antennæ with the second joint transverse, the thorax armed with a lateral spine, the femora slender, almost cylindrical, and the shoulders of the elytra rectangular) are here represented by *Aromia moschata,* often found in the London district on old willows (which are much damaged by its larvæ), and generally known as the "Musk-beetle," on account of its sweet smell; which is, however, much more like otto of roses than musk.

This scent is so strong as to be readily noticed at some distance from trees frequented by the insects;

which may be seen in June flying strongly in the hot sunshine: the males, in which the antennæ are very long, are by far the most active; and it has been remarked that the peculiar odour,—which is strongest in the female, and especially at the coupling time,— acts probably as an attraction to them. A live specimen, imprisoned for a short time in a handkerchief, will impart an agreeable and enduring scent to it.

This insect, which is rather narrow, long, blue or coppery-green in colour, and somewhat shagreened in texture, possesses in a marked degree a habit found in most *Longicornia*, viz. that of making a loud, sharp, squeaking noise, by moving the head and prothorax briskly up and down, the inner part of the hinder margin of the latter rubbing against the smooth part of the front of the mesothorax.

The *Callidiina* are somewhat depressed, and have the head inserted in the thorax almost up to the eyes, the labrum small, the thorax with no lateral spine, the femora nearly always elavate, and the front and hind coxæ usually somewhat approximated.

Three genera are found in England, viz. *Callidium, Hylotrupes*, and *Asemum*. The species of the former are of considerable brightness: they frequent firwood, &c., and thus are liable to get transported from one locality to another in building materials, &c. It has, indeed, been suggested (and with apparent reason) that one, if not more, of the species in this genus, now certainly considered as indigenous, have been in this way introduced from abroad. *C. violaceum*, a dull violet-coloured, flattened insect, was formerly of great rarity, though now very common in many parts of the country; and it is impossible to distinguish British from Canadian examples;—much timber coming to us from North America. Its transformations have been accurately described in the Linnean Transactions, vol. v., by Kirby; from whose account it appears that the larva mines galleries on the surface of felled fir-trees, under the bark, burrowing deeply and obliquely into the solid wood before changing to pupa. Its mandibles are very stout and solid, resembling two sections of a cone applied against each other for the whole of their flattened sides.

C. alni (Plate XIII., Fig. 3) is very small, and elegantly variegated: it occurs plentifully in hedges, &c., both on flowers and in dry twigs.

H. bajulus, a dull blackish species, variegated with greyish down, and having two shining black marks on the thorax, is occasionally taken near London; where its larva has been known to do considerable damage in the timber of houses, even penetrating sheets of lead.

A. striatum,—very dull, entirely black, and sluggish,—occurs in Scotland, settling on freshly-cut pine stumps.

The *Clytina* have the thorax nearly globose, and are represented by one genus, *Clytus*; the species of which somewhat resemble wasps, being mostly black with yellow bands: their larvæ make circular holes in palings and poles, &c. *C. arietis* is very abundant in flowers, &c., about June.

The *Obriina* have the thorax cylindrical, constricted at the base; the antennæ setaceous, never less than the body in length; the clytra entire and parallel, and the femora clavate.

Obrium cantharinum, a small, shining, entirely reddish species, with large eyes, and very long antennæ, is of considerable rarity: *Gracilia pygmæa*, our other representative, duller and darker, occurs not unfrequently on old wood-work, twigs, &c.

The LEPTURIDÆ are closely allied to the *Cerambycidæ*, in that they have the prosternum not or scarcely produced behind the anterior coxæ, and the labrum free and distinct; they differ in having the clypeus longer, often subquadrate, the anterior coxæ conical and strongly prominent, and the eyes (in our genera) always almost entire or feebly emarginate; their head is bent downwards, but not abruptly so, and with a distinct neck; their thorax is narrowed in front, and their elytra are more or less contracted behind.

As compared with their allies, they are more active and diurnal in their habits, and, as a general rule, smaller in size, and with shorter antennæ.

They form two tribes, the *Molorchina* and *Lepturina*; in the former of which the elytra are abbreviated, with the wings exserted; the femora clavate; the front coxæ approximated; and the thorax cylindrical, with a small lateral tubercle.

We possess one genus, *Molorchus*, containing two species; one of which, *M. umbellatarum* (Plate XIII., Fig. 6),—sometimes found in flowers, but much more readily obtained by beating bundles of dead twigs in hedges,—is not uncommon near London. Its small size, narrow appearance, long thin legs and antennæ, short wing-cases and exposed wings, easily distinguish it from any other insect.

The *Lepturina* have the front coxæ much projecting, and usually wide apart; the antennæ rarely longer than the body; the thorax generally almost transverse; and the femora but slightly thickened.

In *Rhagium*,—the species of which are very abundant in pine woods, and which may be found in all their stages under fir-bark, the larvæ eating galleries on the surface,—the antennæ are very short, and the entire insect is flattened, broad, and of a comparatively dull, mottled appearance. The pupæ have rows of short spines across the segments of the abdomen; as in *Cossus* and other wood-feeding *Lepidoptera*.

Toxotus,—a most variable insect, both in size and colour,—has long straggling legs and antennæ, and flies with a considerable noise in the hot sunshine; it is however surpassed, in point of variation, by the common *Strangalia armata* (Plate XIV., Fig. 1; a dark variety), of which it is difficult to obtain two specimens exactly alike; and in the male of which the hinder tibiæ have two conspicuous tooth-like processes on the inner side.

This insect,—which, according to the predominance of colour, may be designated either as yellow with black spots, or as black with yellow,—is abundant during the summer months on the flowers of *Umbelliferæ*, especially at the margins of woods; and is very active both with its legs and wings (at all events when the sun shines), taking to flight readily, and making ludicrous movements in its hurry to escape.

The LAMIIDÆ are divided into two tribes, *Lamiina* and *Saperdina*, in which the head is abruptly and vertically bent down, the antennæ are inserted within the emargination of the eyes, the tibiæ armed with small spurs, and the legs not very elongate.

In the *Lamiina* the femora are distinctly clavate,

the intermediate tibiæ obliquely truncated, and with a setose tubercle on the outer side behind the middle, the thorax is armed with a lateral spine, and the mandibles are short.

In this sub-family some of our largest and most curious *Longicornia* are found; *Lamia textor* and *Astinomus ædilis* being especially remarkable. The former of these is a large, clumsy, convex, dull black insect, found near Bristol, and at Rannoch in Perthshire, on willow-trees and in osier beds, the top shoots of which it is reported to weave together as a nidus.

The other, *A. ædilis* (Plate XIII., Fig. 4), is conspicuous for the enormous length of its antennæ, especially in the male. This, also, occurs at Rannoch, where it may be not uncommonly seen flying across the glades of the Black Forest with its long appendages streaming behind. It loves to settle on felled pine logs, with its antennæ spread out like compasses; from which habit it is termed by the Highlanders "Timberman;" a name, curiously enough, also applied to it in Lapland and Sweden, where it is common. If two males come within range they inevitably fight; for which reason, and also on account of their delicate structure, it is difficult to obtain quite perfect specimens.

The larva makes wide galleries and perforations in pine stumps, forming a nidus with coarse gnawed fragments near the surface, in which it changes to pupa. In this state the antennæ are turned downwards and recurved towards the middle of the head. The larva appears to be full fed at the beginning of the summer, and, after remaining two or three weeks in the pupa state, changes to the perfect state; staying as such in its nest until the following summer.

The species of *Pogonocherus* are very much smaller, having the elytra slightly hairy, generally spined at the apex, and with the front greyish-white. They are beaten out of bundles of old twigs and faggots in hedges.

In the *Saperdina*, which are all more or less cylindrical, the femora are not clavate; and the thorax, which has no spine at the sides, is continuous in outline with the elytra, being, moreover, deeply sinuated on the sides beneath.

Here are situated some of our most handsome species; notably *Saperda scalaris* (Plate XIII., Fig. 5), a very beautifully coloured insect, occurring near Manchester and at Rannoch; it has also been found near Burton-on-Trent.

Of the other *Saperdæ*,—which appear to affect aspens, poplars, and willows,—*carcharias* (found in fenny districts) is remarkable for its large size and uniform yellow-ochreous tint; and *populnea*, a hairy, minutely speckled insect, common near London on young aspens, is readily found in its larval state by the round swollen knobs which it makes in the stems of that tree.

Agapanthia lineatocollis, which may be known by its very long twelve-jointed antennæ, has been taken near Lincoln in numbers on the Cow-parsnip (*Heracleum spondylium*), and *Oberea oculata*, conspicuous by its red thorax, which is furnished with two black tubercles on its disc, used to be found not uncommonly on sallows in the Cambridge Fens, but has not been recorded for many years from its old locality; it has, however, been recently (1889) taken in Norfolk, and one specimen was captured a few years ago near Romney Marshes.

Another genus, *Tetrops*,—of which the single species is also common near London, and easily known by its linear shape, very small size, black head and thorax, and yellowish elytra,—is worthy of notice on account of each of its eyes being absolutely divided into two by the insertion of its antennæ.

The *Longicornia* are, as a rule, so rare in this country, that the young collector will probably be some time before he takes more than this insect, one or two small species of *Grammoptera*, *Clytus arietis*, and a *Rhagium*.

CHAPTER XVIII.

THE EUPODA, OR PHYTOPHAGA (COMMONLY CALLED CHRYSOMELIDÆ).

At the beginning of this section we must now place the *Bruchidæ*, which until comparatively recently have been placed in the *Rhynchophora*; it must be allowed that they are not very closely allied to any other group, but they come nearer to the *Sagrina* than to anything else; the following are their chief characters: head free, produced in front, but with no distinct rostrum, neck usually constricted, antennæ eleven-jointed, not clavate, but often serrate or pectinate; anterior coxæ conical and oblique, contiguous at apex, posterior coxæ large, laminate, reaching the margin of the elytra; pygidium always exposed; abdomen with five free ventral segments, of which the first is the longest; tarsi, as in the *Chrysomelidæ*, with the third joint bilobed, and the fourth very small; the basal joint of the hind tarsi is long and curved, and the hind legs are more or less thickened. Our single genus, *Bruchus*, comprises some small, oblong beetles, usually leaden-black in colour, and variegated with grey or white pubescence, arranged in indistinct bands or spots. Their males are usually distinguished by the denticulation, &c., of the inner side of the middle tibiæ. One species, *B. pisi*, found in peas, is in all probability imported from abroad; but *B. rufimanus*, almost equally large, abounds in bean-fields, &c., in the south of England; all the members of the genus, indeed, being more or less attached to leguminous plants, and consequently noxious to man. Their larvæ live in the seeds, consuming all the internal parts, and changing to pupa within the skin; the perfect insect escaping through a circular hole, previously bitten by the larva for that purpose.

In the CHRYSOMELIDÆ proper there is no rostrum, the antennæ (which are generally much shorter than the body) are straight, never elbowed or clavate, but either filiform, moniliform, or serrate, and with a short basal joint; the head is sunk into the thorax as far as the eyes; the parts of the mouth are but little prominent, the mandibles being short, triangular, and bifid or trifid at the apex, the maxillæ formed of two lobes, of which the inner one is unarmed, and the palpi terminated by a subulate or short joint; the elytra cover the sides of the abdomen, which is composed of five free ventral segments; the femora are sometimes thickened; the tibiæ usually not spurred at the apex, or very slightly so; and the third joint of the tarsi bilobed.

Its members are all essentially vegetable-feeders, very rarely attaining any large size, mostly oval and convex in shape; diurnal in habits, though (except the *Halticina*) slow in their movements; and generally punctate-striate, and of bright metallic hues.

Our species are divided into nine tribes—the *Sagrina, Donaciina, Criocerina, Clythrina, Cryptocephalina, Chrysomelina, Galerucina, Halticina*, and *Cassidina*.*

* Mr. Rye (1st Edition, p. 211) regards these as families.

The SAGRINA (which comprise some very large and splendid exotic insects) are here only represented by a single genus, *Orsodacna;* the few British species of which are of considerable rarity, being usually found in the blossoms of the white-thorn. They are small, narrow, linear insects, exhibiting no particular points for observation.

In this family the apex of the mandibles is entire, without emargination; and the labium is deeply incised, so as to become bilobed.

The DONACIINA have the antennæ long, and inserted before the eyes; the head prominent, and rather constricted behind; the first segment of the abdomen as long as all the rest together; and the legs long and straggling, the femora (and especially the hinder pair) being often much thickened and toothed on the under side.

We possess two genera, *Donacia* and *Hæmonia;* the members of which are exclusively attached to water-plants (as the specific names of many of them import), in the stems of which their naked larvæ are found; the pupæ being enclosed in transparent silken cocoons, attached to the roots or filaments. The *Donaciæ* are all more or less coarsely punctured and metallic above, with fine silky down on the underside; they have a narrow thorax and somewhat flattened elytra, and are usually found in great numbers, being gregarious. Some of the species have a variegated longitudinal metallic stripe on each wing-case;

" *Sagridæ, Donaciadæ,*" &c.; the members of the whole group *Chrysomelidæ* are, however, so closely connected that they cannot with reason be regarded as more than tribes at the most.—ED.

and a few are exceedingly variable in colour, specimens of all shades from dull black to light brass being seen together, the intermediate examples exhibiting beautiful shades of dark and light blue, green, copper, purple, and red: there are, in fact, few prettier objects than the broad leaf of a water-lily, rippled over by the clear stream, and studded with these living gems (which, beautiful in death, are a thousand times more so when alive), basking in the summer sun.

Our other genus, *Hæmonia*, has long straggling legs, the apical joint of the tarsi being very long and prehensile. Both the species are found on water-plants (*Zostera* and *Potamogeton*), even beneath the surface; but *H. Curtisii* (Plate XIV., Fig. 2) is by far the most common. *H. equiseti* has occurred in flood-refuse near Burton-on-Trent, but very few British examples are known. They have the antennæ inserted close together, and the apex of the elytra produced into a spine.

The CRIOCERINA have the eyes emarginate, with the antennæ inserted within their front inner margin; the mandibles truncate at the tip, with two or three acute teeth, and the labium entire.

We possess three genera, *Zeugophora*, *Lema*, and *Crioceris*; the two first of which do not require any especial remark, the only peculiarity about either of them being that *Z. subspinosa*, a little blue-black insect with reddish head and thorax, found on aspens, has a wary habit of folding up its legs and dropping, on the approach of the net.

The species of *Crioceris* are, however, more conspicuous, both from appearance and economy. One of them, *C. merdigera*, of great rarity here, though sometimes occurring near London in the flowers of lilies, is, when alive, of a bright scarlet colour, which fades after death. The eggs of this insect are laid on lily-leaves, and glued together; and the young larvæ, when hatched, feed for some time gregariously, though separating as they grow older. These larvæ defend themselves from the heat of the sun, &c., by covering their backs with their own excrement, gradually pushed from the end of the intestinal canal, the opening of which is situated on the back of the last segment. This coating dries into a hard layer, from which the larva can free itself at pleasure. When full grown it descends to the ground, in which it forms a polished oval cell.

C. asparagi (Plate XIV., Fig. 3), a smaller and much more abundant species, is very prettily marked, and sometimes does considerable damage to asparagus, on which its short, fleshy, grey larvæ feed. This insect has been observed to make a squeaking noise, similar to that of the *Longicornia* above mentioned.

The CLYTHRINA have the head vertical, and the antennæ serrate and short; their larvæ live in hairy, leathery cases, which they drag about, with their head and legs protruding from the narrow end; and have, when taken out of their covering, much the appearance of those of the small *Lamellicornia*.

Our species are by no means common; occurring in woods, where they have been bred from ants' nests. *C. tridentata*, a greyish-brown insect, with blue-black head, thorax, and limbs, has very long front legs; and *C. quadripunctata*, as its name implies, may be distinguished by its four black spots.

The little *Lamprosoma concolor* is so exceedingly unlike its allies, both in size, shape, and colour, as to seem at first sight misplaced in this tribe; by some authors it is placed under a different one, the *Eumolpina*. Its structure will be readily understood from its old generic name, *Oömorphus*, or egg-shaped; and it much resembles certain species of *Phædon* in the *Chrysomelina*.

The CRYPTOCEPHALINA, also, have the head vertical, and sunk in the thorax; the body being cylindrical, and seeming to be truncate in front. Their antennæ are long and filiform; their thorax margined; their pygidium not entirely covered by the elytra, and their eyes kidney-shaped.

Our single genus, *Cryptocephalus*, contains many brilliant species, found on hazel, oak, birch, sallow, &c. They are only to be seen during fine weather, and chiefly in the hottest part of the day, retiring when the sun is overclouded. The approach of the net, and sometimes even the step or shadow of the collector, is enough to make these wary little beauties drop from their leafy perch. Their larvæ are enclosed in cases somewhat like those of *Clythra*, supposed to be formed of earth, but which in one case has been found to consist of the excrement of the larva, moulded into shape with its mandibles.

The sexes vary somewhat in this genus, the males being usually less bulky, and having longer legs and antennæ. In *C. coryli*, found on hazel bushes at Darenth in June, the female is entirely red, while the male has a black thorax.

C. sexpunctatus, found in the same place, and at Cobham, Kent, is elegantly spotted; though the palm of beauty in this respect must be given to *C. decempunctatus*, discovered in 1865 at Rannoch, by Dr. Sharp and the author, on dwarf sallow, and subsequently found by Mr. J. T. Harris and the late Mr. W. Garneys at Chartley Moss, Staffordshire. This species is exceedingly variable: one form being clear yellowish-white, with ten round black spots; another orange with transverse black bands, and a third entirely black. Others of our *Cryptocephali* are wholly of a lovely green; either frosted (*C. aureolus* and *sericeus*; the latter common at Mickleham on *Hieracium*) or dark and shining (*C. nitidulus*, Cobham and Mickleham, birch). Of the smaller species *C. bilineatus* (Plate XIV., Fig. 4) is elegantly banded; it is found commonly by sweeping, &c., at Mickleham.

The CHRYSOMELINA (or "Golden-apple beetles") have the head sunk in the prothorax, but more exposed than in the last family; the antennæ shorter, moniliform, and slightly thickened towards the tips; the legs of equal size; the palpi short; no spurs to the tibiæ; the thorax fitting closely to the base of the elytra; and the body hemispheric or oval. They are found on low plants and shrubs, for climbing on which their broad tarsi are eminently adapted.

We possess several genera and species of this family, many of which are conspicuous for their beauty.

The only large one, *Timarcha lævigata*, sometimes known as "the Bloody-nosed beetle," on account of its habit of distilling a drop of clear red fluid from the mouth when handled, is common in grassy lanes: it is very convex, dull but smooth in texture, and of an uniform blue-black colour, with exceedingly wide tarsi, especially in the male; which, as usual, is rather smaller, not quite so dull, and has longer legs. Its larva is also frequently to be seen clinging to low plants in lanes and on commons: it is of a shining bluish-green colour, very convex, and elevated in the middle.

Chrysomela distinguenda (Plate XIV., Fig. 5) is not uncommon near London, in grassy places, on the flowers of *Antirrhinum*, &c.; the contrast of colour afforded by its dark blue-black elytra, broadly margined with orange, being very effective.

C. menthastri and *graminis*, two of the largest, are especially conspicuous from their somewhat oblong form and uniform rich green metallic hue, which, in *graminis* especially, runs to blue and coppery reflections; but *C. cerealis*, striped longitudinally and alternately with purple, green, gold, and reddish copper, is perhaps the most handsome. It is found at the roots of wild thyme on Snowdon. The commonest species is *C. polita*, abundant in grassy places; it is shining, blue-green, with reddish-brown elytra, round and convex; and it is from the general rotundity and convexity of the members of this section that the name of *Cyclica* has been applied to it.

Of the allied species, *Lina populi* and *tremulæ* deserve notice: both are blue-black with brown wing-cases, and not uncommon on poplar and aspen; the former being distinguished by its larger size, and a small black spot at the apex of its elytra. They are gregarious in their habits; *L. tremulæ* being often found in great numbers and in all its stages on the same tree. The larvæ, which are tuberculated, whitish, and adorned with straight rows of dark-brown spots

P

(somewhat resembling those of the common seven-spot Lady-bird), have a custom of distilling from their mouth, tubercles, and apparently all other available orifices, a peculiar and strong-smelling yellow fluid; also emitted, though in a less quantity, by the perfect insect.

This fluid, similar, but more intense, in odour to that secreted by many Lady-birds, has been stated to be a specific for toothache, if rubbed into the gums; the remedy, however, seems at once so unlikely and nauseous, that nothing but the recollection of chloroform (originally obtained from an acid produced by ants) restrains one from dismissing the idea as absurd.

The pupæ of these insects are also spotted, and attached to leaves and twigs by their tails; having the "mortal coil" of their larva-dom "shuffled off," but still clinging to their extremity.

The oblong species of *Gonioctena*,—some of which are, when alive, bright red with black spots,—are found on aspens; they have a small tooth in the middle of their claws, and the tibiæ also strongly and sharply toothed on the outer side just above the apex.

Gastrophysa, as its name implies, contains insects in which the abdomen is much inflated,—especially in the females; these may be seen crawling slowly on pathways in cornfields, or on the common dock, with their elytra elevated, and abdominal plates widely distended, through the large mass of eggs with which they are loaded.

The remaining genera, usually found on plants near water, demand no comment; except, perhaps, *Phra-*

tora, of which the narrow and uniformly blue or brassy species are exceedingly common on willows, both in the summer on the leaves and trunk, and in winter hybernating beneath the bark in society. The larvæ, also, are gregarious, feeding in rows upon the leaves, of which they devour only one side.

The GALERUCINA are mostly oval and somewhat convex, being generally decidedly widest behind; their legs are nearly uniform, the hind femora being simple, and the front coxæ approximated; their antennæ are of considerable length, closer together at the base than in the *Chrysomelina*, and not thickened at the apex; their head is inserted in the thorax almost up to the eyes, which are entire, the thorax itself being margined at the sides, more or less hollowed out in front, and with produced front angles; the maxillary palpi are thickest in the middle, with the apical joints resembling two cones, united at the base; and the claws have a tooth in the middle.

They are of softer integuments than the *Chrysomelina*, and not so gaily coloured or metallic, though equally diurnal and attached to plants.

Our largest species is *Adimonia tanaceti*, a dull black, sluggish, thickly and coarsely punctured insect, found on the wild tansy, especially in chalky places on the south coast. It exhibits in a marked degree the peculiarity of the family of being widest behind; and its female has somewhat the distended appearance of *Gastrophysa* above mentioned, possessing, also, though in a minor degree, *Lina's* evil habit of distilling and smelling. Of the others in this genus, *A. capreæ* is exceedingly common on osiers, and less so on heath,—a very wide range of food-plant,—and, when feeding on the latter, becomes of a much darker colour; and *A. sanguinea*, found in May-blossom, is of a bright red tint.

The *Galerucæ* are mostly narrow in shape, dull-yellow or brown in colour, roughly granulated, covered with a close powdery grey pubescence, and gregarious; being found in numbers on willows and water-plants. Their larvæ,—which are sluggish, rather elongate, wrinkled, and with lateral tubercles and an anal projection, serving as an extra leg,—live in company, and commit great ravages, often stripping every leaf off the trees, &c., on which they feed.

Agelastica halensis, very common in the south, abounding in grassy places towards the autumn, is our brightest species; it is upwards of a quarter of an inch long, with its broad elytra and the top of its head bright green, more or less running into dark blue, its mouth, thorax, body and legs yellow, and tarsi, antennæ, and tips of tibiæ black.

Phyllobrotica (*Auchenia*), adorned with four spots, and the narrow delicate *Calomicrus circumfusus* (Plate XIV., Fig. 6) are the only species we possess that can be considered as at all variegated in markings; the latter (in which the elytra always gape somewhat) has much the *facies* of certain of the *Halticina*, and lives gregariously on the dwarf furze.

Finally, *Luperus*, elongate, feebly-built, with very large granulated eyes, and exceedingly long and fragile antennæ (especially in the male; whose body, also, is longer), of which the second joint is minute, occurs plentifully on alders, and other marsh-loving trees.

The HALTICINA are at once distinguished from the

other families by their thickened hinder femora, which are formed for jumping; an exercise in which they freely indulge, often to the disgust of the collector, who gets his net half full of some desired species (for they are usually gregarious), and perhaps succeeds in bottling only a dozen, owing to the extreme activity and long leaps of his temporary captives.

Their antennæ are inserted between the eyes, and in the majority, close together; their elytra have the margin sinuated, and their front coxæ are almost transverse, and not approximated.

We possess more than a hundred species of this family, descriptions of which (with many others) will be found in the " Essai Monographique sur les Galérucites Anisopodes (Altises) d'Europe," by M. Allard, Paris, 1861 (extracted from the Annals of the French Ent. Society), and by Herr Weiso in the " Naturgesichte der Insecten Deutschlands," vol. vi., parts 4 and 5 (1886-1888).

They are all small, mostly metallic, strongly punctured, and often gaily coloured; varying from a very convex and globular to an elongate form, but preserving throughout a certain likeness. They frequent all kinds of plants, but one species is generally attached to its particular favourite; Thistles, Hazel, Mallow, Willow, *Mercurialis*, *Salicaria*, *Euphorbia*, *Rubus*, *Nasturtium*, *Thapsus*, *Dulcamara*, *Hyoscyamus*, *Atropa*, *Alliaria*, and the *Cruciferæ* generally, having all their peculiar devourers in this family.

Graptodera contains our largest species; somewhat resembling the *Galerucidæ* in shape; usually of an uniform blue or green in colour: and occurring plentifully on hazel, &c.: *Hermæophaga*, considerably smaller, and very convex, is exclusively devoted to *Mercurialis perennis*, the leaves of which are riddled by it to a large extent: *Crepidodera*, distinguished by the abrupt depression in the middle of the base of the thorax, comprises several insects of bright and metallic colours, *C. helxines, aurata*, and *chloris* being especially bright; of these the first is the largest and broadest, found on poplars, with entirely yellow antennæ and legs (except the hind femora), uniformly coppery, green, or blue, and with the thorax not so roughly or closely punctured as the second, which is smaller, occurs on willows abundantly, has its antennæ, and sometimes its legs, more or less suffused with dark, and its thorax often of a different colour to its elytra. *C. chloris*, found on poplars, is narrower than *aurata*, always unicolorous, and with four joints at the base of its antennæ yellow, the remainder being abruptly black.

The species of *Mantura* are remarkable for their cylindrical shape,—affording a great contrast to the larger and pallid *Sphæroderma*, which resemble nothing so much in structure as half a microscopic orange, with the flat side down.

Aphthona contains some inconspicuous forms, somewhat resembling certain of the genus *Thyamis*, from which they may be distinguished by the basal joint of their hinder tarsi being much shorter.

The species of *Phyllotreta* are especially addicted to the destruction of cruciferous plants; certain of them being known as the "Turnip-flea" or "-fly," on account of their ravages upon that vegetable, the leaves of which are both mined by their small elongate dotted larvæ, and devoured by the perfect insect. They are mostly black; often having on the elytra yellowish-white stripes, which are sometimes divided into spots. The male of *P. nodicornis*, a linear bronze-coloured insect, most abundant on *Reseda lutea* (wild mignonette), is remarkable for the abrupt, flattened, and exceedingly conspicuous plate formed by the fourth joint of its antennæ; and *P. ochripes* (Plate XV., Fig. 1), found on the *Alliaria*, is the most gaily ornamented in the genus. The striped species are often very troublesome to beginners, but are readily separated by the following characters:—*vittula*, very small and the most parallel, has an almost straight stripe, which is *abruptly* and obliquely sloped inwards at its upper extremity by the shoulder; *undulata*, larger, and rather less straight-sided, has the stripe gently hollowed out or waved in the middle on the outer side, and slightly and gradually sloped off at the shoulder; *nemorum*, usually considered as the "Turnip-flea," though not nearly so common as *undulata*, is more coarsely punctured and larger still, and has yellow tibiæ,—the same parts in the latter insect being infuscated; *tetrastigma* is largest of all, very shining black, more convex, and with its stripes (which are of a darker yellow) much contracted in the middle, often quite divided, and forming four large spots; *sinuata*, very rare (occurring in Suffolk on horse-radish), resembles a small *undulata*, but has the stripe notched very abruptly both in the middle of the outer side, and at the shoulder; *ochripes* has entirely yellow legs, and the fifth joint of the antennæ enlarged in the male; and *brassicæ*, the least of all, has four yellow spots, and resembles a very small *tetrastigma*, being, however, more globose. In this species, also, the fifth joint of the antennæ is somewhat thickened in the male.

The species of *Plectroscelis* and *Chætocnema* have their hinder tibiæ armed with a tooth on the outer side below the middle; and *Thyamis*, a genus of large extent, may be known by the elongate basal joint of its hind tarsi, which is about half the length of its tibiæ. Although its members are usually of dull-yellowish colours, there is one, *T. dorsalis*, of great beauty, being intensely black and shining, with the thorax and a broad sharply-defined margin all round the elytra bright yellow; it occurs somewhat rarely at Mickleham, Weymouth, and in the Isle of Wight.

Psylliodes is more robust, compact, and inclined to an elongate-oval in outline; the basal joint of its hind tarsi is elongate, but differs from that of *Thyamis* and its other allies in being inserted not at, but above the apex of its tibiæ, which is sloped off: here, also, the antennæ are more distant at the base.

Of the remaining genera *Apteropeda* and *Mniophila* are conspicuous for their extreme rotundity and convexity; *A. graminis* (Plate XV., Fig. 2), either bronze or bluish-green in colour, being abundant in autumn among all kinds of wild plants, and *M. muscorum*,—more like a black seed, or a little round *Acarus*, than a *Haltica*,—occurring in moss in many localities.

The CASSIDINA, or Tortoise-beetles, are entirely unlike any other British *Coleoptera* (except, perhaps, *Thymalus limbatus*), on account of their broad, flattened bodies. Their head is hidden beneath the thorax, which is semicircular, and overlaps the elytra; the parts of the mouth are feeble, situated at the under-side of the head, and received at rest into a projection of the prosternum; the antennæ straight, short, and slightly thickened towards the apex, but with the last joint pointed; and the legs contractile, projecting slightly beyond the elytra, with simple unspurred tibiæ, and short broad tarsi, of which the third joint is deeply bilobed, and encloses the apical joint.

They are found during the summer months on thistles, wild mint, &c.; and, on account of their extremely quiescent nature, slightly convex upper surface, and flat under-side, resemble certain *Cocci* rather more than beetles. Our species are mostly bright green (not metallic) when alive, fading after death to a much duller colour: many of them are prettily variegated with brown speckles or red stains (*Cassida sanguinolenta*, Plate XV., Fig. 3); and one, *C. vittata*, found very rarely,—I believe on ragwort,—is banded alternately with deep black and bright red.

A few, found chiefly on the sea-coast, are most beautifully and broadly striped on each wing-case with gold; but this appearance, requiring a certain amount of moisture, fades with the life of the creature. It has been stated that glycerine, applied under the elytra, will not only retain the lustre in fresh examples, but renew it in old ones: I have, however, tried this plan without success. Varnishing the outside is of no avail, as it is from the inside that the colour proceeds.

One of these adorned insects, *C. oblonga*, occurs plentifully on the south coast, on *Salicornia*, in tufts of grass, &c. Its lovely green ground-colour is relieved by slightly pink edges, and the golden stripe partakes also of the hues of the emerald.

The larvæ in this family have an ingenious but unpleasant habit of forming their excrement into an umbrella, as in *Crioceris*. They are broad and flat, with short legs; beset on the sides with long setose spines, and having a long fork bent forwards, and arising rather above the anal orifice, by means of which they retain their excrement as a shelter. The pupæ, also, are broad and flat, with spined appendages on the sides, and the thorax dilated, spined, and covering the head.

The transformations of *C. viridis,*—a very common species on thistles,—may readily be observed.

CHAPTER XIX.

THE HETEROMERA.

This section comprises thirteen families, the *Tenebrionidæ, Lagriidæ, Cistelidæ, Melandryidæ, Pyrochroidæ, (Œdemeridæ, Mordellidæ, Scraptiidæ, Rhipidophoridæ, Anthicidæ, Xylophilidæ, Meloïdæ,* and *Pythidæ* (or *Salpingidæ*), in all of which the front and middle tarsi have five joints, and the hinder pair only four. Some few aberrant species in other sections also exhibit this tarsal formula, either in one or both of their sexes; but they cannot easily be confounded with any of the *Heteromera*, on account of their own unmistakable family likeness, and of wanting other characters which are nearly always found in this section, such as the kidney-shaped eyes, exserted and clavate maxillary palpi, moniliform un-elbowed antennæ, and bifid mandibles. The missing joint in the *Heteromera*, moreover, is merged in the elongate basal joint; whereas in other heteromerous species it is usually the fourth joint that is wanting or undeveloped.

We possess but a meagre list of species belonging to this section, which is very extensively represented in tropical countries; and it is worthy of notice that only one known genus (an exotic one, *Heterotarsus*) departs from the standard with regard to the joints of the tarsi; and in *that* the same proportions are preserved (4, 4, 3),—the apparently missing joints being represented by a slight constriction.

Thomson has divided this section into two tribes, the *Globicoxæ* and *Conicoxæ;* in the former of which (amongst other characters) the anterior coxæ are globose or ovate, and the thorax is mostly margined, whilst in the latter, the anterior coxæ are long, conic and exserted, the thorax being very rarely margined. The *Globicoxæ* comprise all except the *Pyrochroidæ, Meloïdæ, Œdemeridæ, Anthicidæ, Xylophilidæ* and the *Rhipidophoridæ.*

The typical *Heteromera* (*Melasoma*, Latr.) are of darkling and sluggish habits, black or obscure in colour, hard and wingless. It has been ingeniously remarked that the fact of the eyes in these light-shunning species being but slightly elevated above the surface of their head affords an indication of their habits; and this is borne out, to a certain extent, by the utter absence of eyes in certain cave-frequenting *Coleoptera;* and, *per contra*, by the large size and extreme prominence of the same organs in many diurnal species; but in this theory, as in many others equally good at first sight, exceptions occur so often that it is very difficult to turn it to any practical benefit.

Others of the section are eminently active, gaily coloured, soft, with ample wings, and frequent flowers: many occur in rotten wood, flour, or sandy places; and one or two species are parasitic in their habits. Perhaps the best known are the "cellar-beetle" (*Blaps*), "Mealworm" (*Tenebrio*), "Cardinal" (*Pyrochroa*), "Oil beetle" (*Meloe*), and "Spanish-fly," or "Blister-beetle" (*Lytta*).

The TENEBRIONIDÆ are characterized by having the anterior coxal cavities closed behind, the tarsal claws simple, the anterior coxæ globose, rarely oval, not prominent, and the penultimate joint of the tarsi very rarely bilobed and spongy beneath; the abdomen has five ventral segments of which the first three are more or less closely connected; the form is very variable; the family may be divided into the following ten tribes, which are by some authors regarded as separate families:— *Blaptina, Crypticina, Pedinina, Opatrina, Trachyscelina, Bolitophagina, Diaperina, Tenebrionina, Ulomina,* and *Helopina.*

The *Blaptina* have the last joint of the maxillary palpi hatchet-shaped, the epipleuræ of the elytra wide, and the hind femora long; they are represented here by one genus (*Blaps*) of three species, all of which are large, somewhat flat, dull black, with the elytra soldered together and pointed behind. They are found (sometimes in great numbers) in kitchens, outbuildings, stables, churchyards, &c., and are very slow in their movements, sedately lifting one long leg at a time, and only crawling about at night. They have a peculiarly foul smell, which is difficult to get rid of, and are indiscriminately known as the "churchyard beetle." Their larvæ closely resemble the common "meal-worm;" and instances have been recorded of their having been discharged (once in large numbers) from the human stomach.

Our commonest species is *B. mucronata,* formerly called *mortisaga;* the latter, however, is much rarer, only occurring in the north of England, and readily distinguished by the longer process at the apex of its elytra, and by its thorax being more evidently punctured and more contracted behind.

The *Crypticina* are here represented solely by *Crypticus quisquilius* (Plate X., Fig. 2), a small, black, shining species found in some numbers on sandy banks at Deal. It has slender legs and tarsi, the hinder femora not reaching far beyond the elytra, of which the epipleuræ are narrow. It is usually winged, but individuals occur in which the wings are either imperfectly developed or absent. In this family there is a narrow projection between the anterior coxæ.

The *Pedinina* have the eyes divided into two by the lateral margin of the head; they include one British species, *Heliopathes gibbus*, abundant in hot sandy places by the sea. It is deep-black in colour, shining, oblong, of clumsy shape, with coarsely punctured elytra, the epipleuræ of which are conspicuously ridged at the shoulder, the anterior tibiæ are triangular, and the three basal joints of the front tarsi strongly widened in the male, in which sex the posterior femora are fringed beneath.

The larva is filiform, cylindrical, whitish, with a brown head and thorax, and strong fossorial front legs: the head and tail are slightly hairy, and the apex of the abdomen is furnished with eight erect tubercles.

The *Opatrina* have the tarsi simple in both sexes, and present numerous other smaller differences from the *Pedinina*, with which they are sometimes associated. Our two species have the eyes divided, and the clypeus deeply notched (as in *Heliopathes*); but in *Opatrum* the maxillary palpi have the last joint hatchet-shaped, whilst in *Microzoum* it is almost ovate. Both are dull black and somewhat depressed; and occur in similar places to the *Pedinina*. *O. sabulosum* much the larger of the two, is common on the south coast.

The *Trachyscelina* never have the last joint of the maxillary palpi hatchet-shaped; their antennæ are short, and the projection between their coxæ is triangular. In *Trachyscelis*, a doubtful British genus, the antennæ are shorter than the head and distinctly clubbed, and the eyes are sunk in the thorax, the sides of which, and the elytra, are fringed with long hairs. In *Phaleria* the antennæ are longer than the head, and not clubbed; the eyes are more free, and there are no lateral fringes. *P. cadaverina*, a clear yellowish convex insect, with a suffused black patch in the middle of each elytron, occurs in decaying animal matter, and at the roots of maritime plants, in sandy places on the coast; being common at Shoeburyness, at the roots of *Sedum*.

The *Bolitophagina*, in company with several of the succeeding families, have their tarsi clothed on the under side with short hairs; a similar structure being only exhibited by the *Pedinina* among the preceding families of this section. Their antennæ are partly received in repose into a transverse furrow of the head; the labial palpi are widely separated at the base; and the apical joint of the maxillary palpi is not hatchet-shaped.

They live entirely in boleti, and are apparently gregarious.

Bolitophagus crenatus, in which the eyes are divided, and the thorax crenulated at the sides, is dull black in colour, and has strong rows of punctures alternating with linear elevations, on its elytra. It is found in the north of England, and is much larger than the commoner *Heledona agaricola*, a convex, oval, dull dirty brown insect, in which the eyes are of the normal structure, and the thorax is not roughened at the sides. As in many fungus- and wood-feeders, individuals of both these species sometimes occur in which the colour is much lighter than usual.

The *Diaperina* present a considerable resemblance to certain of the *Chrysomelidæ*, from which their five-jointed front and middle tarsi will at once distinguish them. They are metallic, smooth, and more or less bright in colour, with their eyes not entire and their antennæ gradually widened to the apex. In *Diaperis* the basal joint of the hind tarsi is short, whilst in the other genera it is much elongated. *D. boleti*, a very convex, shining, black species, with the apex of the elytra and the two transverse bands yellow, is one of our rarest species, no instance of its capture having been recorded for many years. Its larva is blind, and feeds on boleti growing on the trunks of trees, enclosing itself in a cell with a silky lining before undergoing its final metamorphoses.

Scaphidema, smaller, more depressed, and brassy, has its intercoxal projection wide, quadrangular, and truncated in front. It occurs not uncommonly near London among dead leaves, and at the bottoms of hedges. Its larva, as in the genus next mentioned, has two miunte spines at the apex of the abdomen, and lives in *Boleti* under bark, making no cell to change in. It has three ocelli on each side of its head. *Platydema*, the larva of which has four ocelli on each side, is exceedingly like a *Chrysomela*, and is found in the New Forest, but rarely.

The *Tenebrionina* here are represented by one genus,

Tenebrio, the two species of which are known in their larval state as "the meal-worm," a favourite food for singing-birds. It has been remarked that meal-worms obtained from the east end of London usually produce *T. obscurus*; whilst those from the west end produce *T. molitor*. The two larvæ appear to be superficially much alike, except that in *T. obscurus* the colour is darker, and the last segment is rather longer, with more diverging terminal projections; the pupæ are not enclosed in a cocoon, and have the six first segments of the abdomen furnished with flattened parallel, truncate appendages, the last segment being bifurcate. The larva of *T. molitor* is eyeless, elongate, nearly cylindrical, rather attenuate behind, light yellow in colour, with fine thin hairs on the sides, and marked with partly confluent minute dark spots on the upper side; the apical segment is conical, and terminates in two slightly diverging projections, having a minute black spine on each side.

The perfect insects are dull pitchy-brown, elongate, and rather flat, specimens often occurring of a light reddish-brown colour. The inner lobe of their maxillæ is armed with a horny hook; the apical joint of their maxillary palpi hatchet-shaped; the eyes largest on the under surface, and the anterior tibiæ curved (especially in the male). They sometimes fly to lamps, &c.; attracted, like moths, by the light.

The *Ulomina* are here represented by a few inconspicuous insects, of which the majority are doubtless imported, being found in flour, merchandise, &c. They have no trochantins to the intermediate femora; and their eyes (which are in nearly all the species almost divided into two on each side) have their greater bulk on the lower surface, except in *Hypophlœus*. The perfect insects and larvæ of *Gnathocerus cornutus* (the male of which has its head armed with conspicuous and sharp projections) are often found in bakers' shops, where also *Tribolium ferrugineum* occurs: the latter, however, sometimes exists in its larval state in neglected collections of insects, which are liable to attack from many other enemies, such as *Anthrenus*, *Dermestes*, *Psocus*, the larvæ of certain *Tineæ*, and—worst of all—the lazy, footless, white, fat "mite," which so often cleans out all the ligaments of specimens, leaving the mere outer husk, ready to fall to pieces on being manipulated, and often pierced in more than one place by its voracious tenant. A single application of benzine to any insect supposed to be so infested will destroy the parasite, which usually signifies its presence by dropping a little heap of fine yellow dust underneath the specimen on which it is feeding: nevertheless, a second or third dose should be administered on a future occasion, as the fluid has no effect upon any *eggs* which may happen to have been deposited in the body of the insect.

Both *Gnathocerus* and *Tribolium* are small, flat, yellow beetles; but the species of *Hypophlœus* are very different, both in shape and habits, presenting a certain likeness to *Rhizophagus*, on account of their linear cylindrical form. They are found under bark, or in galleries, where their larvæ (as in the last-mentioned genus) prey on the larvæ of certain wood-feeding beetles: *H. bicolor*, a pretty little red species with the apical half of the elytra black, is found not uncommonly under elm bark, where its larvæ feed on those of certain *Scolyti*. The species of *Alphitobius* sometimes resemble certain of the *Dermestidæ*; they are black in colour, and are probably imported, being found in warehouses, &c., where their larvæ feed in flour, &c.

The *Helopina* are in England only represented by a single genus, *Helops*, in which the inner lobe of the maxillæ has no hook, the antennæ are slender, elongate, with their penultimate joints longer than their width, and the eyes transverse and narrow. Our species present a certain superficial resemblance in miniature to the form of *Blaps*, and this is most shown in *H. cæruleus*, the largest of them, a slowly-moving beetle, dull blue in colour, sometimes found in clusters under the bark of old felled trees, where its larva (which considerably resembles that of *Tenebrio*, and has spines on the apical segment) feeds on rotten wood. *H. striatus*, by far the most common, is abundant in woods, &c., in tufts of grass at the roots of trees, under bark, in rotten wood, moss, &c.; its larva is the only one of the genus which has been noticed to possess ocelli. Another species, *H. pallidus* (Plate X., Fig. 3), is found at the roots of grass, &c., in sandy places on the south coast (Southend, &c.), often much below the surface. In all these the males are not so robust as the females, with longer antennæ, and the basal joints of the front and middle tarsi more dilated.

The LAGRIIDÆ are here only represented by one genus and species, *Lagria hirta*, an insect utterly unlike any of its allies, being very hairy, with a narrow thorax, a neck to the head, long black antennæ and legs, and somewhat inflated elytra, which are widest and shortest in the female. It is very soft and sluggish, black, with yellowish elytra, and abounds towards the middle of summer in hedges, &c. Its elongate larva, flat and white beneath, convex and yellow above, spotted with black, and tufted with yellow hairs along the sides, has been found under dead leaves at the foot of old oak-trees; but its food is not known, though it is supposed to be carnivorous.

The absence of any pectination to the under side of the claws of the tarsi distinguishes this species from any of the *Cistelidæ*; its projecting, approximated, conic anterior coxæ separate it from the *Tenebrionidæ* and their allies, and the structure of the cotyloid cavities into which these coxæ fit is different from that of all the other *Heteromera*, as they are not open on any side.

The CISTELIDÆ have the claws of the tarsi pectinated on the under side; the mentum supported by a neck; the apical joint of the maxillary palpi very large; the mandibles with a projection on the inside of the base; the labrum distinct; distinct intermediate trochantina; long legs, slender tibiæ, which are evidently spurred at the apex; and the penultimate joint of the tarsi often apparently bilobed. Their eyes are kidney-shaped, and always entirely free, not being encroached upon by the front angles of the thorax; and are larger in the males than in the females; in the former sex the antennæ, also, being always the longest.

Their larvæ are very slender, more or less cylindrical, and having the apical segment hollowed beneath and furnished with a kind of plate, directed backwards, and ending in two slender appendages: they are found in rotten wood.

Five of our seven species occur in flowers or on

bushes, &c., in the hot sunshine; one of the others, *Mycetochares bipustulata*, a small, very agile insect, black, with a yellow shoulder-spot to the elytra, lives in rotten cherry-wood, &c., and, when found (for it is of rare occurrence), is generally seen in some numbers. The remaining species, *Eryx atra*, is nocturnal in its habits, frequenting old willow-trees, on which it is more often seen by lepidopterists,—who hunt by night for moths,—than by coleopterists. It is a dull black, oval, convex insect; rather large, but, like all its allies, of very delicate texture. Its larva, preparatory to undergoing metamorphosis, forms a cell composed of woody fibres glued together, and is the only one of this family known to take any such precaution.

In *Cteniopus* and *Omophlus*, both found about maritime plants, the males have the last abdominal segment considerably excavated; and in *Cistela* the antennæ are rather strongly serrated.

The MELANDRYIDÆ have the head not constricted behind and received into the thorax as far as the eyes, which are either entire or emarginate, the mandibles short, the antennæ eleven-jointed (except in *Conopalpus* in which they are ten-jointed), the thorax not narrower at base than at apex and not narrower at base than elytra, and the anterior coxal cavities open behind; the elytra cover the abdomen, which is composed of five free ventral segments; the species are very variable in size and colour; the family may be divided into two tribes, the *Tetratomina* and the *Melandryina*; in the former of which the last four joints of the antennæ form a very abrupt strong and distinct club, whereas in the latter the antennæ are, as a rule, filiform or very gradually thickened, only in one or two cases forming a rather strong but not abrupt club.

The *Tetratomina* are very unlike their neighbours, having the facies of certain species of *Cis*, and of some of the *Dermestidæ*. Their head is much bent down, being scarcely visible from above; their anterior coxæ are cylindrical, transverse, separated by a projection of the prosternum, and with their cotyloid cavities widely open behind.

All the species are small, rather cylindrical, and strongly punctured, and are found in partly decayed wood. One (*Tetratoma Desmarestii*, occurring at Coombe Wood, and elsewhere) is blackish-green; another (*T. fungorum*) is blue-black, with a red thorax; and the remaining one (*T. ancora*, recently taken in some numbers in old stumps near Highgate) is testaceous, spotted and banded with brownish-black. All of them must be considered rare. *T. fungorum* superficially resembles certain species of *Triplax*, but the latter genus can be easily known by the *three*-jointed club to its antennæ, and the lesser number of joints to its tarsi.

The position of this family is anything but firmly established, and it appears to have been placed in its present place chiefly *faute de mieux*.

The *Melandryina* have the labial palpi very short, and the maxillary palpi much developed, often with the joints indented, and with the apical joint very large. The claws of their tarsi are simple; and the upper part of the prothorax is not continued until it is confused with the sides, but is distinctly separated by a margin.

They have no neck to the head, which is bent down

and sometimes not visible from above, though the eyes are never encroached upon by the thorax; and the clypeus is never distinctly separated by a suture from the rest of the head.

They are somewhat elongate, narrow, usually hard, not clothed with much pubescence, and more or less convex.

In *Orchesia* (*O. undulata*, Plate X., Fig. 4; found in white-thorn flowers in the New Forest) the antennæ are rather thickened at the apex, the spurs to the tibiæ are very long; the anterior coxæ are not approximated; and the penultimate joint of the hind tarsi is very long and entire,—the two latter characters being also shared by *Hallomenus*. The species of both of these genera are bred from the fungoid matter growing on old wood, and from boleti, in which their smooth fleshy larvæ are found. *Orchesia*, wherein the hinder coxæ are large, flat, square, and transverse, and the spurs to the hinder tibiæ very long and pectinated beneath, possesses the power of skipping about in a ludicrous manner.

With the exception of *Melandrya caraboides*,—a species very variable in size (as in most wood-feeders), flat, hard, blue-black, shining, with the elytra rather widened behind,—none of this family can be considered common, though many of them occur in some numbers when they are met with. *M. caraboides* lives in its earlier stages in old willow stumps; and the perfect insect may be seen with its head projecting from the mouth of the burrow made by the larva, into which it rapidly backs on an attempt being made to capture it. It flies readily, and with a metallic sound, in the hot sunshine; alighting on felled trees, and readily tucking up its legs and falling to the ground on the approach of the collector.

The species of *Abdera*,—small, cylindrical, and banded with pale testaceous,—have the penultimate joint of the tarsi truncate, and very small spurs to the tibiæ; they are found in dead boughs of trees, and in the short half-rotten stumps left on trees where boughs have been broken off. *Hypulus quercinus*, a narrow, elegantly spotted and banded insect, with robust antennæ, occurs in old wood in some numbers when found, for it is very local; and the fragile *Conopalpus* may be taken under the same conditions as *Abdera*, though it has been also found in flowers, where it might readily be passed over for a pallid *Telephorus* by the incipient Coleopterist. In this genus the antennæ have only ten joints, and the apical joint of the maxillary palpi is very narrow and elongate.

Osphya bipunctata, exceedingly local, being only found in flowers, &c., at Monk's Wood, has very much the general appearance of a *Telephorus*, but with the hinder femora in the male much inflated and arched, as in *Œdemera*; the two sexes, also, differ considerably in size and colour; the male being usually the largest and black, and the female testaceous. As in many instances before noticed, these marked sexual disparities exhibit several modifications; undevoloped males occurring in which the inflation of the hinder femora disappears, the size is diminished, &c.

In the PYROCHROIDÆ the head is exsorted, horizontal or almost horizontal, and is strongly constricted a short distance behind the eyes, which are emarginate; the anterior coxal cavities are broadly open behind and confluent, and the prosternum is long before the anterior coxæ, which are furnished with a distinct trochantin, and are elongate, subcylindrical, and very projecting.

The species of *Pyrochroa*, commonly known as "Cardinal beetles," are bright scarlet or brickdust-red in colour, moderately large, with serrate or pectinate antennæ, pedunculate mentum, acutely bifid mandibles, elytra not covering the sides of the abdomen, and long legs. They are very active and rapacious; flying readily and strongly in the hot sunshine, and often simulating death when captured. The largest, *P. coccinea*, is distinguished by its black head; it is not uncommon in woods in the south. I have found it, in all its stages, in great numbers under the bark of a felled tree at Darenth, in Kent.

The ŒDEMERIDÆ are elongate, slender, with thin legs and antennæ, no abrupt neck to the head, simple hooks to the tarsi, the mandibles flattened and bifid at the apex, and the penultimate joint of the tarsi bilobed. Their larvæ live in rotten wood, and resemble those of the Longicorns, to members of which section the perfect insects also present a certain likeness.

Nacerdes melanura, not unlike a large *Telephorus*, is found at the seaside; it is testaceous with the apex of the elytra black, and is especially noteworthy from the fact of its male possessing twelve joints to the antennæ, though the female has the normal number. It flies strongly in the hot sunshine, and is often taken on old posts on the shore; the larvæ even living in timber that is periodically covered by the tide.

Oncomera (*Dryops*) *femorata*, the largest of the family, is a very graceful, slender insect, with very long and thin antennæ. Its male is distinguished by the peculiar formation of the hinder legs, which have the femora much inflated and arched, and the tibiæ angulated at the base. It is nocturnal in its habits, and occurs somewhat freely at ivy blossom and sallow bloom, both in the autumnal and spring months.

In *Œdemera cœrulea* (Plate XI., Fig. 2), a small metallic, bright blue or green species, found abundantly in flowers during the summer months, in the hot part of the day, the male exhibits a similar formation of the hinder legs to that of *Oncomera*.

The MORDELLIDÆ are, perhaps, the most readily distinguishable of any of the section, owing to their strong family likeness. They are mostly small, widest in front, contracted behind, with the pygidium exposed, and often ending in an absolute spine; broadest and convex on the upper side, but shelving down to a comparative ridge on the lower surface (resembling nothing so much in shape as one of the small segments of a peeled and divided orange); with the thorax and head bent down, the latter so much so as to be often quite invisible; the legs getting larger from front to rear, closely articulated, flattened, and with long spurs to the hinder tibiæ. They are found most frequently in the flowers of *Umbelliferæ*, and are very active in their movements, having an especially irritating habit of slipping away on an attempt being made to capture them. When caught, they are not the easiest beetles to mount on card,—as may readily be guessed from their structure.

The family falls naturally into two tribes, the *Mordellina*; in which the apex of abdomen is produced into a more or less strong spine or style, and the *Anaspina*, in which it is simple; several of the species of *Anaspis* may be beaten in swarms from any hawthorn bush in blossom in May and June.

The family SCRAPTIIDÆ contains the genus *Scraptia*, which has usually been classed with the *Melandryidæ*, or placed in an exceedingly imperfectly characterized family called the *Pedilidæ;* its position is extremely doubtful, but the general formation of the head and thorax appears to place it near *Anaspis;* the species are small and fragile, and are found in rotten wood; they are extremely rare, and represented in but very few of our collections.

The RHIPIDOPHORIDÆ are closely allied to the *Mordellidæ;* they contain here a single genus and species, *Metœcus paradoxus* (Plate X., Fig. 6), a most remarkable insect, both on account of its form and habits; and in which (and its allies not found here) commences a certain degradation in the development of the parts of the mouth;—the mentum being slender and confused with the ligula, the labial palpi apparently composed of only one joint, the lobes of the maxillæ rudimentary, and the mandibles short and not toothed internally.

It differs from the *Mordellidæ* in having the lobes of its maxillæ soldered together at the base, with the last joint of their palpi not hatchet-shaped, no membranous plate to the inner side of the mandibles, and its antennæ flabellated; but otherwise presents numerous points of affinity, and great superficial resemblance. It is much larger than any other of the family; the female being the largest, and usually having blue-black elytra (which are attenuated and gaping, allowing the wings to be seen) instead of reddish-testaceous.

The thorax is very strongly arched on each side of the hinder margin, and produced in the middle; the hooks of the tarsi are bifid; and the third and following joints of the antennæ in the male are divided into double fan-like rays.

The perfect insect is found (according to Lacordaire) sometimes on flowers, or at the exuding sap of trees, and I possess a specimen taken under bark, in Scotland; but its real home is in the nests of the common Wasps (*Vespa rufa* and *vulgaris*), in which, also, it undergoes its transformations; and it has been observed by Mr. S. Stone (who has for a long period accurately observed the economy of certain coleopterous parasites on *Hymenoptera*) that the larger larvæ (from which the females are produced) are found with, and feed on, the female wasp grubs,—the *fact*, but not the *object* of such association having been long before known.

The ANTHICIDÆ present a certain external resemblance to some of the smaller *Geodephaga*: they are delicately built, of slender shape; with thin legs and antennæ, the penultimate joint of the tarsi bilobed, the head suddenly contracted into a narrow neck, the eyes entire, and the hinder coxæ separated by a projection of the abdomen.

Notoxus monoceros (Plate X., Fig. 5), an elegant, downy, little species, very variable in its markings, occurs plentifully in sandy places, both at the seaside and inland. Its thorax is produced in the middle into a stout horn, which projects over the head (Fig. 5 *a*).

The species of *Anthicus* are all very small, and have been fancifully compared to ants, both on account of their colours, small size, shape, and activity. They are most abundant at the seaside, but are often common inland in heaps of garden refuse, &c. One of them (*A. instabilis*) has the hinder tibiæ in the male suddenly enlarged into a rounded plate at the apex.

The XYLOPHILIDÆ contain our two genera, *Euglenes* and *Xylophilus*, which are often classed as one genus; they may be distinguished by having the penultimate joint of the tarsi minute, and hidden within the lobes of the preceding joint, which is strongly bilobed; the head is constricted immediately behind the eyes, which are large and notched; in *Euglenes* the male has very large eyes and long antennæ; from which circumstance, added to general facies and habits, it sometimes calls to mind certain of the smaller *Ptinidæ*.

The MELOÏDÆ have a very abrupt neck to the head, and each of the hooks of the tarsi divided into two, as if with an additional and slender hook on its lower surface.

In *Meloë* (the Oil-beetles) the metasternum is very short, with the intermediate coxæ overlapping those of the posterior legs, the elytra strongly reflected at the sides, short, overlapping, and gaping at the apex, and no wings.

One or two of the species are well known, being often seen in very early spring on heaths, commons, and lanes, especially on the buttercup. They are large, blue-black, heavy, bloated-bodied creatures, crawling slowly, and exuding a clear yellow oil from their joints when handled, which was formerly used for medicinal purposes. When dried, the normal distension of the body disappears, the abdomen shrinking up beneath the elytra in a wrinkled unsightly knot: specimens for the cabinet should, therefore, be stuffed with wool,—an easy operation, if an incision be made in the lower side of the body, and its contents taken out. The males are often very small; and, in some cases, have the sixth and seventh joints of the antennæ enlarged and suddenly bent, so that the apex appears deformed.

The transformations of these insects are, perhaps, the most wonderful of any that are yet known to us; and it is chiefly on account of somewhat similar habits in their earlier stages that the *Stylopidæ* have been recently considered as coleopterous.

The female of *Meloë* deposits from two to four separate batches of minute yellow eggs, some thousands at a time, though the number diminishes with each laying. These eggs are glued together, and deposited in small holes in the ground, dug by the parent beetle. After an interval of from three to six weeks, according to the temperature, the young larvæ are hatched, and are extremely like minute *pediculi*, or bird-lice, being yellow, elongate, parallel, flattened, with rather long legs, and four long hairs at the apex of the last segment. They appear to remain torpid for some time; but, when once roused by sufficient warmth, exhibit extraordinary activity in traversing low plants, chiefly *Ranunculaceæ* or *Chicoraceæ*. From these they attach themselves, often in great numbers, to the hairy covering of bees as they settle on the flowers of their temporary lodgings; and also, sometimes, to certain hairy *Diptera*, or two-winged flies, which closely resemble wild bees. In the latter case it is an unfortunate attachment for the larvæ; as the *Diptera* make no nest or provision for their offspring, so that the would-be parasite necessarily perishes of starvation : and it is probably the chance of this, added to the many fortunate contingencies required before the larvæ can be safely landed within reach of their food, that causes such an enormous number of eggs to be laid by the parent beetle. As it is, all the perfect insects of this genus, seen by one observer in his lifetime, would bear a ridiculously small proportion to the number of eggs laid by one specimen.

When carried by the unconscious bee to its nest, the *Meloë* larva devours the egg therein contained, changes (without leaving the shell of the latter) into a second form,—not unlike the larva of a *Lamellicorn* beetle in miniature, being arched, cylindrical, with toothed mandibles and stout legs,—and then subsists on the food intended by the bee for its own young. After some time this second form of the larva changes its outer covering, which is not entirely shed, but remains wrinkled together at the hinder apex of its body : it is then arched, distinctly composed of thirteen segments, attenuated at the extremities, and motionless. From this *false pupa* (and probably after passing the winter) a third form of the larva appears, similar to the second ; but from this point it is only by analogy with the transformations of *Sitaris muralis*, an allied insect (Plate XI., Fig. 1), that we can form an idea of its final metamorphosis.

The latter insect (which has large wings) is in its earlier stages, and indeed during all its life, a parasite upon certain mason bees of the genus *Anthophora*, common in old walls near London (the Rev. A. Badger having taken the first British specimen of the beetle at Chelsea). In this species the larva undergoes less vicissitudes than in *Meloë*, as the eggs (two or three thousand at a time) are deposited by the female at the entrance of the hole burrowed by the *Anthophora;* and, after passing through the stages above mentioned, and taking no food in its third form, changes into a pupa of the ordinary Coleopterous type, from which, in about a month, the perfect insect appears,—the entire changes occupying nearly two years. In the case of *Sitaris*, of which the perfect beetle is always found in or about the burrows of the bee, the entire scheme of life is readily credible, even if it had not been accurately observed; but in *Meloë* there still remains an awkward gap for which an account is required, viz. the passage of a heavy, slow-going, large beetle from the nest of the bee to the common or meadow where it is always found.

Particulars of the discoveries as to this insect are to be found in Mr. Newport's paper in the Linnean Transactions, vol. xx. p. 297, and vol. xxi. p. 167; also in M. Fabre's " Mémoire sur l'Hypermétamorphose et les mœurs des Méloïdes," 'Annales des Sciences Naturelles,' ser. 4, vol. vii. 1857, p. 299; and in Lacordaire, Col., vol. v. 2nd part, 651.

Our remaining species, the well-known " Blister-beetle" or " Spanish-fly" (*Lytta vesicatoria*), the old *Cantharis*, is very different in shape, &c., to the members of either of the preceding genera,—being elongate, cylindrical, with long legs and antennæ, and bright metallic-green in colour. It is occasionally taken in the southern and south-eastern counties, but can scarcely be considered as truly indigenous.

The PYTHIDÆ or SALPINGIDÆ have the anterior coxal cavities open behind, the head prominent, free, and not strongly and suddenly constricted behind the eyes, which are entire, and the thorax (except in *Mycterus*), subovate or cordiform, narrowed in front and behind, and often narrower at base than at apex; the elytra are rounded at apex and cover the abdomen, which has five free ventral segments; the family may be divided into three tribes, the *Pythina*, *Salpingina* and *Mycterina*; the first of these may be distinguished from the other two by the fact that the intermediate coxæ have a very distinct trochantin, as well as by the large depressed form; and the *Salpingina* may be known from the *Mycterina* by the side pieces of the mesosternum not attaining the intermediate coxæ, as well as by having the thorax much narrower at base than at apex, whereas in *Mycterina* it is broader.

The *Pythina* comprise the single genus *Pytho; P. depressus*, hitherto found only in Perthshire under firbark (where also occurs the larva, which has two strong hook-like projections on the upper side of the last segment) is very depressed, metallic, usually blue or green, but sometimes nearly testaceous, and with two strong depressions on its thorax. Both the perfect insect and larva are carnivorous, feeding upon other subcortical species.

The *Salpingina*, on account of some of their members possessing a rostrum, afford a passage to the next section, wherein such prolongation of the head is constant, and with which they have been associated by old authors.

Their antennæ are thickened at the apex, the last joint of their maxillary palpi is not hatchet-shaped, their mandibles do not project beyond the labrum, and their body is smooth.

R

They are all small and shining, and are found under bark, or by beating dead twigs.

Rhinosimus viridipennis (Plate XI., Fig. 3) is perhaps the most elegant of the family; it occurs not uncommonly in old hedges near Darenth.

The best transition, however, to the *Rhynchophora* is formed by the *Mycterina*, which greatly resemble that group in general appearance, and also as regards the characters of the rostrum, intermediate coxæ, scutellum, &c.; *Mycterus curculionoides*, taken in England many years ago by Mr. T. V. Wollaston, and, more recently, near Oxford, by Mr. Gunning, is found abroad on flowers (chiefly *Umbelliferæ*); and it has been remarked that, like certain of the *Curculionidæ*, and in particular those of the genus *Larinus* (to which it has some resemblance in form), it is covered with a yellowish pubescence which is renewable during life, after having been rubbed off.

CHAPTER XX.

THE RHYNCHOPHORA OR WEEVILS.

This group, which has usually been included under the so-called *Tetramera*, is now regarded as forming a section apart from all the others, characterized by the abnormal structure of the head and thorax, of which latter the posterior lateral parts are nearly always soldered together on the central line of the under-surface; they have been regarded as the most archaic of the Coleoptera.

The *Rhynchophora* (often termed, as a group, *Curculionidæ*) are usually convex and hard; they have the head elongated in front into a rostrum or beak,—sometimes short and thick, and at others very long, thin, and arched,—bearing the organs of the mouth at its apex. Their antennæ are inserted on the rostrum, generally short, and in far the greater number of species elbowed (having a long basal joint), and clubbed at the apex; they vary in the number of their joints from eight to twelve, and are inserted on the sides of the rostrum, in two cavities or *scrobes*, which assume the form of pits or furrows. These cavities often cause two side-pieces to appear on the upper side of the apex of the rostrum, called winglets, or *pterygia*, which are greatly developed in *Otiorrhynchus* and its allies. With one exception, the parts of the mouth are, comparatively, of little assistance in classifying these insects, the ligula and palpi (except in a few instances) exhibiting but little variation, and the maxillæ being usually single-lobed; the mentum, however, affords a great diversity of structure, being either abruptly truncate at its base, or provided with a neck, and in either case received into a more or less deep emargination of that part of the head that supports it. This neck is wide, but of very little depth, in the species with a short rostrum; but in those that have a long rostrum it is elongate, and, in proportion to its elongation, the mentum is reduced, so as to appear sometimes entirely absent. The mentum, varying thus in development, either wholly covers the maxillæ (except sometimes at their base), or leaves them free; and it is upon this structure that Lacordaire has based his classification of the section, which he primarily divides into the *Adélognathes* (in which the maxillæ are entirely, or for the greater part, hidden by the mentum), and *Phanérognathes* (wherein they are completely uncovered).

Of the remaining characters in the *Rhynchophora*, it may suffice to say, that their mandibles (which are short and robust) vary considerably in shape; their prothorax is very rarely margined at the sides, which are usually merged imperceptibly with the pronotum; their tibiæ are very rarely toothed externally, and often spurless at the apex; and their abdomen is composed of five segments, whereof the two first are very often soldered together, and the third and fourth usually shorter than the others.

By Schönherr (whose "Genera et Species Curculionidum," 8 vols., Paris, 1833-1845, has long been the text-book of Coleopterists devoted to this section), the *Rhynchophora* are divided into two sub-sections, the *Orthoceri*, in which the antennæ are not elbowed, with the basal point slightly elongated; and the rostrum has no distinct lateral grooves for the reception of the basal joints of the antennæ;—and the *Gonatoceri*, wherein the antennæ are more or less distinctly elbowed, the basal joint being usually elongated, and always received into a canal at the side of the rostrum. The latter sub-section is separated into two groups, the *Brachyrrhynchi*, having the rostrum short, straight, and thick, with the antennæ inserted near its extremity, and mostly twelve-jointed; and the *Mecorrhynchi*, in which the rostrum is cylindric or filiform, more or less elongated (being seldom shorter than the thorax), and with the antennæ inserted before or near the middle, never near the mouth orifice.

The late Mr. Walton has published many papers in the "Annals and Magazine of Natural History" (1844), in which are descriptions of, and useful remarks upon, many of our species of Weevils.

As before remarked, all the *Rhynchophora* are vegetable feeders; and, although comparatively harmless in their perfect state, there is not one part of any tree or plant, or its product, that their larvæ do not attack.

These larvæ, of which the grub of the nut-weevil (*Balaninus nucum*), so often found in filberts, &c., is a good type,—are fat, fleshy, and cylindrical; slightly attenuated in front and recurved behind, with a round horny head, and no legs, which are represented by tubercles or callosities set with short bristles. Although usually adhering to one particular plant (whether attacking its leaves, flowers, shoots, roots, bark, fruit, or timber), they are sometimes promiscuous feeders; and many (as the nut-weevil), on becoming full-grown, drop to the earth, in which they undergo their final changes, whilst others remain attached to the plant, &c., on or in which they have hitherto existed,—usually forming a cocoon.

The aforesaid nut-weevil (but only in its larval stage), and the corn-weevil, *Calandra granaria* (most probably an imported insect), of the British species,—and the splendid exotic "Diamond Beetle," *Entimus imperialis*, so often employed as an object for the microscope,—are, perhaps, the most generally known members of this section.

The question of the Classification of the *Rhynchophora* is one that must be considered far from settled; in all probability the series will be found to comprise more than a hundred thousand species; it is obvious therefore that, with our extremely limited fauna, we are not in a position to discuss it to any extent; the best known recent works on the subject are "The Classification of the *Rhynchophora*," by Dr. Leconte and Dr. Horn, and the extra volume of the French "Annales," by M. Bedel, which has just been published:—"Faune des Coléoptères du bassin de la Seine, Rhynchophora," Paris, 1888; Dr. Leconte and Dr. Horn divide the group into three great sections, on the composition of the pygidium in the sexes, and the structure of the underside of the clytra; certain details of their work are, however, more valuable than their general system; and, as far as our fauna at least is concerned, we cannot do better at present than follow, with certain modifications, the system of M. Bedel; the series may then be divided into four families, the *Rhinomaceridæ* (or *Nemonychidæ*), *Platyrrhinidæ* (or *Anthribidæ*), *Curculionidæ*, and *Scolytidæ*.

The RHINOMACERIDÆ are distinguished by having the maxillary palpi of the ordinary form and flexible, the labrum distinct, and the antennæ straight; the anterior coxæ are conical, and the pygidium is covered by the elytra; the rostrum is long and enlarged in front; the antennæ are long and slender with the club long, loose, and scarcely marked, and the scrobes are absent or superficial; the family appears to bear a strong affinity to the *Mycterina*, which conclude the *Heteromera*.

Rhinomacer attelaboides is a slender and elegant insect, clothed with rather long greyish pubescence. M. Perris has observed that its female deposits her eggs in the catkins of the male flowers of the pine, of which the presence of the larva prevents the expansion. This species is found not uncommonly in certain parts of Scotland; it frequents Conifers, and its male is remarkable for possessing two little tufts of yellowish hairs on the second and third abdominal segments.

The PLATYRRHYNIDÆ (or ANTHRIBIDÆ) have the antennæ eleven-jointed, and terminated by a short, abrupt three-jointed club, the eyes not notched, short transverse scrobes to their wide, deflexed rostrum, the pygidium not exposed, and the second joint of the tarsi bi-lobed; they differ from the *Rhinomaceridæ* (which, in many points, they closely resemble) by having the anterior coxæ globose, and the pygidium more or less uncovered. The males are usually distinguished by the superior length of their antennæ.

These insects are all of considerable rarity, and of some beauty, though not peculiar for delicacy of outline. They frequent old wood, dead twigs, &c., and are usually found in the early part of summer.

Brachytarsus scabrosus (Plate XI., Fig. 4) is occasionally taken in May-blossom in the London district, also occurring sparingly in the north, where it is replaced by *B. varius*, which is not so brightly coloured, and very rare in the south. The larvæ of both of these species appear to be parasitic upon *Cocci*.

The species of *Tropideres* are of great rarity here; though sometimes beaten out of dry dead hedges, or taken from rotten wood: they somewhat resemble the next-mentioned insect in miniature, but have the basal joint of the tarsi much longer in proportion.

Anthribus albinus, a handsome brown and white insect, is remarkable for having the antennæ in the male as long as the body, and has usually been regarded as connecting the *Rhynchophora* with the *Longicornia*, to certain species of which section it presents a close resemblance.

Platyrrhinus, a large, exceedingly broad, flat, strong, black-brown-and-white mottled insect, occurs rarely near London, and chiefly in the western counties (being not uncommon near Cheltenham); it lives upon *Sphæria*, and other fungi growing on ash-trees, &c., burrowing also in the rotten wood, or lurking under loose bark, and having a particularly comical way of elevating itself by its front legs, though usually of sedate appearance.

The little *Choragus Sheppardi* is peculiar, on account of its power of jumping, although its hind femora are not widened. It is beaten out of dead hedge-sticks at

Deal, Southend, Wickham, and elsewhere. Through its curious appearance this insect has been at different times considered as allied to *Cryptocephalus*, *Cis*, and *Anobium*.

The CURCULIONIDÆ, by far the largest of the family in point of numbers, may be separated from the two preceding families by the shape of the maxillary palpi, which are short, thick, rigid and conical, with the joints gradually diminishing in size to apex; from the *Scolytidæ* they differ in the well-developed rostrum, and the fact that the legs are not formed for burrowing into wood, as in the latter group; they may be subdivided into four sub-families, viz. *Attelabinæ* (or *Rhynchitinæ*) *Apioninæ*, *Otiorrhynchinæ* and *Curculioninæ*.

The ATTELABINÆ have the rostrum more or less elongate and enlarged in front; the antennæ straight, with the scape short, and with a more or less distinct club; the pygidium almost always exposed; the anterior coxæ conical, cylindrical, exserted and contiguous, and the central projection of the first ventral segment acuminate at apex; the segments of the abdomen are uneven in length.

Some of these insects are exceedingly beautiful, having the brightest metallic hues of blue, golden, green, red, or copper, and many are very pubescent.

Attelabus and *Apoderus* are each represented by a single species, which are bright red, and are not uncommon in woods in many localities in early summer. *Attelabus curculionoides*, the shorter, more convex and smooth of the two, infests young oaks; its female rolling up their leaves into a thimble-like mass, in which she deposits her eggs. *Apoderus coryli* is found on hazel; its larva, conspicuous in this section for the possession of large dorsal tubercles, living in cylindrically rolled-up leaves of that plant.

The species of *Rhynchites* differ from the two just mentioned, in having the external border of the mandibles cut out into large teeth, and the tibiæ, as a rule, simple and not toothed on their internal margin. *Rhynchites betuleti*, a very lovely species, found not uncommonly at Darenth on the hazel, pierces the top shoots of that plant so as to arrest their growth, after having deposited an egg in them. Other species have been observed to lay an egg in the recently-formed fruit of wild trees, afterwards duly making an incision below, so as to impede its proper development, the larva finding sufficient nourishment before the fruit falls to the ground. *R. æquatus* (Plate XI., Fig. 5) is occasionally found in profusion in the flowers of the whitethorn.

With these insects terminates the division *Isotoma* of Thomson, distinguished by the connate abdominal segments, of which the second and third are nearly equal, the antennæ straight, &c.: his other division, *Anisotoma*, has the three apical segments free, the second being much longer than the third, the antennæ usually elbowed, &c.

The APIONINÆ have the rostrum long, arched, cylindrical, and sometimes subulate (i.e. suddenly contracted before the apex), with its scrobes more or less distant from the mouth, and the antennæ inserted towards its middle, or base; the head more or less elongate behind the eyes; the trochanters very large, and separating the femora and the coxæ;* the scutellum

* This peculiarity is also found in *Nanophyes*, and Bedel

very small; the elytra covering the pygidium; the tibiæ not spined at the apex; and the hooks of the tarsi free.

The species of *Apion* are very numerous, chiefly frequenting clover, trefoil, &c. Their larvæ have varied habits, the majority living in the seeds of *Leguminosæ*, some forming a kind of gall on the twigs or leaves of plants, others making galleries in their stems, and some even attacking their roots.

The antennæ in this genus are composed of twelve joints, the club, which apparently has but three joints, exhibiting, under a high power, a minute fourth one at the apex. The rostrum has on the under side two deep antennal grooves, converging from the points of insertion of the antennæ; their use is to receive and protect the basal joints of the antennæ.

Certain of the yellow-legged species are usually very troublesome to beginners, not only on account of their minute specific differences, but because the sexes vary somewhat. Mr. Walton (p. 39 of his paper above mentioned) points out the assistance to be derived in this respect from the coloration of the coxæ and trochanters, in which many species differ sexually. One of the most curious in the genus is called (and rightly so) *difforme*; its male has the basal joints of the antennæ much dilated, the basal joint of the front tarsi hooked, the middle legs elongate, the hinder legs bent, dilated, flattened, and generally distorted, and a spine to the epigastrium. It is usually found on furze, *Polygonum*, &c.

therefore joins this genus with *Apion*, under the sub-family *Apiidæ*; it is, however, much more closely connected with *Cionus*.

The OTIORRHYNCHINÆ are distinguished by the fact that the perfect insect as it emerges from the pupa is provided with a pair of false mandibles, which soon fall off, but may sometimes be noticed in fresh specimens; a scar, however, is always left at the apex of the rostrum, so that the fact of their having existed is not difficult to determine; in *Cænopsis fissirostris* these deciduous mandibles are large and hooked, and in many species they appear to be conspicuous.

The characters of the various tribes into which this sub-family has been divided need not here be discussed, as they are somewhat abstruse: *Otiorrhynchus* and its allies (which include *Phyllobius, Trachyphlœus,* &c.) have the basal joint of the antennæ reaching beyond the back of the eyes, the funiculus with usually seven joints, and the rostral scrobes variable, but never at the same time linear and directed downwards, the rostrum itself being short, stout, and nearly horizontal. In many of the genera the winglets, or lateral projections at the apex of the rostrum, are much developed.

Such of their larvæ as are known are moderately elongate, fleshy, feebly tuberculated at the sides, set with short hairs, and legless; and the pupæ do not appear to be enclosed in a cocoon.

In *Phyllobius*, which much resembles *Polydrosus*, the scutellum and wings are present, the hooks of the tarsi are soldered, and the scrobes of the rostrum are nearly always very short. The species are very abundant on nettles, &c., and, when fresh, are thickly clothed with bright golden green scales, which, however, readily rub off. One of them, *P. argentatus,* is a common object for the microscope, owing to the beauty of its covering;

another, *P. viridicollis*, found in Scotland, is equally remarkable in spite of its peculiar abraded appearance.

In *Trachyphlœus* and its allies the scutellum is wanting, or very small, and the wings absent, the hooks of the tarsi are free, the antennæ robust, and the scrobes of the rostrum lateral, deep, slightly arched, and reaching to the eyes.

The species are mostly small, oval, and convex, strongly set with short stout bristles, often arranged in lines, and frequently thickly covered with earthy matter, which adheres so firmly as to disguise their outline and punctuation. They are found in sandy places, at the roots of grass, in moss, &c., and are very slugglish.

The species may generally be distinguished *inter se* by the toothing and shape of the front tibiæ.

In *Otiorrhynchus* the antennæ are long, usually slender, and often inserted at the apex of the rostrum; the scutellum is wanting, or very small; the wings are absent; the winglets to the sides of the rostrum at the apex strong; the scrobes deep, visible from the upper side in front, but rectilinear and evanescent behind; the body convex, ovate, seldom thickly clothed with scales, and usually dull in colour; and the tarsi spongy beneath, with the apical joint long and the hooks free. The males are, for the most part, smaller and less globose than the females.

The larvæ of *O. sulcatus*, a common metropolitan insect, have been observed to do considerable damage to potted plants, &c., by gnawing round the upper part of the roots.

The different species are found in hedges, under stones, in moss, sand-pits, &c., and at the roots of grass on sand-hills. *O. picipes* (Plate XII., Fig. 1) is one of the most abundant, frequently doing considerable damage to young trees and plants; it may be obtained in profusion by beating white-thorn hedges in spring.

Some of our species, found in mountainous parts of the north, and others peculiar to the south coast, are shining black, and many of them congregate under stones, especially on turf-walls. Dr. Stierlin, in his "Revision of the European *Otiorrhynchi*," Berlin, has fully described our species (amongst others).

Strophosomus, and its allies (which as here regarded, for simplicity's sake, answer in great measure to the old family *Brachyderidæ*, and include *Polydrosus*), have the antennæ elbowed, with the basal joint variable in length, the funiculus usually seven-jointed, the scrobes of the rostrum generally linear, and directed downwards, the rostrum being short and stout, and not received into any groove of the prosternum; the mandibles are usually slender, the scutellum is absent or very small, and the elytra cover the pygidium.

There is nothing particularly noteworthy in this family, which consists of moderate-sized, mostly dull-coloured insects, many of which are apterous. The species of *Strophosomus*, globular in shape, with prominent eyes, usually abound on hazel and oak, some being also found on heaths; one of those latter, *S. limbatus*, has the appearance of being entirely denuded of scales.

Some of the *Polydrosi* are beautifully clothed with bright-green metallic scales, and are often mistaken for *Phyllobii*, from which they differ in their longer and thinner legs and antennæ, and the possession of long and distinct rostral grooves for the anteunæ.

The sub-family CURCULIONINÆ contains by far the majority of the *Rhynchophora*, and is made up of very divergent forms, many of which exhibit relationships to other families; they are, however, all connected by the fact that the mandibles have no scar (left by deciduous mandibles) at the anterior external angle of the rostrum; they have been divided into a large number of tribes (which probably will have to be reduced), the chief of which may briefly be noticed.

The *Sitonina*, distinguished by having the mandibles thickly punctured and pubescent on their surface, not toothed and curved at apex, contain the single genus *Sitones*, which comprises many species, especially noxious to clovers and trefoils, many of them abounding at all times of the year; the commonest is *S. lineatus*. They are small, rather elongate, greyish or brownish insects, which are very troublesome to beginners, owing to their great likeness to one another. They have been fully described by the author in the *Entomologist's Monthly Magazine*, vol. ii.

The *Gronopina* have a more or less distinct excavation in the prostornum for the reception of the rostrum, the scrobes of which are linear and arched; the eyes large, depressed, entirely covered in repose by the lobes of the prothorax, which are very prominent; the metasternum very short; and the tarsi spinose, or hairy beneath, never spongy.

We possess but one genus and species, *Gronops lunatus*, in which the second joint of the antennæ is very elongate; it is a small dull-white or grey insect, strongly ribbed, with a narrow thorax, wiry legs, and a more or less extensive dark lunated mark on each elytron. It is not uncommon in sandy places on the coast, and near London. The characteristic prothoracic canal is in this insect of a very superficial nature.

The *Hyperina* are chiefly distinguished by their life history, in which they can only be compared with the *Cionina*. The species of *Hypera* (*Phytonomus*), in which the funiculus of the antennæ is seven-jointed, are often very abundant in clover-fields, &c.; they are moderately large, oval, with a globular thorax, and prettily clothed with variegated scales and hairs. *H. trilineatus*, found commonly on *Leguminosæ* in many districts, is perhaps one of the most elegant. (Plate XI., Fig. 6.)

Their larvæ live on the outer side of the leaves of plants, of which they devour the parenchyma; they have two or three rudimentary eyes on each side of the head. Possessing no legs, they fix themselves to their support with a viscous fluid secreted by a retractile process, situate in the front part of the back of the last abdominal segment. When full grown they cover themselves with a coarse network, composed of threads of the same fluid, which hardens on exposure to the air. A cocoon is thus formed (often found on water plants, &c., in wet places, where some of the species are abundant), in which the transformations of the insect take place.

The little *Limobii* exactly resemble the members of the preceding genus, except that their antennæ have but six joints to the funiculus; and it should be remarked that many other genera are accompanied by similar imperfect reproductions of their structure.

The *Lixina* comprise some of our most conspicuous species.

In *Cleonus* the rostrum is longer than the head, robust, slightly arched, angulated, and sculptured on the upper side, with the antennæ inserted near its apex, and the scrobes moderately separated, but not joined on the under side; the tarsi spongy beneath, more or less flat; the tibiæ with a dagger-like spine at the apex; and the body oblong, cylindrical, and pubescent. Our species are large, variegated with grey or reddish scales, and found in waste places; they feed in the stems of thistles, &c., some of them being of excessive rarity. As in all the other members of this family, their integuments are exceedingly hard.

The species of *Lixus* are usually very elongate, cylindrical, and narrow, with the grooves in the rostrum of very variable formation, but, as in *Larinus*, directed downwards, and usually commencing between the middle and the apex. In the latter genus they meet beneath.

The *Lixi* are rare in this country, being found chiefly on the south coast. They live in water-plants, &c.; one of them, and that the most beautiful, *L. bicolor*, breeding in thistle-stems at Deal. When freshly disclosed this insect is clothed with very thick and bright scarlet and yellow down, which (as in the other members of the genus) readily rubs off, so that it is difficult to obtain good specimens for the cabinet. According to M. Lacordaire, they are able during life to renew this plumage to a certain extent.

Another species, *L. paraplecticus*, is noteworthy on

account of its very elongate, thin, pointed appearance, reminding one of the "walking-stick" insects. Very different to this are the allied *Larinus* and *Rhinocyllus*; squat, stumpy, and ovate; found in thistle flowers, &c., on the coast. The latter, which is slightly hairy, was formerly considered a specific for toothache; the genus *Antiodontalgicus* having been formed for its reception.

Alophus triguttatus has been associated with *Cleonus*, but is now placed among the Otiorrhynchidæ; it is not uncommon near London, being often found basking in the sun on hot walls; the white V-shaped mark behind renders it conspicuous.

The *Hylobiina* have the rostrum moderately long, deflexed, sub-cylindrical, rather arched, and mostly not very stout. They have the tibiæ armed at the apex on the inner side with a strong hook.

They are mostly of considerable bulk; the smallest, *Tanysphyrus lemnæ*, is now placed in a separate tribe; it is found in wet marshy places, and exhibits a great resemblance to the structure of its larger brethren. *Hylobius abietis*, large, black, with yellow interrupted band-like spots, is now abundant in the south of England, though formerly very rare; it commits great ravages in pine woods, and has been transported in building-timber from Scotland, where it is exceedingly common.

In *Molytes* the elytra are very convex and rounded, the whole insect being black, shining, and smooth, or, at most, with a few patches of yellow or grey hairs. Both our species inhabit chalky districts. *M. germanus* is, perhaps, the largest of our British weevils.

Liosomus, a more fraction of *Molytes* in size, reproduces exactly its superficial characters, differing, however, in the rostral scrobes, the structure of its antennæ, and the shortness of the spurs to its tibiæ. It abounds in wet places.

Plinthus, found in dry situations on chalk by the coast (Dover, &c.), and less commonly in grass, &c., inland, is of very different shape from any of the preceding, being more linear, with no scutellum, the rostrum longer than the head, and slightly contracted at the base, &c. ; it is very strongly and coarsely punctured, the punctures being often filled up with chalk, so that the normal dull pitchy-black colour of the insect is disguised.

Pissodes, resembling *Hylobius*, though on a smaller scale, frequents pine forests ; one species, *P. pini*, abounding in many parts of Scotland, where I have seen the female with her rostrum deeply buried into the soft part between the outer bark and solid timber of fresh-cut fir-trees. In the hole thus formed an egg is deposited, the larva proceeding from which eats galleries under the bark until it is full grown, when it closes its retreat with particles of wood, frass, &c., and changes to pupa. The perfect insects are very prettily marked, being rich brown with golden-yellow spots : like *Hylobius*, they cling very tightly to the fingers when handled.

The *Erirrhinina*, as usually constituted, consist of a somewhat heterogeneous assemblage ; a considerable number of them have now been referred to separate tribes ; their antennæ are either cloven- or twelve-jointed, with the club usually four-jointed ; their anterior legs are approximated at the base, and the greater part are winged, and have the scutellum more or less distinct.

Erirrhinus (sometimes divided into two genera,—*Notaris*, wherein, amongst other characters, the femora are unarmed; and *Dorytomus*, wherein they have a strong tooth on the under side) comprises several small common species, mostly found in wet places or on willows, poplars, &c. The rostrum in all these is elongate and arched, and they are usually yellowish or dull brown in colour, slightly variegated with ill-defined lighter spots. Their larvæ are chiefly found on water-plants, those of *E. festucæ* (not uncommon on the towing-path near Hammersmith) living in the stems of *Scirpus*, of which it devours the pith.

Those of another species (*E. vorax*, common in the perfect state on poplars, upon which it may be detected lurking in chinks of the bark, and remarkable for the great length of the front legs in the male) have been found in the pods of laburnum, feeding on the seeds; and the larva of a third (*E. tæniatus*) lives in the catkins of the sallow, which it mines for their entire length, and forms a cocoon for itself with the silky fibres peculiar to the seeds of that tree.

The species of *Anthonomus*, in which the rostrum is slender and usually long, the eyes very prominent, and the prosternum very short, are small, moderately convex, and sometimes adorned with short variegated pubescence of a pinkish-grey tone relieved by a darker band. Some of them are well known to commit great havoc upon apples and pears, the female insect boring a hole with her slender rostrum into the young buds, and then depositing an egg into it, the larva proceeding from which subsists upon the young blossom (and occasionally the fruit), and forms a kind of cocoon with the petals, wherein it undergoes its changes. Other species infest the elms, bramble, &c., in like manner.

In *Anoplus*, comprising *A. plantaris*, a small black insect, common on birch in summer, the tarsi have no last joint or onychium.

In *Orchestes* (so named for its jumping habits) the head is very little projecting; the rostrum bent back on the under surface in repose; the eyes are very close on the upper side, and very often contiguous; and the posterior legs saltatorial, their femora being often enormously developed. It has six joints to the funiculus of the antennæ, whilst in the closely allied *Tachyerges* there are seven.

Their larvæ are elongate, flat, with no tubercles, and mine in the leaves of different trees, eating the parenchyma. When full grown they enclose themselves in an oval silky cocoon, the pupa having the thorax produced in front into two strong projections, and the abdomen ending in two double-jointed projections, with several acute tubercles on the last segment beneath.

Certain insects of the genera *Tychius* and *Sibynes* —the former found chiefly on the vetch and its allies, and the latter in dry sandy places—are conspicuous for their dense covering of light-coloured scales, being often beautifully spotted or banded. In the former genus the funiculus of the antennæ consists of seven joints, whilst in *Microtrogus*, which very closely resembles some of its members, it consists of only six. These three genera are now usually united together under one tribe, *Tychiina*, which is characterized by having the posterior margins of the second segment of the abdomen produced at each side, and extending over the third segment to the base of the fourth.

Bagöus, *Lyprus*, and *Hydronomus* are all water-plant frequenters, frequently found in mud or even under water, and very often so encased with crusted dirt as to be difficult to distinguish. They have short antennæ, and very slender tarsi, of which the third joint is not bilobed, and slightly (if at all) wider than the preceding, the apical joint being long. The first and second of these genera have the prosternum slightly excavated, whilst in the latter it is level. For this reason they have been separated widely in arrangements; but they are in reality very closely allied. *Lyprus*, which is very attenuate, and spider-like about the legs, has but six joints to the funiculus.

In *Orthochætes* and *Trachodes* (the former found in moss and the latter in old twigs or in rotten wood) the scutellum and wings are absent. Both of them are set with stiff bristles.

The species of *Magdalinus*,—small, oblong, parallel, dull black or bluish insects,—are found in the spring and early summer about dead wood in hedges, &c., or on young trees. They are chiefly conspicuous for the close punctuation of their thorax, and the occasionally spindle-shaped development of the antennæ in the male. One species has been reared from larva found in burrows under the bark of willow-trees; and the female of another, *M. carbonarius*, found in Scotland, has been observed to introduce its eggs into sickly branches of pine-trees, the larva eating its way along the pith for a considerable distance. After undergoing its metamorphosis, the perfect insect escapes by means of a gallery gnawed by the larva through the solid wood, but not penetrating the outer bark.

The *Cryptorrhynchina* and *Ceuthorrhynchina* have the rostrum bent downwards, and received into a more or less distinct canal on the under side. The anterior legs are nearly always distant at the base.

The genus, *Cryptorrhynchus*, contains one species, *lapathi* (Plate XII., Fig. 3), not uncommon on willows, into the trunk of which its larva bores, making large cylindrical holes. It has been noticed that this insect, when alarmed, makes a creaking noise by rubbing the base of its prothorax against the front of the mesothorax.

The species of *Acalles*,—dull brown, slightly variegated, with strong ridges and spines,—are found in old twigs, hedges, &c. They have a peculiar habit of simulating death, contracting their legs continuously with the under side of the body; and one of them has been observed to make a stridulating noise similar to *Cryptorrhynchus*.

In *Cœliodes* the rostrum is received into a canal between the front and middle pair of legs; its species are small, convex, and "dumpy;" one of them, *didymus*, a dull brownish-black insect, variegated with white scales, and having a white spot on each side of the elytra, is most abundant on nettles.

Rhytidosomus and *Orobitis* are both peculiar, on account of their globular form; the latter—a dark blue shining insect, found on a pretty species of vetch—having a habit of applying its legs close to its body. Packed up in this manner, it has all the appearance of a ripe seed of the common wild blue hyacinth, and its size seems much increased when it unfolds its long straggling limbs; it is remarkable as having the posterior coxæ reaching to the base of the second ventral segment, and dividing the first, which is very short, into three separate parts.

Mononychus pseudacori, a larger, awkward-looking, dull black creature, with a white spot beneath the scutellum, has very clumsy legs,—of which the tibiæ are obtusely and coarsely toothed on the outer side below the middle,—and only a single claw to the apical joint of each tarsus. Its larva feeds in the pod of the wild iris, and is taken in August, chiefly in the Isle of Wight.

In *Litodactylus* and its allies, all more or less attached to water-plants (some even oxisting under water, on *Myriophyllum*, and swimming with their hind legs in the same fashion as the *Dytiscidæ*), the rostrum is short and thick, the scutellum inconspicuous, and the eyes large and prominent; and in *Ceuthorrhynchus*, a very extensive genus of small convex species, the rostrum is long, arched, and slender. Some of this genus (which is divided into two sections, the first having the femora simple beneath, whilst in the second they are toothed) are prettily variegated with white scales; others are metallic blue, or set sparingly with short stiff bristles.

Many of them are very abundant, and do considerable damage to culinary vegetables, either—as perfect insects—by piercing holes in them, or—as larvæ—by forming gall-like excrescences on their roots. As is frequently the case, there is another genus (*Ceuthorrhynchidius*), closely resembling this, in which there are six instead of seven joints to the funiculus.

The *Cionina* and *Gymnetrina* have the antennæ ten- or nine-jointed, short, the funiculus composed of five joints, and the club of three or four. They are all small; and (except *Mecinus*, which is elongate and cylindrical) "squat" and rounded; in the former family the second, third, and fourth segments of the abdomen are produced into a point on each side at apex.

The species of *Cionus* are all beautifully variegated; they frequent *Verbascum* and its allies, often in great numbers, the different species sometimes occurring in company. Their larvæ, which are small, convex, and spotted, devour the entire parenchyma of the leaves, but do not touch the ribs and stem: they appear to make an open network cocoon. *C. blattariæ* (Plate XII., Fig. 4) is, perhaps, the prettiest, and is not uncommon. In repose, with its legs contracted, it affords an exact representation of a small patch of bird-droppings.

Nanophyes, a much smaller and elegantly banded insect, occurs (locally) in great profusion on low plants of *Salicaria*; and the species of *Gymnetron* and *Miarus* especially frequent *Veronica*, *Antirrhinum*, and *Campanula*. They are mostly small, short-ovate, dull black, and set with rows of short yellowish hairs.

The *Barina* have the front legs distant at the base, and the breast flat. We possess but one genus, *Baris*, containing certain small, elongate, cylindrical beetles, mostly glabrous, but in some cases very slightly clothed with pubescence, which readily rubs off. They frequent *Lepidium*, *Reseda*, &c., and superficially resemble the species of *Mecinus*, which have but five joints to the funiculus.

The tribe *Balaninina* is very remarkable from the fact that its members, which all belong to one genus, are distinguished not only from all the other *Rhynchophora*, but from all known Coleoptera, by the fact that the mandibles have a vertical instead of a horizontal motion.

In the genus *Balaninus* the rostrum is very long, slender, and arched, sometimes nearly as long as the body, and the prosternum considerably elongate between the front coxæ. To it belongs the "nut-weevil" before mentioned, the larva of which is so well known. The female deposits a single egg in the nut when the latter is very young, and has been stated to use her long beak as a drill in that operation. The larva, which leaves the vital part of the fruit until the last, when arrived at its full growth, bores a hole through the shell and drops to the ground, into which it burrows prior to turning into pupa.

Other species operate in a similar way upon acorns (*B. glandium*), and the kernels of certain wild *Pruni* (*B. cerasorum*, found in the perfect state on birch). The larvæ of one of the smallest, *B. brassicæ*, have been observed to live in red galls on the leaves of willows, the formation of which has even been attributed to this insect, though it appears most probable that they are the work of one of the *Hymenoptera*. Another, *B. villosus* (Plate XII., Fig. 2, head and rostrum sideways, 2*a*), not uncommon on the oak, has been reared from larvæ found in galls formed by a *Cynips* on the leaves of that tree.

The *Calandrina* are here represented by one genus, *Calandra*, containing two species, *granaria* and *oryzæ*, both doubtless imported, and the former being known *par excellence* (or *par* the want of it) as *the* Weevil. Here the antennæ are eight-jointed, the basal joint being long, and the apical one forming a large knob; the rostrum is long; the body somewhat flat; the thorax very coarsely punctured, the elytra scarcely covering the apex of the abdomen, and deeply striated, and the tibiæ spined at the apex.

The "Corn-weevil" is small and pitchy-red in colour; it bores a hole with its rostrum in the grain, in which it lays an egg; the young larva afterwards devouring all the contents, and leaving merely the husk, wherein it turns to pupa. It has been observed that if suspected grain be thrown into water, the good will sink, while the infected seeds will float.

The other species, distinguished by its four red spots, attacks rice in a similar way.

The *Cossonina* have short antennæ, of which the funiculus is seven-jointed, the basal joint long, and the club either two-jointed or nearly solid, so that there seem to be nine joints in all; their rostrum, also, is somewhat deflexed; their tibiæ armed at the apex with a stout external hook, and their tarsi slender. They are all distinguished by a certain linear, parallel, flattish, or cylindrical habit, pre-eminently adapted for boring in wood, or existing under bark.

Cossonus linearis (Plate XII., Fig. 5) is very local; but, when found, occurs in great profusion; as, indeed, is the case with most of this family. *Mesites Tardii*, the largest, lives in the wood of ash-trees, &c., at Killarney, Mount Edgcumbe, and elsewhere on the western coast. It has very little the aspect of an

English species, and varies much in size. In the male the antennæ are inserted near the apex of the rostrum, which is dull, enlarged, and suddenly contracted behind their articulation; whilst in the female it is smooth, narrow, and with the antennæ inserted close to the base.

Some of the remaining species,—small, obscure, cylindrical beetles,—are common in half-rotten wood, under fir bark, &c.

The remaining family, the SCOLYTIDÆ (also termed *Hylesinidæ*, or *Tomicidæ*), are by some authors raised to a sectional rank, under the name *Xylophaga*; but, being intimately allied to the *Cossonidæ*, they are generally considered as a division of the *Rhynchophora*, connecting that section with the next.

These insects have been fully described by Erichson, in Wiegmann's Archiv. für Naturg., vol. ii., 1836 (an abstract of which appeared in the "Naturalist" for December of the same year), and also (with others injurious to timber) by Ratzeburg, "Die Forst-Insecten," Berlin, 1837,—a work of considerable value.

They have the head somewhat globular, deeply sunk in the thorax (Plate XII., Fig. 6 *a*; head and thorax of *Hylesinus vittatus*), and produced into the suggestion of a rostrum in front; the antennæ (which have never more than ten joints) elbowed, having a long basal joint, and a more or less flattened club, which is either solid or four-jointed; the front coxæ globose, prominent, and not widely separated; the tibiæ flattened and widened at the apex, hooked at the extremity, fossorial, and usually toothed or crenulated on the outer side; the mandibles short, robust, prominent, and triangular; the maxillæ thin, broad, and spined internally, with their palpi minute and conical; the labrum obsolete; the eyes vertically oblong, and the third joint of the tarsi bilobed, except in *Tomicus* and *Platypus*.

All the species are small, mostly black or dull brown in colour, and usually somewhat oblong, or cylindrical in shape, being especially convex on the upper side.

Many of them are very destructive to trees; their larvæ eating irregular galleries at right angles from a straighter central line; and it is from their habit of always engraving this kind of pattern in their devastations that some of them have been termed " Typographers."

The small, dull black, elongate, cylindrical species of *Hylastes* occur in profusion in the tracks eaten by their larvæ under the bark of decaying or felled pine-trees; they have the club of the antennæ scarcely flattened, the tibiæ distinctly spurred at the apex, and the prosternum excavated in front; whilst in *Hylurgus piniperda*, a larger, more robust insect, found sometimes in still greater profusion, and very injurious to fir-trees, this excavation is obsolete.

The *Hylesini* have an elongate oval club to the antennæ, and the tibiæ obsoletely spurred; they, also, feed on wood. One small species, *H. vittatus* (Plate XII., Fig. 6), is very prettily variegated.

It is, however, to the genus *Scolytus* that the unworthy distinction of destructive ability must be awarded; one of them, *the destroyer, S. destructor*, being notorious for the ravages it inflicts, both in its larval and perfect state, upon elm-trees, especially in the London parks.

Its larvæ are white, fleshy, thick, curved, and footless; with wrinkled backs, hard heads, and powerful mandibles; they feed in gangs; and, although small, are so numerous, that the fate of a tree is sealed when once they obtain a lodgment.

In the perfect insect, which is very elevated, stumpy, and cylindrical, with the head bent downwards and inwards,—the elytra are abruptly and obliquely truncate behind; and in some of the other species the abdomen has a flat horizontal tooth on its second segment beneath; the peculiar slope of the abdomen is, perhaps, one of the best distinguishing characters of the genus.

Xyloterus lineatus (Plate XIII., Fig. 1), an elegantly striped insect, with more pretensions to beauty than its allies, is found (rarely) in Scotland: I have seen it with its head and thorax protruding from its neat circular drill in the solid wood of felled pines; but it is oftener seen than taken, owing to its habit of backing quickly to an indefinite depth into its burrow, on the approach of the bark-knife. In this species the antennæ have a rounded club, whilst in the other (*domesticus*) the club is pointed; in both, each of the eyes is widely divided, the funiculus is four-jointed, and the club solid.

The minute *Hypothenemus eruditus* (an insect Giles Gingerbread, who " on learning fed ") was discovered by Mr. Westwood burrowing in the cover of an old volume, from which strange locality it derives the attribute of erudition conveyed by its name. Both genus and species were then new to science; and the beetle has never, I believe, been found since its original capture.

The *Tomici* have emarginate eyes, five joints to the

funiculus, and the third joint of the tarsi simple; they are sometimes pubescent, and always elongate, narrow, cylindrical, and more or less truncate behind, especially in the male, which sex also often exhibits strong spines on the edges of the truncation. They abound in larch-trees, elms, &c., and their larvæ resemble those of *Scolytus* in miniature; the pupæ differing, however, in the possession of two spines at the apex of the abdomen.

Lastly, *Platypus cylindrus* (Plate XIII., Fig. 2), found rarely here, and chiefly in the New Forest, departs from the others (amongst other characters) in its very short antennæ, which have a long basal joint, a very compressed four-jointed funiculus, and an extremely large, flat, round club; its widened and flattened front femora; very short tibiæ, short hind legs, and extremely long and slender tarsi, which are longer than the femora and tibiæ, and of which the basal joint is longer than all the rest put together, and the third joint is simple. Its larva, which feeds upon oak, differs from that of *Scolytus* in being short and straight, somewhat truncate behind, with a large head and several rows of tubercles on the sides.

It should be remarked that the *Bostrichidæ*, above associated with the *Malacodermata*, present great resemblance to certain of this family; in which, indeed, they have been placed by Latreille and other authors. But in the *Bostrichidæ* the larvæ have legs, which are wanting in those of the *Scolytidæ*; and, although the perfect insect appears in both to have only four joints to the tarsi, yet in the former there are five, the *basal* joint being very small; whilst in the latter the *fourth* joint is obsolete, or confused in the middle of the lobes of the third: the parts of the mouth, moreover, are of a much higher development in *Bostrichus* and its allies. As if to increase the confusion, certain other authors, while separating these two groups widely, apply the *name* of the *Bostrichidæ* to the present family.

CHAPTER XXI.

THE STYLOPIDÆ.

THIS family contains a few species which have been placed by various authors in the *Hymenoptera*, *Coleoptera*, and *Diptera*, and even considered by some as allied to the *Hemiptera*, *Orthoptera*, and *Lepidoptera*; their structure is so degraded that they have lost all resemblance to the other members of the *Coleoptera*, and the extremely minute development of their prothorax seems at first to be much against their location in that order; from the period of their discovery until within the last few years, they were considered by many authorities as a special order *Strepsiptera*, but are now usually regarded as abnormal members of the *Coleoptera*, although Professor Westwood is still of opinion that they should be kept separate; the species are parasitic, in their early stages, in the bodies of various bees and wasps, the footless larva, when full grown, protruding its head between the abdominal segments of these insects, and appearing, at first sight, like a flattened *Acarus*; foreign genera have been discovered, which infest ants and *Homoptera*; they may be characterized as follows :—Male free, with very small and collar-like prothorax and mesothorax, small twisted fore wings, and a large metathorax bearing very large and ample hind wings, which are fan-shaped and hyaline, and longitudinally folded; the mouth parts are metagnathous, or adapted in the larva for biting, and in the imago for sucking; the mandibles are roduced, the maxillæ connate with the labium, and their palpi two-jointed. The female is blind, vermiform, and never quits the bee on which it is parasitic; the larvæ, as in Meloë, have a double form; on being hatched, they are carried by a bee or wasp to its nest, where they bore into a grub, and are transformed from their former more active condition to sluggish footless vermiform larvæ; the species are all small in size, the largest not being a quarter of an inch long; the tarsi have from two to four joints, and the antennæ are often forked or branched.

We possess three British genera, *Stylops*, *Halictophagus*, and *Elenchus*; in the first of these the antennæ have six joints, and the tarsi four; in the second the antennæ have seven joints, and the tarsi three; while in the third the number of joints is five and two respectively. Stylops is not uncommon, at least the female; the male is very seldom met with, but has been taken in some numbers on the wing near London; it flies, apparently, in the early morning, with a very elegant undulating motion; Mr. Dale, in recording his capture of a specimen flying in the hot sunshine over a quick-set hedge in his garden at Glanvilles Wootton, Dorset, says "it looked milk-white on the wing, with a jet-black body, and totally unlike anything else; it flew with an undulating or vacillating motion amongst the young shoots, and I could not catch it until it had settled on one, when it ran up and down, its wings in motion, and making a considerable buzz or hum nearly as loud as a Sesia; it twisted about its rather long tail, and turned it up like a Staphylinus. I put it under a glass, and placed it in the sun; it became quite furious in its confinement, and never ceased running about for two hours."

"By putting two bees (*Andrena labialis*) under a glass in the sun, two Stylops were produced; the bees seemed uneasy, and went up towards them, but evidently with caution, as if to fight, and moving their antennæ towards them retreated; the oddest thing was to see the Stylops get on the body of the bee and ride about, the latter using every effort to throw his rider. A large hole is left in the tail of the bee when the Stylops escapes, which closes up after a time. I have found five species of Andrenæ infested."

Our other two genera are extremely rare; *Elenchus tenuicornis* has been taken by Mr. Dale near Glanvilles Wootton, Dorset, in June (White-down, June 11th, 1830, and Alder Mead, June 27th, 1839); by Mr. Walker at Southgate, by Mr. Kirkby in a spider's web in Suffolk, and by Mr. Templeton at Belfast. *Halictophagus Curtisii* (in the males of which the antennæ are beautifully branched) has been captured by Mr. Dale near Lulworth Cove, and by Sir S. S. Saunders near Folkestone; for several of these particulars I am indebted to the kindness of Professor Westwood, who tells me that in Sir S. S Saunders' collection there is no trace of the male; in *Halictophagus* the nervures of the wings are much more pronounced than in either *Stylops* or *Elenchus*.

INDEX.

Abdera, 232
Acalles, 263.
Achenium, 106.
Acidota, 112.
Acilius sulcatus, 81.
Acoritus, 131.
Acrognathus, 111.
Actocharis Readingi, 97.
Acupalpus exiguus, 68.
Acylophorus, 101.
Adolognathes, 244.
Adelops, 118.
Adephaga, 56.
Adimonia capreæ, 211.
—— sanguinea, 212.
—— tanaceti, 211.
Adrastus, 171.
Ægialia, 155.
Æpys, 71.
Agabus maculatus, 80.
Agapanthia lineatocollis, 200.
Agaricophagus, 117.
Agathidium, 117, 118.
Agelastica halensis, 212.
Agrilus biguttatus, 165.
Agriotes, 171.
Agrypnina, 169.
Aleochara, 94, 95.
Aleocharium, 94.
Alexia pilifera, 128.
Alophus triguttatus, 258.
Alphitobius, 226.
Alula, 34, 81.
Amara fulva, 68.
Ammœcius, 155.
Amphicyllis, 117, 118.
Amphimallus, 158.
Anaspis, 235.
Anchomenus 6-punctatus, 69.
Ancystronycha, 179.

Anisodactylus, 67.
Anisotoma, 117.
—— cinnamomea, 118.
Anisotomina, 117.
Anobiidæ, 187.
Anobium tessellatum, 188.
Anomala Frischi, 160.
Anoplus plantaris, 261.
Antennæ, 30.
Anthaxia, 165.
Anthicidæ, 236.
Anthicus instabilis, 237.
Anthobium, 112.
Anthocomus, 180.
Anthonomus, 260.
Anthophagus alpinus, 112.
Anthribidæ, 247.
Anthribus albinus, 248.
Antiodontalgicus, 258.
Aphides, 125.
Aphidiphagi, 125.
Aphodiina, 154.
Aphodius inquinatus, 155.
Aphthona, 214.
Apion difforme, 251.
Apionina, 250.
Apoderus coryli, 249.
Apteropoda graminis, 216.
Arachnida, structure of, 5.
Aromia moschata, 194.
Arthropoda, 4.
Asemum striatum, 196.
Aspidiphorus orbiculatus, 143.
Astinomus ædilis, 199.
Astrapæus, 101.
Atemeles emarginatus, 95.
Athous hæmorrhoidalis, 170.
Atomaria, 140.
Attolabinæ, 249.
Attelabus curculionoides, 249.

Anchenia, 212.
Antalia, 94, 95.
Axinotarsus, 180.

Badister, 67.
Bagöus, 262.
Balaninina, 266.
Balaninus brassicæ, 266.
—— cerasorum, 266.
—— glandium, 266.
—— nucum, 245, 266.
—— villosus, 266.
Baptolinus alternans, 105.
Barina, 263.
Baris, 265.
Bembidiina, 70.
Bembidium flammulatum, 71.
—— pallidiponne, 71.
—— paludosum, 71.
Benzino, 47.
Berosus, 86.
Bipalmati, 70.
Blaps mucronata, 221.
Blaptina, 221.
Blechrus maurus, 73.
Bledius, 64, 109, 110.
Blister-beetle, 240.
Bloody-nosed beetle, 208.
Bolitobius atricapillus, 99.
Bolitoebara, 95.
Bolitophagina, 223.
Bolitophagus cronatus, 223.
Bombardier beetle, 73.
Books:—
 Allard, *Halticidæ*, 213.
 Bedel, *Faune Col.*, 38, 246.
 Bestimmungs-Tabellen, 39.
 Biologia Centrali-Americana, 39.
 Brauer, *Zool. Studien*, 14.
 Burmeister, *Manual*, 38.
 Candèze, *Elateridæ*, 171.
 Chapuis and Candèze, *Larves*, 39.
 Claus, *Text Book of Zoology*, 2.
 Cox, *Manual*, 37.
 Curtis, *Genera*, 37.
 Dawson, *Geodephaga*, 58.
 Denny, *Psel. et Scyd.*, 120, 121.
 Entomologist, 50.
 Entomologist's Monthly Magazine, 99, 109, 255.
 Erichson, *Ins. Deutschl.*, 38.
 —— *Scolytidæ*, 268.
 —— *Staphylinidæ*, 92.
 Fabro, *Meloë*, 240.
 Fairmaire, *Faune Franc.*, 38.
 Fowler, *Brit. Col.*, 37.
 Gillmeister, *Trichopterygidæ*, 123.
 Kraatz, *Colon*, 118.
 Lacordaire, *Genera*, 39, 240.
 Leconte and Horn, 39, 246.
 Lubbock, *Ants, Bees, and Wasps*, 9, 11.
 Marseul de, *Histeridæ*, 132.
 Matthews, *Myllæna*, 97.
 —— *Trichopterygidæ*, 123.
 McLachlan, *Enc. Brit.*, 10.
 Mollié, *Cis*, 183.
 Mulsant, *Palpicornes*, 84.
 Mulsant and Rey, *Col. Franç.*, 38.
 Murray, *Catops*, 118.
 Newport, *Meloë*, 240.
 Pandellé, *Tachyporini*, 100.
 Perris, *Larves*, 39.
 Putzeys, *Mon. des Clivinas*, 69.
 Ratzeburg, *Forst. Ins.*, 268.
 Regimbart, *Gyrinidæ*, 83.
 Rolleston, *Forms of Animal Life*, 2.
 Schiödte, *De Met. El.*, 39.
 Schmidt, *Histeridæ*, 132.
 Schönherr, *Curculionidæ*, 244.
 Sharp, *Dytiscidæ*, 83.
 —— *Homalota*, 97.
 —— *Eucnemis*, 167.
 Stephens, *Illustrations*, 37.
 —— *Manual*, 37.
 Stierlin, *Otiorrhynchus*, 254.
 Strauss-Dürckheim, 19.
 Thomson, *Skand. Col.*, 39.
 Tournier, *Colon*, 118.
 Walton, *Curculionidæ*, 243.
 Waterhouse, *Gyrophæna*, 96.
 —— *Heteroceridæ*, 145.
 Weise, *Halticidæ*, 213.
 Westwood, *Introduction*, 38.
 Wollaston, *Atomaria*, 140.
Bostrichidæ, 186, 271.

Bostrichus capucinus, 186.
Brachelytra, 89.
Brachinus crepitans, 73.
Brachypterina, 132.
Brachyrrhynchi, 245.
Brachytarsus scabrosus, 248.
—— varius, 248.
Bradycellus, 68.
Broscus, 65.
Bruchidæ, 202.
Bruchus rufimanus, 203.
Bryaxis sanguinea, 121.
Brychius elevatus, 77.
Buprestidæ, 163.
Burying-beetles, 119.
Byrrhidæ, 142.
Byrrhus fasciatus, 142.
Bythinus, 121.
Byturidæ, 138.

Calandra grauaria, 246, 266.
—— oryzæ, 266.
Calandrina, 266.
Callicerus, 96.
Callidiina, 195.
Callidium alni, 196.
—— violaceum, 195.
Callistus lunatus, 66.
Calomicrus circumfusus, 212.
Calosoma sycophanta, 62.
Calyptomerus, 116.
Campylina, 171.
Campylus linearis, 171.
Cantharis, 240.
Carabidæ, 61.
Carabinæ, 61.
Carabina, 61.
Carabus monilis, 62.
—— nemoralis, 62.
—— nitens, 62.
—— violaceus, 62.
Cardinal-beetle, 233.
Carpophilina, 133.
Carpophilus hemipterus, 133.
Cassida oblonga, 217.
—— sanguinolenta, 217.
—— viridis, 218.
—— vittata, 217.
Cassidina, 217.
Catops, 118.

Cebrionidæ, 171.
Cellar-beetles, 69.
Cephalochorda, 8.
Cerambycidæ, 194.
Cerambycina, 194.
Cercus pedicularius, 132.
Cercyon, 87.
Cerylon, 130.
Cetonia ænea, 161.
—— aurata, 161.
Cetoniina, 160.
Ceuthorrhynchidius, 264.
Ceuthorrhynchina, 263.
Ceuthorrhynchus, 264.
Chætarthria seminulum, 86.
Chætocnema, 216.
Chafers, 146.
Chilocorus, 127.
Chlænius vestitus, 66.
Choleva, 118.
Cholevina, 118.
Choragus Sheppardi, 248.
Chrysomela cerealis, 209.
—— distinguenda, 209.
—— graminis, 209.
—— menthastri, 209.
—— polita, 209.
Chrysomelidæ, 203.
Chrysomelina, 208.
Churchyard-beetle, 221.
Cicindela campestris, 60.
—— germanica, 60.
—— sylvatica, 61.
Cicindelidæ, 59.
Cicones variegatus, 130.
Cionina, 265.
Cionus blattariæ, 265.
Cissidæ, 183.
Cis boleti, 184.
Cistela, 229.
Cistelidæ, 228.
Clambina, 116.
Clambus, 116.
Claviger foveolatus, 120.
Clavigeridæ, 120.
Clavipalpi, 129.
Cleonus, 257.
Cleridæ, 181.
Clerus formicarius, 181.
Clivina collaris, 64.
Clypeus, 30.

Clythra quadripunctata, 206.
—— tridentata, 206.
Clythrina, 206.
Clytina, 196.
Clytus ariotis, 196.
Cnemidotus, 77.
Coccidula scutellata, 127.
Coccinella hieroglyphica, 126.
—— obliterata, 126.
—— oblongo-guttata, 126.
—— ocellata, 126.
—— 18-guttata, 126.
—— 19-punctata, 126.
—— 13-punctata, 126.
—— 22-punctata, 126.
Coccinellidæ, 125.
Cockchafer, 158.
Cœlenterata, 3.
Cœliodos didymus, 263.
Colenis, 117.
Coleoptera, *definition of*, 10, 16.
—— *divisions of*, 51—55.
—— *metamorphosis of*, 16, 17.
—— *structure of*, 29—36.
Collecting, 48.
Collecting-bottle, 42.
Colon, 118.
Colydiidæ, 129.
Colydium, 130.
Comazus, 116.
Conicoxæ, 220.
Conipora, 142.
Conopalpus, 229, 232.
Coprina, 153.
Copris lunaris, 153.
Corn-weevil, 246, 267.
Corticaria, 137.
Corylophidæ, 123.
Corylophus cassidioides, 121.
Corymbites cuprous, 171.
—— pectinicornis, 171.
Corynetes, 181, 182.
Cossonina, 267.
Cossonus linearis, 267.
Coxa, 33—35.
Creophilus maxillosus, 102.
—— v. ciliaris, 103.
Crepidodera aurata, 214.
—— chloris, 214.
—— helxines, 214.
Criocerina, 205.

Crioceris asparagi, 206.
—— merdigera, 206.
Crustacea, *structure of*, 4.
Cryptarcha, 134.
Crypticina, 222.
Crypticus quisquilius, 222.
Cryptobium fracticorne, 106.
Cryptocephalina, 207.
Cryptocephalus aureolus, 208.
—— bilineatus, 208.
—— coryli, 207.
—— 10-punctatus, 208.
—— nitidulus, 208.
—— soriceus, 208.
—— sex-punctatus, 207.
Cryptohypnus dermestoides, 170.
Cryptophagidæ, 139.
Cryptophagus scanicus, 140.
Cryptopleurum, 87.
Cryptorrhynchina, 263.
Cryptorrhynchus lapathi, 263.
Cteniopus, 229.
Cucujidæ, 138.
Curoulionidæ, 249.
Curculioninæ, 245.
Cybistor, 81.
Cychramina, 134.
Cychramus, 134.
Cychrus rostratus, 63.
Cyclica, 209.
Cyclonotum, 87.
Cyphonina, 173.
Cyrtusa, 117.

Dascillidæ, 173.
Dascillina, 173.
Dascillus cervinus, 173.
Dasytina, 180.
Death-watch, 188.
Deinopsis, 97.
Doleastor, 111.
Dermostes lardarius, 142.
Dermostidæ, 141.
Devil's coach-horse, 88.
Diachromus germanus, 67.
Diamond-beetle, 246.
Dinodus cœrulescens, 107.
Diaperina, 224.
Diaperis boleti, 224.
Dichirotrichus obsoletus, 67.

INDEX. 281

Diglossa, 97.
Dinarda, 95.
Diphyllus lunatus, 139.
Diptera, 11.
Dissection, 20.
Diversimani, 65.
Dolopius, 171.
Donacia, 204.
Donaciina, 204.
Dorcatoma, 188.
Dorcus, *eye of*, 30.
—— parallelopipedus, 151.
Dorytomus, 260.
Drilidæ, 177.
Drilus flavescens, 177.
Dromius, 73.
Dryops, 233, 234.
Drypta dentata, 73.
Dung-beetles, 153.
Dyschirius, 64, 110.
Dytisci complicati, 78.
—— fragmentati, 78.
Dytiscidæ, 77.
Dytiscus marginalis, *abdomen of*, 36.
—— ——, *head of*, 30, 31.
—— ——, *larva of*, 17, 80.
—— ——, *pupa of*, 17.
——, *thorax of*,
—— —— mesothorax, 33.
—— —— metanotum, 34.
—— —— metasternum, 35.
—— —— pronotum, 32.
—— —— prosternum, 33.
Dytiscus punctulatus, 79.

Echinodermata, 4.
Elaphrina, 63.
Elateridæ, 168.
Elaterina, 169.
Elater sanguinolentus, 169.
Elenchus tenuicornis, 275.
Elmina, 144.
Elytra, 33.
Emus hirtus, 103.
Encephalus complicans, 96.
Endomychidæ, 127.
Endomychus coccineus, 128.
Engis humeralis, 129.
—— rufifrons, 129.

Ennearthron, 184.
Enopliides, 181.
Entimus imperialis (*exotic*), 246.
Epimera, 33—35.
Episterna, 33—35.
Epuræa, 133.
Erirrhinina, 259.
Erirrhinus festucæ, 260.
—— tæniatus, 260.
—— vorax, 260.
Eros Aurora, 175.
Erotylidæ, 129.
Eryx atra, 229.
Eubria palustris, 174.
Eucnemidæ, 166.
Eucnemis capucina, 167.
Eugleues, 237.
Eunmicrus tarsatus, 119.
Euplectus Karstenii, 122.
—— nanus, 122.
—— signatus, 122.
Eupoda, 202.
Euryporus, 100.
Eusphalerum, 112.
Evæsthetinæ, 107.
Examination *of insects*, 20, 21.
Exochomus, 127.

Femur, 33.
Fungicola, 189.

Galeruca, 212.
Galerucina, 211.
Gastrophysa, 209.
Genus, *definition of*, 19.
Geodephaga, 56.
Geodromicus, 111.
Georyssidæ, 143.
Georyssus pygmæus, 143.
Geotrupes stercorarius, 153.
—— vernalis, 157.
Geotrupina, 155.
Gibbium, 188.
Globicoxæ, 220.
Glow-worm, 175.
Gnathocerus, 226.
Gnorimus, 160, 161.
Gonatoceri, 245.
Gonioctena, 209.

Gracilia pygmæa, 197.
Graptodora, 213.
Gronopina, 255.
Gronops lunatus, 255.
Gum-tracaganth, 44.
Gymnetrina, 265.
Gymnetron, 265.
Gymnusa, 97.
Gyrinidæ, 81.
Gyrinus, 30, 82.
—— bicolor, 82.
Gyrophæna, 94—96.

Habrocorinæ, 99.
Habrocorus, 99.
Halictophagus Curtisii, 275.
Haliplidæ, 76.
Haliplus obliquus, 77.
Hallomenus, 231.
Halticina, 212.
Haploglossa, 95.
Harpalinæ, 64.
Harpalus ruficornis, 67.
Hedobia imperialis, 187.
Heledona agaricola, 224.
Heliopathes gibbus, 222.
Helophorus rugosus, 85.
Holopina, 227.
Helops cœrulous, 227.
—— pallidus, 227.
—— striatus, 227.
Hemiptera, 13.
Hermæophaga, 213.
Heteroceridæ, 144.
Heteromera, 52, 220.
Heterothops, 101.
Hister bimaculatus, 131.
Histeridæ, 130.
Holoparamecus, 137.
Homaliinæ, 111.
Homalium, 31, 112.
—— planum, 112.
Homaloplia, 159.
Homalota gregaria, 97.
Homœusa, 95.
Hoplia philanthus, 159.
Hopliina, 159.
Hydaticus, 79.
Hydnobius, 117.
Hydradephaga, 75.

Hydræna, 85.
Hydrobius fuscipes, 86.
Hydrochus, 86.
Hydronomus, 262.
Hydrophilidæ, 84.
Hydrophilinæ, 84.
Hydrophilus piceus, 85.
Hydroporina, 78.
Hydroporus rivalis, 78.
Hylastes, 269.
Hylecœtus dermostoides, 183.
Hylosinidæ, 268.
Hylesinus vittatus, 268, 269.
Hylobiina, 258.
Hylobius abietis, 258.
Hylotrupes bajulus, 196.
Hylurgus piniperda, 269.
Hymonoptera, 11.
Hypera trilineata, 256.
Hyperina, 256.
Hyphydrus ovatus, 79.
Hypocyptus, 98.
Hypophlœus bicolor, 226.
Hypothenemus cruditus, 270.
Hypulus quercinus, 232.

Ilyobates, 96.
Insecta, 6, 9, 10, 14.
Intrancatipennos, 64.
Ipina, 134.
Ips ferruginous, 134.
Ischnoglossa, 95.

Keeper's tree, 49.

Labial palpi, 31, 32.
Labium, 31.
Labrum, 30.
Laccophilus, 78.
Lacon murinus, 169.
Lady-birds, 125.
Læmophlœus, 138.
Lagriidæ, 227.
Lagria hirta, 227.
Lamellicornia, 146.
Lamiidæ, 198.
Lamiina, 198.
Lamia textor, 199.

INDEX.

Lamprosoma concolor, 207.
Lampyridæ, 175.
Lampyris noctiluca, 175.
Langelandia anophthalma, 130.
Laparosticti, 152.
Larinus, 242, 257, 258.
Larvæ, 17, 58, 59, 76, 80, 82, 83, 85, 91, 126, 131, 134, 142, 147, 151, 164, 165, 170, 173, 175, 176, 192, 194, 199, 207, 217, 222, 224, 225, 238, 239, 245, 250, 256, 261, 266, 267, 269, 271, 273.
Lasia globosa, 127.
Lathridiidæ, 136.
Lathridius lardarius, 137.
—— nodifer, 137.
Lathrimæum, 112.
Lathrobium, 106.
Lobia chlorocephala, 72.
—— crux-minor, 72.
Leistus, 63.
Lepidoptera, 11.
Leptacinus formicetorum, 105.
Leptinidæ, 116.
Leptinus testaceus, 116.
Lepturidæ, 197.
Lepturina, 197.
Lestova, 111.
Licinus silphoides, 66.
Ligula, 31, 32.
Limexylonidæ, 182.
Limexylon, 183.
Limnobius picinus, 86.
Limnichus, 142.
Limobius, 256.
Lina populi, 209.
—— tremulæ, 209.
Liodes, 117, 118.
Lionychus quadrillum, 73.
Liosomus, 259.
Litodactylus, 264.
Lixina, 257.
Lixus bicolor, 257.
—— paraplecticus, 257.
Longicornia, 190.
Loricera, 64.
Loricerina, 64.
Lucanidæ, 146, 147.
Lucanus corvus, 149.
Ludius ferrugineus, 170.
Luperus, 212.

Lycidæ, 175.
Lycoperdina bovistæ, 128.
Lyctidæ, 185.
Lyctus canaliculatus, 186.
Lyprus, 262.
Lytta vesicatoria, 240.

Magdalinus carbonarius, 262.
Malachius, 180.
Malacodermata, 172.
Malthinus, 180.
Malthodes, 180.
Mandibles, 30.
Mantura, 214.
Maxillæ, 31.
Maxillary palpi, 31.
Meal-worm, 221.
Mecinus, 265.
Mecorrhynchi, 245.
Megarthrus, 112, 113.
Megastornum, 87.
Melandrya caraboides, 231.
Melandryidæ, 229.
Melandryina, 230.
Melasis buprestoides, 167.
Melasoma, 220.
Meligethes, 133.
Meloë, *transformations of*, 238.
Meloidæ, 237.
Melolontha, 158.
Melolonthina, 158.
Melyridæ, 180.
Mentum, 31, 32.
Mesites Tardii, 267.
Mesonotum, 34.
Mesosternum, 34.
Mesothorax, 33.
Metanotum, 34.
Metasternum, 35.
Metathorax, 34.
Metœcus paradoxus, 235.
Mezium, 188.
Miarus, 265.
Micralymma brevipennis, 112.
Micraspis, 127.
Micropeplinæ, 114.
Micropeplus, 90, 114.
—— margaritæ, 114.
—— tesserula, 114.
Micorrhagus, 167.
Microtrogus, 261.

Microzoum, 222.
Miscodera arctica, 65.
Mniophila musoorum, 216.
Mollusca, *structure of*, 7.
Molorchina, 197.
Molorchus umbellatarum, 197.
Molytes, 258.
Mononychus pseudacori, 264.
Monotomidæ, 136.
Mordellidæ, 234.
Musk-beetle, 194.
Mycetæa hirta, 128.
Mycetocharis bipustulata, 229.
Mycetophagidæ, 141.
Mycetophagus multipunctatus, 141.
Mycetoporus, 99.
Mycterus curculionoides, 242.
Myllæna, 94, 97.
Myriapoda, *structure of*, 6.
Myrmocoxenus vaporariorum, 130.
Myrmedonia funesta, 95.

Nacerdes melanura, 233.
Nausibius, 138.
Nebriina, 63.
Nebria complanata, 63.
—— livida, 63.
Necrobia, 182.
Necrophaga, 115.
Necrophorus mortuorum, 119.
Nemosoma elongata, 136.
Nets; sweeping, 41.
—— umbrella, 41.
—— water, 42.
Neuroptera, 11.
Nitidulidæ, 132.
Nitidulina, 133.
Nossidium pilosollum, 123.
Notorus, 78.
Notiophilus, 63.
Notoxus, 236.
Nudobius lentus, 105.
Nut-weevil, 245, 266.

Oberea oculata, 200.
Obrium, 195.
Obrium cantharinum, 196.

Occiput, 30.
Ocelli, 30, 111, 113.
Octotemnus, 184.
Ocypus compressus, 104.
—— cyaneus, 104.
—— morio, 104.
—— olens, 88, 103.
Ocyusa, 95.
Odacantha melanura, 73.
Œdemera cœrulea, 234.
Œdemeridæ, 233.
Oil-beetles, 237.
Oligota, 97.
Olophrum, 112.
Omophlus, 229.
Omosita, 133.
Oncomera femorata, 233.
Onthophagus, 154.
Onthophilus striatus, 131.
Oomorphus, 207.
Opatrina, 222.
Opatrum sabulosum, 222.
Opilus, 182.
Orchesia undulata, 231.
Orchestes, 261.
Orectochilus villosus, 82.
Orobitis, 263.
Orsodacna, 204.
Orthoceri, 245.
Orthochætes, 262.
Orthoptera, 11.
Osphya bipunctata, 232.
Othius, 104.
Otiorrhynchidæ, 252.
Otiorrhynchus picipes, 254.
—— sulcatus, 253.
Oxypoda, 97.
Oxyporinæ, 109.
Oxyporus rufus, 109.
Oxytolinæ, 109.
Oxytolus, 110.

Pædorina, 105.
Pædorus caligatus, 106.
Palpi, 31.
Palpicornia, 84.
Panagæus, 67.
Paraglossæ, 32.
Paraplenra, 35.
Parnidæ, 144.
Parnina, 144.

Paromalus, 131.
Patollimani, 65.
Patrobus, 71.
Pea-beetle, 202.
Pectinicornes, 148.
Pedilidæ, 235.
Pedinina, 232.
Pelobiidæ, 77.
Polobius Hermanni, 77.
Pentamora, 52.
Perileptus areolatus, 71.
Phalacridæ, 124.
Phaleria cadavorina, 223.
Phanerognathes, 244.
Philhydrida, 84.
Philonthus, 102, 104.
Phlœobiinæ, 113.
Phlœobium clypeatum, 113.
Phlœocharinæ, 113.
Phlœocharis subtilissima, 113.
Phlœophilus Edwardsi, 181.
Phlœopora, 95.
Phosphænus homipterus, 176.
Phratora, 209.
Phyllobius argentatus, 252.
—— viridicollis, 253.
Phyllobrotica, 212.
Phyllopertha horticola, 160.
Phyllotreta brassicæ, 215.
—— nodicornis, 218.
—— ochripes, 215.
—— sinuata, 215.
—— tetrastigma, 215.
—— undulata, 215.
—— vittata, 215.
Phytonomus, 256.
Phytophaga, 202.
Piestinæ, 113.
Pins, 46.
Pissodes pini, 259.
Platydema, 224.
Platypus cylindrus, 130, 271.
Platyrrhinidæ, 247.
Platyrrhinus, 248.
Platystethus, 110.
Plectroscelis, 216.
Pleurosticti, 152.
Plinthus, 259.
Podabrus, 179.
Pogonocherus, 200.
Pogonus, 71.

Pogonus luridipenuis, 72.
Polydrosus, 254.
Post-scutellum, 33.
Præsentum, 33.
Prionidæ, 193.
Prionocyphon, 174.
Prionus coriarius, 193.
Pristonychus, 69.
Prognatha quadricornis, 113.
Pronetum, 32.
Prostornum, 32, 33.
Proteininæ, 112.
Prothorax, 32.
Protozoa, 2.
Psammobius, 155.
Psammœchus, 138.
Psolaphidæ, 120.
Pselaphus dresdensis, 121.
—— Heisii, 121.
Pseudopsis sulcatus, 113.
Pseudotrimora, 54.
Psylliodes, 216.
Ptenidium apicale, 123.
Pterosticbus niger, *labium of*, 32.
Pterosticbus cupreus, 70.
—— madidus, 70.
—— picimanus, 70.
Pterygia, 243.
Ptilinus pectinicornis, 188.
Ptinella, 123.
Ptinidæ, 187.
Ptinus germanus, 187.
Pupa, 17.
Pygidium, 35.
Pyrochroa coccinea, 233.
Pyrochroidæ, 232.
Pythidæ, 240.
Pytho doprossus, 241.

Quadripalmati, 67.
Quediina, 100.
Quedius auricomus, 102.
—— brevis, 101.
—— cruentus, 102.
—— dilatatus, 101.
—— lævigatus, 102.
—— lateralis, 101.
—— scitus, 102.
—— truncicola, 102.

Relaxing-jar, 44.
Rhagium, 198.
Rhagonycha, 179.
Rhinocyllus, 258.
Rhinomacer attelaboides, 247.
Rhinomaceridæ, 247.
Rhinosimus viridipennis, 242.
Rhipidophoridæ, 235.
Rhizopertha pusilla, 186.
Rhizophagina, 135.
Rhizophagus, 132, 135.
Rhizotrogus solstitialis, 158.
Rhopalodontus, 184.
Rhynchitos æquatus, 250.
—— betuleti, 250.
Rhynchophora, 243.
Rhynchota, 13.
Rhytidosomus, 263.
Rose-beetle, 161.
Rostrum, 243.
Rove-beetles, 88.
Rutelina, 159.

Sagrina, 202, 204.
Salpingidæ, 240.
Salpingina, 240.
Saperda carcharias, 200.
—— populnea, 200.
—— scalaris, 200.
Saperdina, 200.
Saprinus, 131.
Sarrotrium, 130.
Scaphidema, 224.
Scaphidiidæ, 140.
Scaphidium, 140.
Scaphisoma, 140.
Scarabæidæ laparosticti, 152.
—— pleurostioti, 152.
Scaritina, 64.
Scirtes hemisphæricus, 174.
Scolytidæ, 268.
Scolytus destructor, 269.
Scopæus, 106.
Scraptia, 235.
Scraptiidæ, 235.
Scrobes, 243.
Scutellum, 33, 34.
Scutum, 33.
Scydmænidæ, 119.
Scymnus, 127.

Securipalpes, 125.
Serica brunnea, 158.
Sericina, 158.
Sericosomus, 171.
Setting, *directions for*, 45, 92.
Sexton-beetles, 119.
Shard-born beetle, 155.
Sibynes, 261.
Silphidæ, 116.
Silphina, 119.
Silvanus, 138.
Sinodendron, 151.
Sitaris muralis, 239.
Sitonina, 255.
Sitones lineatus, 255.
Skip-jacks, 162.
Soronia grisea, 134.
—— punctatissima, 133.
Spanish-fly, 240.
Species, *definition of*, 19.
Spercheus emarginatus, 84.
Sphæridiinæ, 86.
Sphæridium, 87.
Sphæriidæ, 124.
Sphæritina, 119.
Sphæritos, 119.
Sphærius acaroides, 124.
Sphæroderma, 214.
Sphindus dubius, 184.
Sphodrus, 69.
Spiraoles, 36.
—— *in larva*, 17.
Squeaker, 77.
Stag-beetle, 149.
Staphylinidæ, 88.
Staphylinina, 102.
Staphylininæ, 100.
Staphylinus cæsareus, 103.
—— erythropterus, 103.
—— fulvipes, 103.
Stenina, 107.
Stenolophus elegans, 68.
Stenus Guynemeri, 108.
—— Rogeri, 108.
Sternoxi, 162.
Sternum, 33.
Stilicus fragilis, 107.
Strangalia armata, 198.
Strepsiptera, 273.
Strophosomus, 254.
Stylopidæ, 273.

INDEX.

Stylops, 274.
Sulcicolles, 127.
Sunius, 106.
Sunshiners, 68.
Symbiotes latus, 128.
Synaptus, 171.
Syntomium, 111.

Tachinus, 98.
Tachyerges, 261.
Tachyporinæ, 97.
Tachyporus, 99.
Tachypus flavipes, 71.
—— pallipes, 71.
Tachyusa, 95.
—— constricta, 96.
Tanyspbyrus lemnæ, 258.
Tarsus, 33.
Telophoridæ, 178.
Telephorus clypeatus, 179.
Tolmatophilus, 139.
Tenebrio molitor, 225.
—— obscurus, 225.
Tenebrioides, 136.
Tenebrionidæ, 221.
Tenebrionina, 224.
Torodus, 130.
Tetramera, 52, 190, 243.
Tetratoma ancora, 230.
—— Desmarestii, 230.
—— fungorum, 230.
Tetratomina, 230.
Tetrops, 201.
Thinsophila, 95.
Thorax, 32.
Throscidæ, 165.
Throscus dermestoides, 166.
Thyamis dorsalis, 216.
Thymalus limbatus, 136.
Thysanura, 9.
Tibia, 33.
Tiger-beetles, 59.
Tillus elongatus, 181.
Timarcha lævigata, 208.
Timberman, 199.
Tomicidæ, 268.
Tomicus, 270.
Tortoise-beetles, 217.
Toxotus, 198.
Trachodes, 262.

Trachyphlœus, 253.
Trachys, 165.
Trachyscelina, 223.
Trecbina, 71.
Tribolium ferrugineum, 226.
Trichius fasciatus, 147, 161.
Trichodes, 182.
Trichonyx, 122.
Trichophya pilicornis, 99.
Trichophyinæ, 99.
Trichopterygidæ, 122.
Trichopteryx atomaria, 123.
Trimera, 52.
Tripalmati, 68.
Triphyllus, 141.
Triplax russicus, 129.
Tritoma bipustulata, 129.
Trochauter, 33—35.
Trogina, 157.
Trogophœus, 110, 111.
Trogosita mauritanica, 136.
Trogositidæ, 135.
Tropideres, 248.
Trox, 157.
Tunicata, 7.
Turnip-flea, 215.
Tychius, 261.
Tychus, 122.
Typhæa, 141.
Typhæus vulgaris, 156.

Ulomina, 225.

Vermes, 3.
Vortex, 30.

Water-beetles, 75.
Weevils, 243.
Whirligigs, 82.
Whirlwigs, 82.
Wing, 34.
Winglet, 34, 81.
Wire-worm, 170.

Xantholininæ, 104.
Xantholinus fulgidus, 105.
—— tricolor, 105.

Xylophaga, 268.
Xylophilidæ, 237.
Xylophilus, 237.
Xyloterus domesticus, 270.
—— lineatus, 270.

Xylotrogi, 182.

Zabrus gibbus, 58, 69.
Zeugophora subspinosa, 205.

PLATE II.

1. Callistus lunatus.
2. Anchomenus sexpunctatus.
3. Pterostichus picimanus.
4. Amara fulva.
5. Dichirotrichus obsoletus.
6. Bembidium pallidipenne.

Plate II

PLATE III.

1. Dytiscus punctulatus (*male*).
2. Agabus maculatus.
3. Hydroporus rivalis.
4. Haliplus obliquus.
5. Pelobius Hermanni.
6. Gyrinus bicolor.
    - 6 *a. Head of ditto, seen laterally.*
    - 6 *b. Antenna of ditto.*
    - 6 *c. Hind leg of ditto.*

Plate III

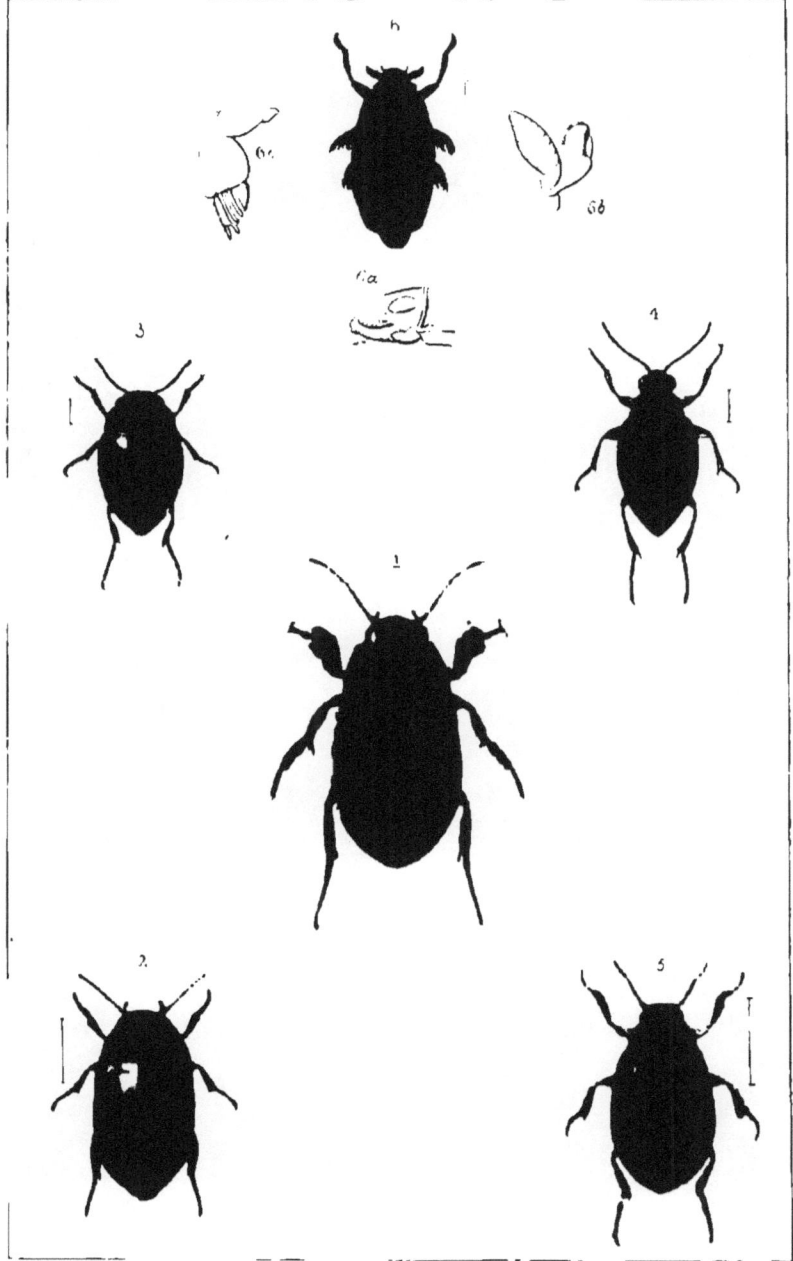

PLATE IV.

1. Atemeles emarginatus.
2. Bolitobius atricapillus.
3. Quedius cruentus.
4. Creophilus maxillosus.
5. Xantholinus fulgidus.
6. Pæderus caligatus.

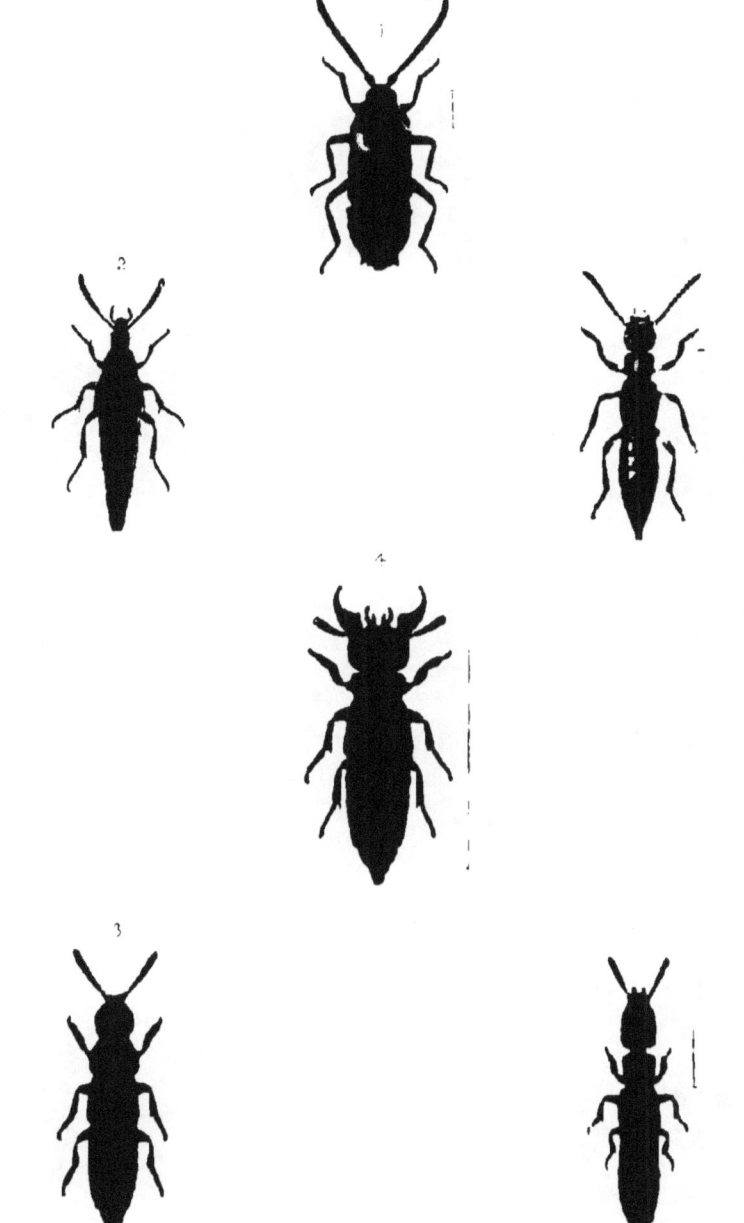

PLATE V.

1. Dianöus cœrulescens.
2. Oxyporus rufus.
3. Homalium planum.
4. Phlœobium clypeatum.
5. Prognatha quadricornis.
6. Micropeplus margaritæ.

PLATE VI.

1. Necrophorus mortuorum.
2. Eumicrus tarsatus.
3. Anisotoma cinnamomea.
4. Hister bimaculatus.
5. Soronia punctatissima.
6. Cicones variegatus.

Plate VI.

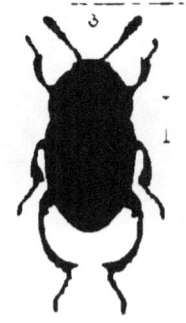

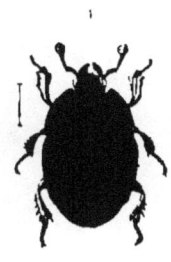
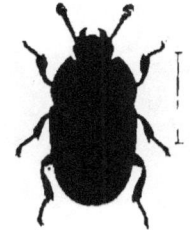

PLATE VII.

1. Cryptophagus scanicus.
2. Mycetophagus multipunctatus.
3. Byrrhus fasciatus.
4. Helophorus rugosus.
5. Hydrobius fuscipes.
6. Trichius fasciatus.

PLATE VIII.

1. Phyllopertha horticola.
2. Typhæus vulgaris.
3. Aphodius inquinatus.
4. Dorcus parallelopipedus.
5. Agrilus biguttatus.
6. Melasis buprestoides.

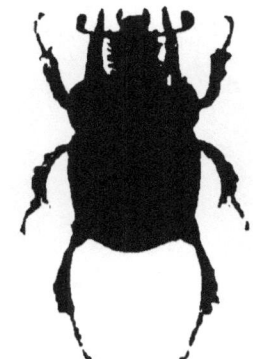
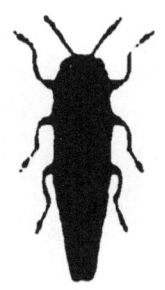

PLATE IX.

1. Elater sanguinolentus.
2. Eros Aurora.
3. Drilus flavescens (*male*).
4. Telephorus clypeatus.
5. Clerus formicarius.
6. Hylecœtus dermestoides (*male*)

Plate IX.

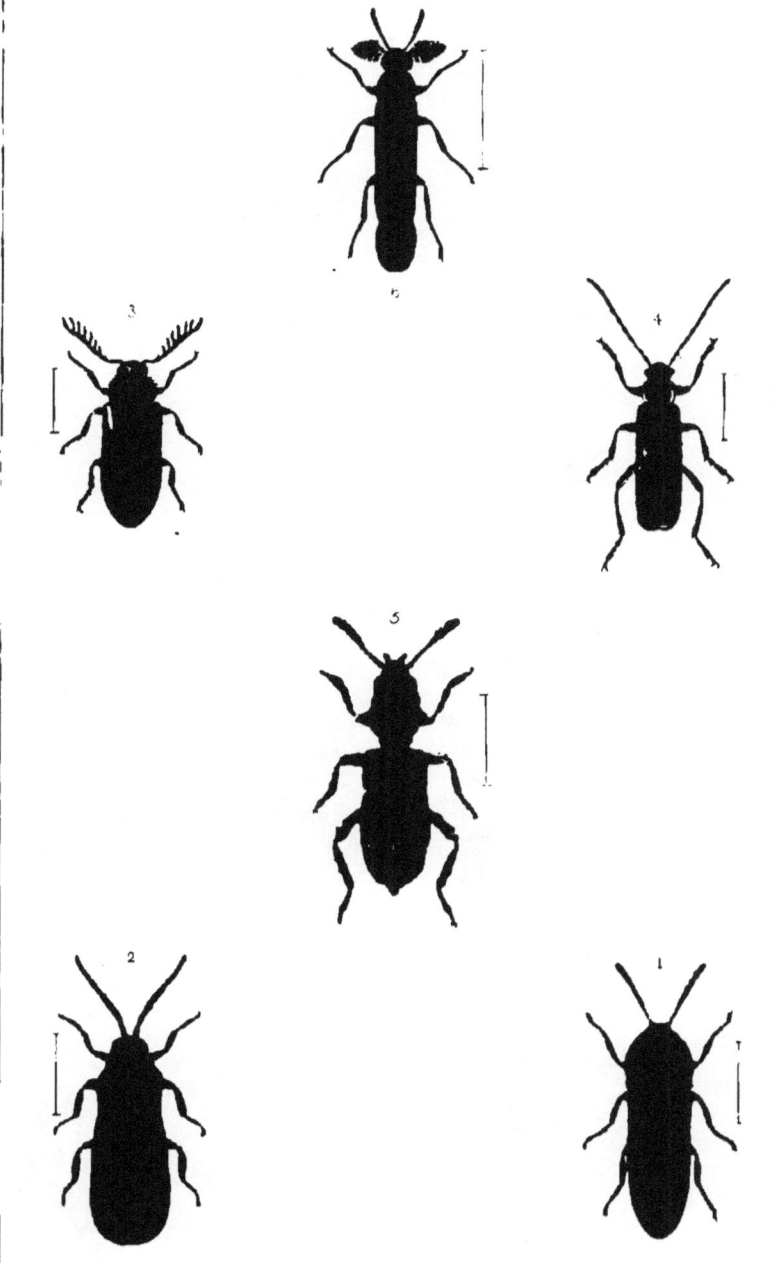

PLATE X.

1. Hedobia imperialis.
   - 1 *a. Head and thorax of ditto, viewed laterally.*
2. Crypticus quisquilius.
3. Helops pallidus.
4. Orchesia undulata.
5. Notoxus monoceros.
   - 5 *a. Head and thorax of ditto, viewed laterally.*
6. Metœcus paradoxus (*male*).

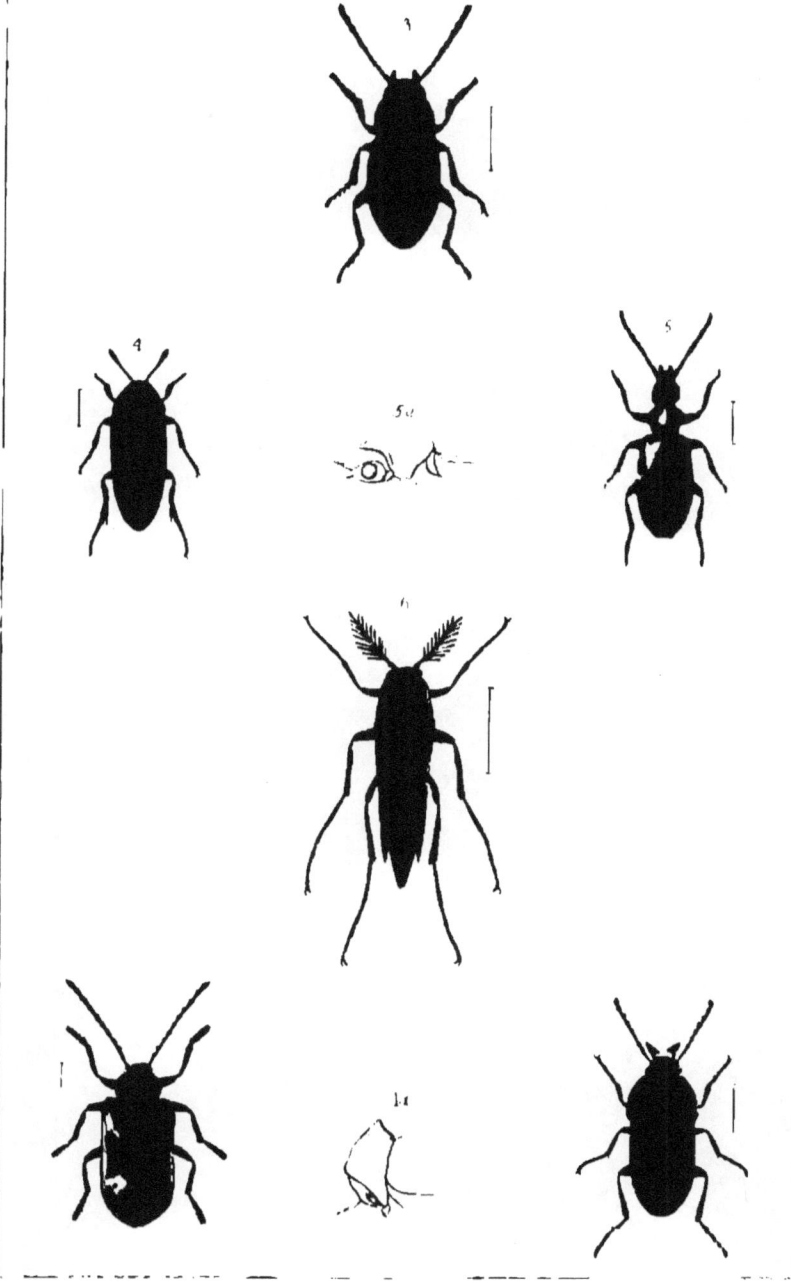

Plate X.

PLATE XI.

1. Sitaris muralis.
2. Œdemera cœrulea (*male*).
3. Rhinosimus viridipennis.
4. Brachytarsus scabrosus.
5. Rhynchites æquatus.
6. Hypera trilineata.

Plate XI.

PLATE XII.

1. Otiorrhynchus picipes.
2. Balaninus villosus.
    2 a. Head of ditto, viewed laterally.
3. Cryptorrhynchus lapathi.
4. Cionus blattariæ.
5. Cossonus linearis.
6. Hylesinus vittatus.
    6 a. Head of ditto, viewed laterally.

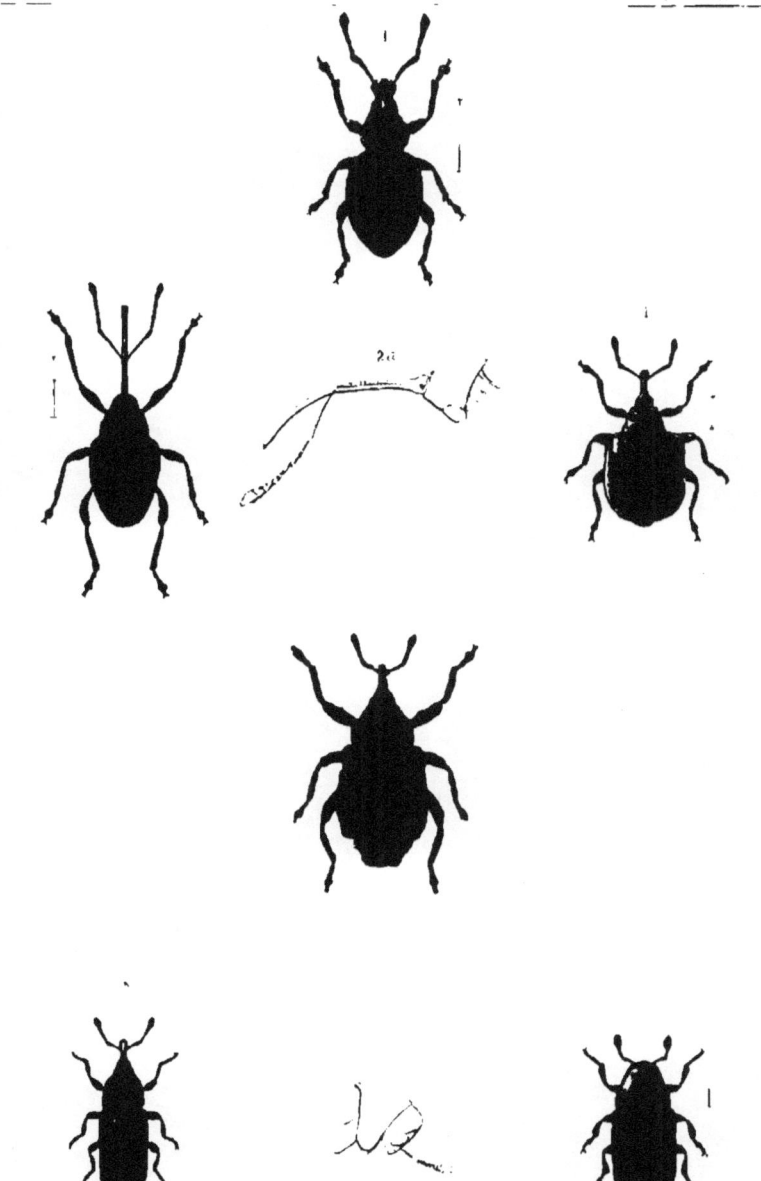

PLATE XIII.

1. Xyloterus lineatus.
2. Platypus cylindrus.
3. Callidium alni.
4. Acanthocinus ædilis (*male*).
5. Saperda scalaris.
6. Molorchus umbellatarum.

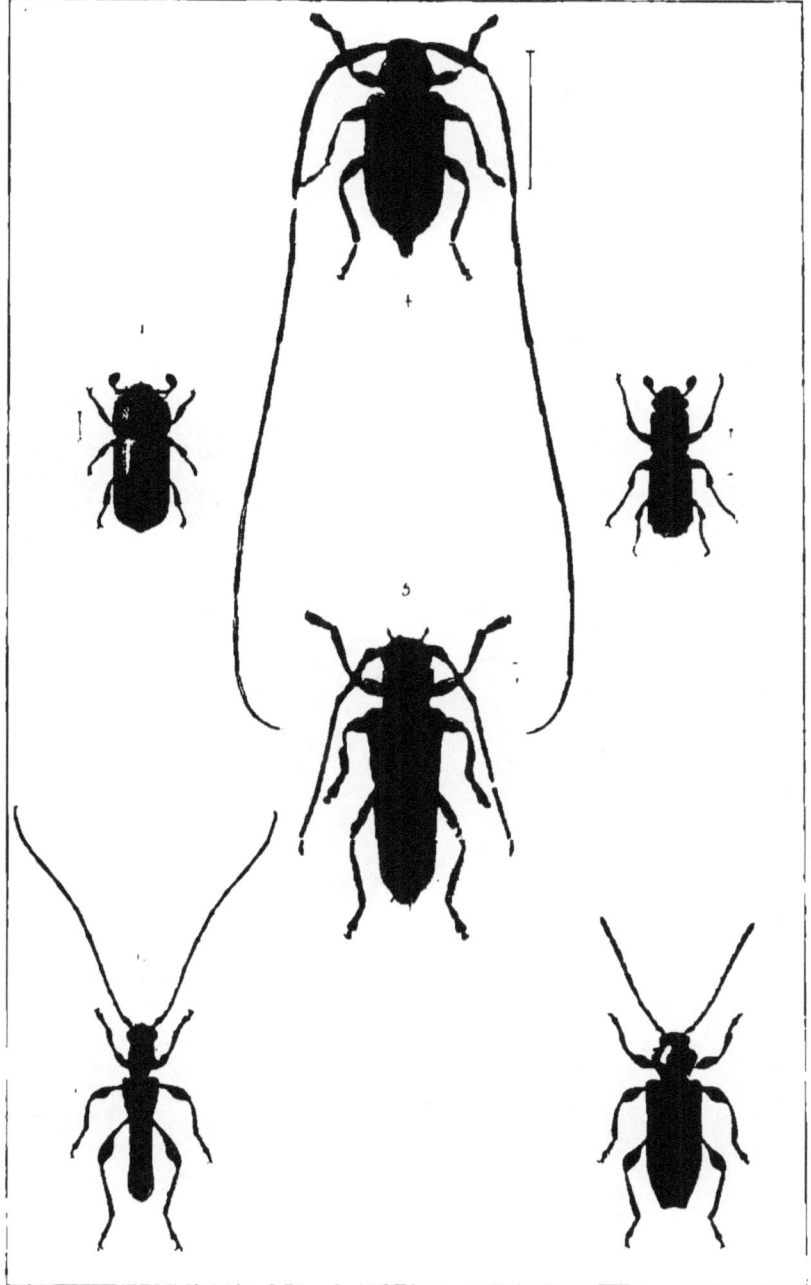

PLATE XIV.

1. Strangalia armata (*var.*).
2. Hæmonia Curtisii.
3. Crioceris asparagi.
4. Cryptocephalus bilineatus.
5. Chrysomela distinguenda.
6. Calomicrus circumfusus.

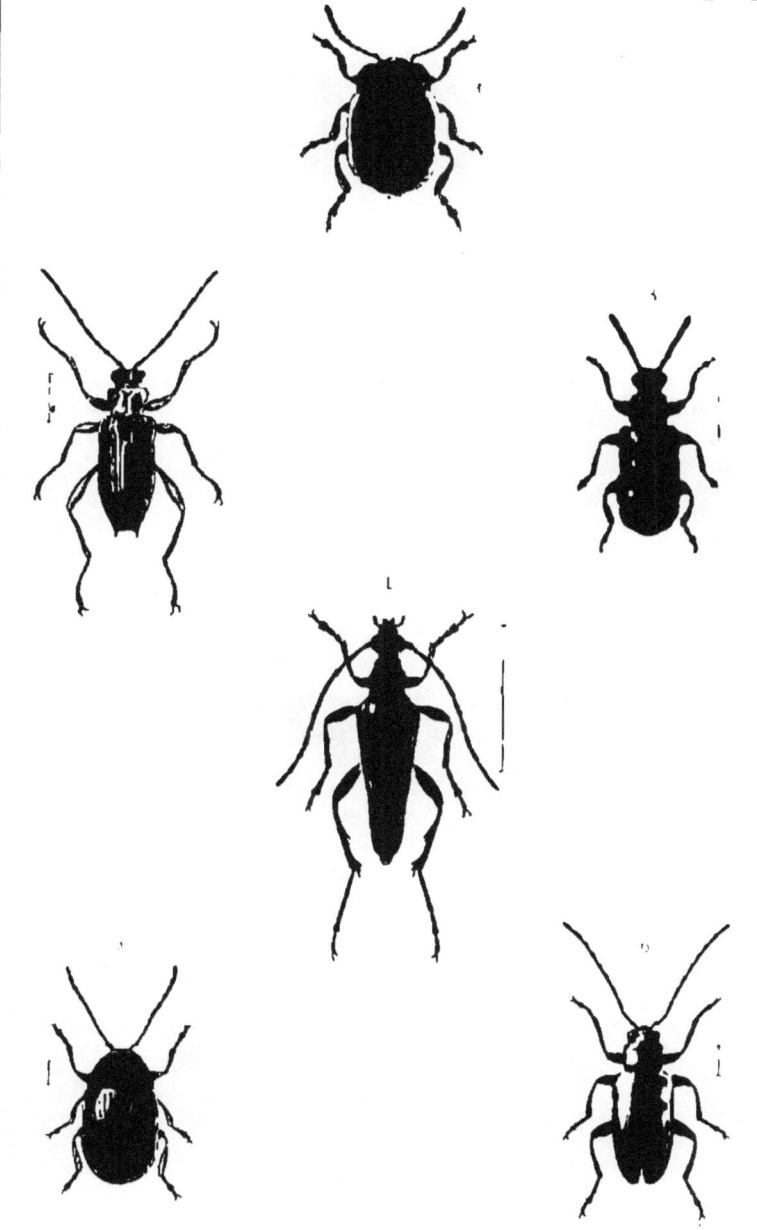

PLATE XV.

1. Phyllotreta ochripes.
2. Apteropeda graminis.
3. Cassida sanguinolenta.
4. Tritoma bipustulata.
5. Coccinella 22-punctata.
6. Endomychus coccineus.

Plate XX

3

2

c

4

PLATE XVI.

1. Corylophus cassidioides.
2. Ptenidium apicale.
3. Lathridius lardarius.
4. Psclaphus Heisii.
5. Euplectus nanus.
6. Claviger foveolatus.

Plate XV.

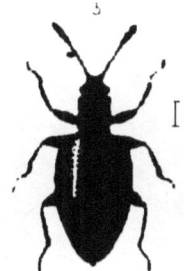

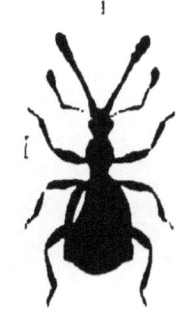
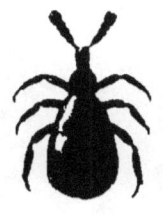

www.ingramcontent.com/pod-product-compliance
Lightning Source LLC
Chambersburg PA
CBHW020240240426
43672CB00006B/592